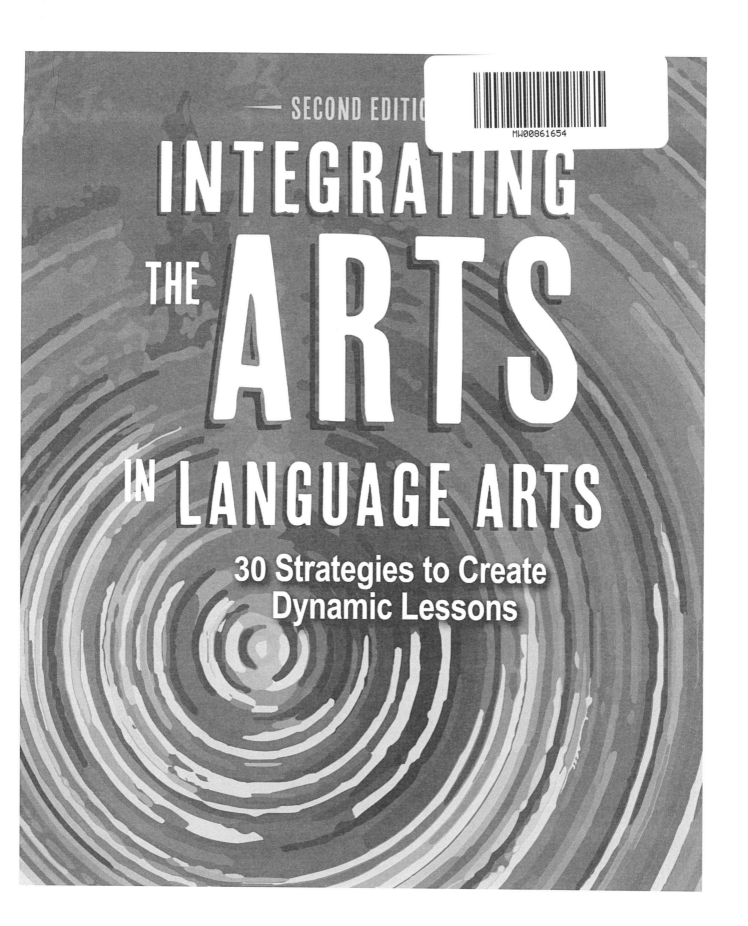

SECOND EDITION

INTEGRATING THE ARTS

IN LANGUAGE ARTS

30 Strategies to Create Dynamic Lessons

Jennifer M. Bogard, Ph.D.

Lisa Donovan, Ph.D.

Contributing Authors

Louise Pascale, Ph.D.
Professor Emerita, Creative Arts in Learning
Lesley University

Celeste Miller, M.F.A.
Choreographer, Associate Professor of Dance
Grinnell College

Dana Schildkraut
Arts Integration Specialist,
Berkshire Regional Arts Integration Network
Massachusetts College of Liberal Arts

Publishing Credits

Corinne Burton, M.A.Ed., *Publisher*
Aubrie Nielsen, M.S.Ed., *EVP of Content Development*
Véronique Bos, *Creative Director*
Cathy Hernandez, *Senior Content Manager*
Sara Johnson, M.S.Ed., *Editor*
Laureen Gleason, *Editor*
David Slayton, *Assistant Editor*

Consultants

Tom Lee
Storyteller and Arts Educator
www.tomleestoryteller.net

Amy Ludwig VanDerwater
Writer and Writing Teacher
www.amylv.com

Mary Ann Cappiello, Ed.D.
Associate Professor of Language and Literacy
Lesley University

Mary C. McMackin, Ed.D.
Professor Emerita, Language and Literacy
Lesley University

Ann Piper, M.Ed.
School Library Media Specialist

Brittany Williams, M.Ed.
Art Educator
Newbury Elementary School, Massachusetts

David Williams, M.Ed.
Grade 5 Teacher
Newbury Elementary School, Massachusetts

Special thanks for the love and support of Rob Bogard, and Rick, Alex, and Jack Donovan.

Image Credits: p. 80, courtesy of the Art Institute of Chicago; p. 125, courtesy of National Gallery of Art, Washington, DC; p. 142, courtesy of A. Carmisciano; p. 143, courtesy of N. Joyce; p. 147, courtesy of Louise Pascale; p. 178, courtesy of Dana Schildkraut; p. 187, courtesy of Jennifer Bogard and Lisa Donovan; p. 198, courtesy of Christine Flood; all other images from iStock Photo and/or Shutterstock.

Standards

A Division of Teacher Created Materials
5482 Argosy Avenue
Huntington Beach, CA 92649-1039
www.tcmpub.com/shell-education
ISBN 978-0-7439-7032-7
© 2022 Shell Educational Publishing, Inc.

Table of Contents

Preface

Welcome to the second edition of the Integrating the Arts series! Now, more than ever, educators are experiencing what the arts have always offered: instructional approaches for social-emotional learning and culturally responsive teaching that value students' funds of knowledge and lived experiences.

This series of books was launched initially to share more widely the success of arts integration in transforming classrooms and to foreground effective and easy-to-implement ideas. Since the first editions were published, educators have reached out telling us their stories and experiences using these strategies with their students.

We're so grateful for the feedback we received from educators. We loved hearing how you could flip through the books with your colleagues at planning time and choose a lesson to implement that afternoon or the next day. The practical aspect of the books was a highlight of the feedback. We learned that the lessons were versatile and worked with a wide variety of topics and learning targets. You'll find this continues to be a focus in our latest work, where we offer even more learning experiences for your classroom.

Here's what you'll find new and different in the second edition:

- inclusion of diverse perspectives and culturally responsive strategies that invite students to tap into their individual ideas and lived experiences
- a variety of student examples
- carefully selected ideas for mentor texts of multiple genres and modalities
- suggestions for the inclusion of primary sources
- several new strategies to bring to your classroom
- call-out boxes to highlight key insights and ideas
- resources for finding texts that bring diverse voices to your classroom
- a new structure in the movement chapter that provides additional details for classroom implementation
- a focus on the elements and key vocabulary of each art form
- updated standards

Dig in and enjoy! Let the power of the novelty of the arts bolster deep engagement with your content areas. We hope you create, experiment, and explore the artistic strategies alongside students, curating your own portfolio of creative work.

. . . .

"The arts help children develop creative problem-solving skills, motor skills, language skills, social skills, decision-making skills, risk-taking skills, and inventiveness."
—Sharuna Segaren (2019, para. 20)

. . . .

The Importance of Arts Integration

Study after study points to compelling evidence of the significant outcomes linked to arts integration. According to the President's Committee on the Arts and the Humanities, "studies have now documented significant links between arts integration models and academic and social outcomes for students, efficacy for teachers, and school-wide improvements in culture and climate. Arts integration is efficient, addressing a number of outcomes at the same time. Most important, the greatest gains in schools with arts integration are often seen school-wide and also with the most hard-to-reach and economically disadvantaged students" (2011, 19). According to the *New Jersey Arts Integration Think and Do Workbook*, "the key benefits of arts integration primarily fall into four categories: improving student academic achievement, student social emotional development, teacher practice, and classroom culture" (Bruce et. al. 2020, 21). Now more than ever, integrating the arts into our teaching creates opportunities for deep engagement and connection and an opportunity for our students to find relevance in course content to their lives.

The Ford Foundation funded a study led by researchers from Lesley University's Creative Arts in Learning Division and an external advisory team. The study involved research with more than two hundred Lesley alumni teaching across the country who had been trained in arts-integration strategies. Findings from the study suggest that arts-integrated teaching provides students with a variety of strategies for accessing content and expressing understanding of what they have learned that is culturally responsive and relevant to their lives. This leads to deep learning, increased student ownership, and engagement with academic content. Not only does arts integration engage students in creativity, innovation, and imagination, it renews teachers' commitment to teaching (Bellisario and Donovan with Prendergast 2012).

> "The key benefits of arts integration fall into four categories: improving student academic achievement, student social emotional development, teacher practice, and classroom culture."
>
> —Eloise Bruce et al. (2020, 21)

Really then, the question becomes this: How can we provide students with access to the arts as an engaging way to learn and express ideas across the curriculum?

Arts integration is the investigation of curricular content through artistic explorations, where the arts provide an avenue for rigorous investigation, representation, expression, and reflection of both curricular content and the art form itself (Diaz, Donovan, and Pascale 2006). This book provides teachers with concrete strategies to integrate the arts across the curriculum. Arts-integration strategies are introduced with contextual information about the art form (storytelling, drama, poetry, music, visual arts, and creative movement).

The Importance of Arts Integration *(cont.)*

Each art form provides you with innovative strategies to help students fully engage with and connect to different content areas. Storytelling connects us with our roots in the oral tradition and can heighten students' awareness of the role of story in their lives. Drama challenges students to explore multiple perspectives of characters, historical figures, and scientists. Poetry invites students to build a more playful, fresh relationship with written and spoken language. Music develops students' ability to listen, to generate a sense of community, and communicate and connect aurally. Visual art taps into students' ability to observe critically, envision, think through metaphor, and build visual literacy in a world where images are pervasive. Creative movement encourages students to embody ideas and work conceptually.

Providing students with the opportunity to investigate curriculum and express their understanding with the powerful languages of the arts will deepen their understanding, heighten their curiosity, and bring forward their voices as they interact more fully with content and translate their ideas into new forms. This book is a beginning, a "way in."

We invite you to see all this for yourself by bringing the strategies shared in this book to your classroom and watching what happens. We hope this resource leaves you looking for deeper experiences with the arts for both you and your students.

. . . .

"Early-career teachers attribute much of their differentiation ability to the arts-integration class. They also report the joy it brings to both teaching and learning, even within a crowded instructional day."

—Jamie Hipp and Margaret-Mary Sulentic Dowell (2021, para. 8)

. . . .

What Does It Mean to Integrate the Arts?

We believe that a vital path to encouraging students to become literate in the twenty-first century is the integration of the English language arts and the arts. Active involvement in the arts can help students develop and use creative and purposeful expression in language, explore different perspectives, and internalize new ideas and ways of thinking. Yellin, Jones, and DeVries assert that critical comprehension happens when the reader is "able to integrate [their] own thinking with the information from the text," giving them the opportunity to visualize events in the text and to "respond creatively through art, music, drama, and writing" (2007).

Listening, speaking, reading, writing, viewing, and visual representation are important components of the English language arts (Yellin, Jones, and DeVries 2007). Skills in reading, writing, speaking, listening, language, and media and technology determine what it means to be literate in the twenty-first century. Albers and Harste make the point that "in light of this changing world of texts and the diverse student population, there is a need to redefine literacy" (2007, 8).

Mary Clare Powell, poet and former director of the Lesley University Creative Arts Division, agrees, noting that "the arts help teachers become multilingual, because the arts are many languages. You can say things in music that you cannot translate into words: when you dance a concept, it is not the same as when you speak about it. The visual arts are their own particular language, not a shortcut for words" (1997).

This book harnesses the power of the arts to provide you with engaging strategies to help students access curriculum, explore content, and represent their learning. We will guide you in the use of the arts and provide a context in which language arts ideas take shape and deepen, while the arts inform and enrich the lives of your

The Importance of Arts Integration *(cont.)*

students. We do not want you to do this in a tangential manner or just on an enrichment basis. Rather, we want you to use arts integration as an approach to teaching the most prevalent standards in your English language arts curriculum and to do so frequently. In teaching ideas through artistic explorations, you will help your students develop skills and knowledge in both disciplines. We will share strategies that are flexible enough to be used across content strands and grade levels.

> The arts can lead to "deep learning" in which students are more genuinely engaged with academic content, spend more time on task, and take ownership of their learning.
>
> —Kerrie Bellisario and Lisa Donovan with Monica Prendergast (2012)

Why Should I Integrate the Arts?

Reading, along with mathematics, continues to dominate classroom instruction and mandated assessments. Government-led initiatives such as the Common Core State Standards and No Child Left Behind underscore the importance of English language arts skills throughout all subject areas. Teachers of all subjects share the responsibility and have a role in this interdisciplinary approach to teaching literacy. With our curriculum dominated by reading and mathematics, little room is left for the arts. Yet as educators, we want to teach the whole child. Students need both the arts and academic disciplines. Research suggests that academic achievement may be linked to the arts (Kennedy 2006). As Douglas Reeves notes, "the challenge for school leaders is to offer every student a rich experience with the arts without sacrificing the academic opportunities students need" (2007, 80). By integrating the arts with English language arts, we place language arts ideas within rich settings and provide students with access to the arts. In fact, the arts can lead to "deep learning," in which students are more genuinely engaged with academic content, spend more time on task, and take ownership of their learning (Bellisario and Donovan with Prendergast 2012).

The Importance of Arts Integration *(cont.)*

Rinne et al. (2011) identify several ways in which arts integration improves long-term retention through elaboration, enactment, and rehearsal. Specifically, when learners create and add details to their own visual models, dramatize a concept or skill, sing a song repeatedly, or rehearse for a performance, they increase the likelihood that they will remember what they have learned. This retention lasts over time, not just during the span of the unit. Through arts integration, students eagerly revisit, review, rehearse, edit, and work through ideas repeatedly and in authentic ways as they translate ideas into new forms.

As brain research deepens our understanding of how learning takes place, educators have come to better appreciate the importance of the arts. The arts support communication, emotional connections, community, and higher-order thinking. They also are linked to increased academic achievement, especially among at-risk students. Eric Jensen (2001) argues that "the arts enhance the process of learning. The systems they nourish, which include our integrated sensory, attentional, cognitive, emotional, and motor capabilities, are, in fact, the driving forces behind all other learning." Lessons and activities that integrate English language arts and the arts provide a rich environment in which all students can explore English language arts ideas—particularly those students who need new ways to access curriculum and express understanding. These lessons and activities also provide another source of motivation.

Teaching through the arts provides authentic differentiated learning for every student in the classroom. As former director of Harvard's Mind, Brain, and Education program Todd Rose (2012) notes, all learners learn in variable ways. The Center for Applied Special Technology (n.d.) suggests that in meeting the needs of variable learners, educators should expand their teaching to provide universal design. That is, teachers should include strategies that "are flexible and responsive to the needs of all learners" by providing "multiple means of engagement, methods of presentation of content and multiple avenues for expression of understanding." The integration of the arts provides opportunities to address all three universal design principles.

For example, the process of enacting a scene from a text provides a meaningful opportunity for metacognition, or "what a child knows about [their] own thinking and how the child is able to monitor that thinking" (Yellin, Jones, and DeVries 2007). Imagine students who, as they prepare to enact a scene from a book, determine what parts of the reading are unclear, go back through the text and reread, visualize the events, and visualize themselves performing the scene. Arts integration benefits students not only by deepening their connection to content and fostering interdisciplinary learning in the arts and English language arts but also by promoting what the Partnership for 21st Century Learning (2019) researchers note as the 4 Cs: creativity, critical thinking, communication, and collaboration. Arts integration brings these significant benefits to learning and engages teachers and students in curiosity, imagination, and passion for learning.

Arts and the Standards

Connections to College and Career Ready Standards

College and Career Ready Standards for English Language Arts (2010) include seven descriptions that characterize the "literate individual." Through the standards in reading, writing, speaking, listening, and language, students exhibit the following capacities:

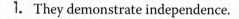

1. They demonstrate independence.

2. They build strong content knowledge.

3. They respond to the varying demands of audience, task, purpose, and discipline.

4. They comprehend as well as critique.

5. They value evidence.

6. They use technology and digital media strategically and capably.

7. They come to understand other perspectives and cultures.

These practices are intended to be interwoven with the content standards and can be thought of as the habits of mind we want to develop in our students. As students represent English language arts ideas in artistic forms, they are involved in applying and demonstrating these seven capacities.

Artistic Habits of Mind

In addition to language arts habits of mind, arts integration will help students develop artistic habits of mind (Hetland et al. 2007). With these habits of mind, students will be able to:

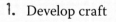

1. Develop craft

2. Engage and persist

3. Envision

4. Express

5. Observe

6. Reflect

7. Stretch and explore

8. Understand the art world

Although these habits were identified in an investigation of visual arts practices, they are relevant for the practice of all the arts.

The skills that the arts develop are valued in every field. The arts develop these skills naturally as students explore and translate ideas into artistic forms. Researcher Lois Hetland notes that "it is these qualities—intrinsic to the arts—that are valued in every domain but not necessarily taught in those subjects in school. That's what makes the arts such potent resources for teaching valued dispositions— what the arts teach well is not used uniquely in the arts but is valuable across a wide spectrum of contexts" (2009, 37).

Arts and the Standards *(cont.)*

Classroom Environment

Whether you are in a virtual learning space or face-to-face, a safe classroom environment is vital for language arts ideas and artistic expressions to flourish. Learners must feel comfortable to make mistakes, critique the work of others, and celebrate success. Think back to groups to which you have presented new ideas or creative works. How did you feel as you waited for their reactions? What was it about their behavior that made you feel more or less comfortable? What was it about your thinking that made you feel more or less safe? Such reflections will lead you to ways you can help students feel more comfortable sharing their ideas. As teachers, we must be role models for our students as we model our willingness to take risks and engage in new ways of learning. You will find that the arts by their nature invite risk taking, experimentation, and self-discipline, as well as encourage the development of a supportive learning community.

Developing a learning community in which learners support and respect one another takes time, but there are things you can do to help support its development:

- **Establish clear expectations for respect.** Respect is nonnegotiable. As students engage in creative explorations, it is crucial that they honor one another's ideas, invite all voices to the table, and discuss the work in ways that value each contribution. Self-discipline and appreciation for fellow students' creative work are often beneficial outcomes of arts integration (Bellisario and Donovan with Prendergast 2012). Take time for students to brainstorm ways in which they can show one another respect and react when they feel they have not been respected. Work with students to create guidelines for supporting the creative ideas of others and agree to uphold them as a group.

- **Explore several icebreakers** during the first weeks of school that encourage students to get to know one another informally and begin to discover interests they have in common. As students learn more about one another, they develop a sense of themselves as individuals and as a classroom unit and are more apt to want to support one another. Using fun, dynamic warm-ups not only helps students get their brains working but also builds a sense of community and support for risk taking.

- **Tell students the ways in which you are engaged in learning new ideas.** Talk about your realizations and challenges along the way, and demonstrate your own willingness to take risks and persevere.

- **Find ways to support the idea that we all can act, draw, sing, rhyme, and so forth.** Avoid saying negative things about your own art or language arts skill levels, and emphasize your continuous growth.

- **Draw out students' ideas by asking open-ended questions.** Ask how, why, in what ways? These prompts encourage students to articulate, refocus, or clarify their own thinking.

- **Encourage risk taking.** Give students the experiences they need to build confidence and express themselves in new ways. Encourage students to reflect on their own goals and whether they think they have met them.

- **Emphasize process over product.** Enormous learning and discovery take place during the creative process. This is as significant as the final product and often even more so.

How This Book Is Organized

Strategies

The strategies and model lessons in this book are organized within six art modalities:

1. Storytelling
2. Drama
3. Poetry
4. Music
5. Visual Arts
6. Creative Movement

Within each modality, five strategies are presented that integrate that art form with the teaching of language arts. The strategies are not intended as an exhaustive list but rather as exemplary ways to integrate the arts into language arts.

Although we have provided a model lesson for each strategy, these strategies are flexible and can be used in a variety of ways across a variety of content areas. These models will give you the opportunity to try out the ideas with students and envision many other ways to adapt these strategies for use in your teaching. For example, we explore painter Georgia O'Keeffe's decision to move to New York City in our drama strategy of monologues, but you may prefer to integrate the monologue strategy with other areas of language arts, such as the exploration of a historical character's decision during a significant world history event. The strategy of found poetry can be used to explore primary source letters, photographs, oral histories, the environment around us, and more. As you become familiar and comfortable with using the strategies, you may combine a variety of them across the art modalities within a lesson.

For example, you might have students begin with writing a monologue but then draw out words and phrases to create a poem that distills the main ideas the character is exploring or create a movement phrase that depicts twists and turns in the monologue. The goal is to make the choices that best fit you and your students.

How This Book Is Organized *(cont.)*

Organization of the Lessons

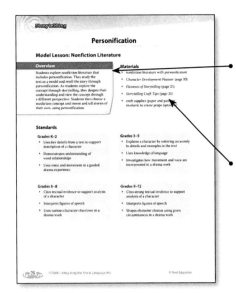

Each model lesson begins with an **overview**, followed by the list of standards addressed. Note that the standards involve equal rigor for both language arts and the arts.

A list of **materials** you will need is provided.

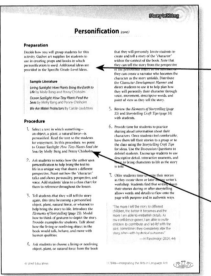

A **preparation** section follows with ways you can better ensure a successful learning investigation. Ideas may relate to grouping students, using props to engage learners, or practicing readings with dramatic flair.

The **procedure** section provides step-by-step directions on how to implement the model lesson.

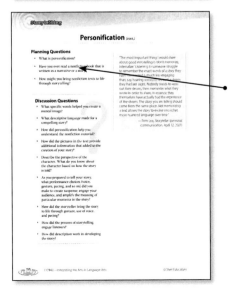

Each model lesson includes **questions** that you can ask as students work. The questions serve to highlight students' reasoning in language arts, stimulate their artistic thinking, or debrief their experience.

How This Book Is Organized (cont.)

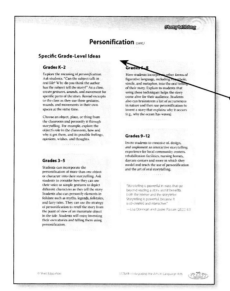

Organization of the Lessons (cont.)

Specific grade-level ideas follow with suggestions on how to better meet the needs of students within the K–2, 3–5, 6–8, and 9–12 grade levels. They may also suggest other ways to explore or extend the ideas in the model lesson at these levels. Read all of the sections, as an idea written for a different grade span may suggest something you want to do with students.

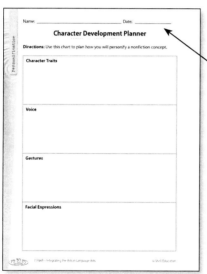

Reproducibles are provided for all applicable model lessons. Often in the form of graphic organizers, the reproducibles are designed to help students brainstorm ideas, organize and record their thinking, or reflect on their learning. Reproducibles are also available as digital downloads in PDF form (see page 260).

How This Book Is Organized (cont.)

How to Use the Lessons

These strategies can be used to teach language arts in any K–12 classroom with any language arts curriculum. A strategy lesson can be implemented as a way to deepen or expand the exploration of a topic, or, if you have the flexibility, expanded to several days or a week. You may choose to use the strategy lesson within your language arts lesson, in combination with time assigned to the arts, or when considering storytelling or poetry, perhaps in conjunction with other content areas.

You may wish to focus on one art form at a time to help yourself become familiar with using that art modality to teach language arts. Or you may want to look through the content index and explore models that relate to what you are teaching now or are about to teach. Over time, you will become familiar with the strategies and find that you choose to integrate them on a regular basis. If integrating arts and language arts is new to you, consider working with another teacher to explore the ideas together. Collaborate with teachers of art, dance, drama, or music in your school system to draw from their expertise in deepening the artistic work.

Working with Text Sets

We know the power of mentor texts and have recommended books that work well with particular strategies within each lesson, and we also encourage you to draw from a variety of texts such as newspapers, web-based resources, cooking recipes, and primary and secondary sources. Think of artistic work as text, as it provides worlds to be explored (e.g., painting, musical scores, plays, choreographed work, and poems). This gives students the opportunity to engage with a variety of complex texts. Engaging in the arts promotes the kind of "close reading" that complex text requires (Varlas 2012).

For each lesson, we encourage working with text sets and resources from multiple genres and modalities. Cappiello and Dawes (2013) discuss "multimodal, multigenre" text sets, explaining that a text set draws from various modalities, including print, audio, photographs, artifacts, webcams, and podcasts. By multigenre, they suggest diverse forms of writing, such as blogs, in addition to traditional genres, such as books and magazines. Text sets may include nonfiction, fiction, poetry, and more to present a wide view of one topic and the approaches of multiple authors.

The recommended resources on the following page are filled with book suggestions and ideas.

How This Book Is Organized (cont.)

Recommended Resources

1. *The Classroom Bookshelf:* A *School Library Journal* Blog

www.theclassroombookshelf.com

This site is an absolute treasure trove of current book reviews for children's and young adult literature. Every review features teaching ideas and related grade-level resources, focusing on "literacy in diverse contexts" to help students learn about the world around them. Cocreators Dr. Mary Ann Cappiello, Dr. Erika Thulin Dawes, and Dr. Grace Enriquez, along with Dr. Katie Cunningham and Dr. Denise Dávila, reveal the many ways teachers can use "multigenre, multimodal print and digital texts" as they plan their lessons and units together to inspire learning in and out of the classroom.

2. **Teaching with Trade Books**

www.teachingwithtradebooks.com/home

This resource, for pre-K–12 educators and librarians, is amazing for many reasons (the inclusion of webinars, blogs, articles, book reviews, resources in children's and young adult literature, and more). We especially appreciate the following two items in relation to choosing books for the lessons in this text: the comprehensive list of websites featuring award-winning texts, curated by cocreators of this website, Dr. Mary Ann Cappiello and Dr. Erika Thulin Dawes, and the text set resources that provide groups of multimodal, multigenre text around related topics such as the text sets called *Monarch Butterfly Text Set, New York City Tree Text Set, Text Sets on Artists and Art*, and more.

3. **Library of Congress**

www.loc.gov

This is our go-to website for including primary sources about any and every topic in our arts-integrated lessons! The immense offering of digital collections is such a gift for teachers and learners. There are many items specifically created for educators, such as Teacher Resources, Lesson Plans, Primary Source sets (including examples created for specific grade levels and topics), and Professional Development. We especially appreciate the primary source text set on Found Poetry—which presents suggested images, letters, music, and more by subject— the thinking behind using primary sources in your classroom, creating found poetry with the primary sources, and more.

4. **Academy of American Poets**

www.poets.org

This incredible website features a wide variety of poems and poets; *Poem-a-Day; National Poetry Month; American Poets* magazine; and many resources geared specifically toward teachers, including *Teach This Poem* and *Materials for Teachers*. Be sure to watch the video called "A Teacher's Guide to Poets.org," in which Richard Blanco—poet and education ambassador for the Academy of American Poets—shares an inspiring talk to welcome you into the world of resources on this website.

5. **Poetry Foundation**

www.poetryfoundation.org

Here you will find a wide variety of poems, poets, collections, *Poem of the Day*, articles, podcasts, videos, and more. For example, the collection called *Poems on Immigration* includes the topics of immigration and immigrant life, poems about refugees and exile, poems on borders and crossings, articles, audio, and video. In the "History and Mission" section of this invaluable website, the independent organization seeks to "discover and celebrate the best poetry and to place it before the largest possible audience." The Poetry Foundation also publishes *Poetry* magazine.

How This Book Is Organized *(cont.)*

6. Poetry Out Loud

www.poetryoutloud.org

You and your students can watch recitation videos of, and listen to, poets performing poetry out loud. This website also features the lesson plans for teachers such as *Line Dancing*, in which students explore how line breaks in poetry affect the performance out loud; collections of poems by theme such as feathered friends, historical poems, cityscapes, and more. We especially appreciate the *Tips on Reciting* section and the expansive glossary called *Poetic Terms*.

7. The Poem Farm

www.poemfarm.amylv.com

Poet Amy Ludwig VanDerwater is the creator of this exciting resource. As Amy states on her website, "the Poem Farm is a safe place for students to explore poems, and it's a place for teachers to find poetry teaching ideas." We especially appreciate how students can search for collections of poems by topic (poems about making things, poems about writing, memory poems, and so on) and for collections of poems that feature a technique (personification, alliteration, repetition, interesting endings, and more). This gives students an opportunity to immerse themselves in an expiration of craft and meaning. Also featured are peeks into notebooks and visual journals from a wide variety of writers.

8. Museum Websites (local, regional, national, international)

Bring the collections and ideas of your local museum, and museums beyond, into your arts-integrated lessons in this book. Museum websites present digital works of art ranging from paintings, photographs, sculptures, historical artifacts, and much more. We invite you to visit *School Library Journal's* blog *The Classroom Bookshelf* and find the blog entry called "Using Online Museum Resources for Literacy Learning" to explore how to fully access the wealth of resources in museums during virtual and in-person learning.

9. Google Arts and Culture

artsandculture.google.com

This global resource brings art from over two thousand museums to your laptop. The site includes virtual tours of museums, exhibitions, and artist collections. We especially appreciate the quick access to diverse artists and traditions that can fuel student research, provide rich artistic work to enhance any curriculum, and enhance a variety of teaching resources.

10. Jacob's Pillow Archives: Dance Interactive and Online Database

www.jacobspillow.org/archives

This robust offering of online archives, videos, essays, and podcasts documents the history of dance at Jacob's Pillow. The site provides access to "documentation of the ongoing activities of Jacob's Pillow and Audience Engagement programing" including exhibitions and talks that explore various aspects of dance history. We especially appreciate access to footage of dance through the Jacob's Pillow Dance Interactive. This resource documents "hundreds of artists who have appeared at the Pillow from the 1930s to the present day, . . . and offers carefully-chosen excerpts from the Archives' extensive video collection accompanied by contextual information, plus an extensive section of multimedia essays that include talks, photos, and other exclusive content organized into various themes."

How This Book Is Organized (cont.)

Assessment

"Data-driven decision-making," "documentation of learning," and "meeting benchmarks" are all phrases that refer to assessment practices embedded in our schools. Assessment has become a time-consuming activity for all involved in education, and yet the time and effort spent does not always yield what is needed to improve learning. As you think about how to assess lessons and activities that integrate language arts and the arts, it is important to stop and consider how to best use assessment to increase learning for students. Chances are that in addressing that goal you also will be documenting learning in ways that can be shared with students, parents, administrators, and other interested stakeholders.

We encourage you to focus on formative assessment—that is, assessment that is incorporated throughout the process of learning. This assessment will inform your instructional decisions during the process of teaching. The purpose of this assessment is to provide feedback for learners and teachers along the way, in addition to feedback at the end. As such, we are interested in the data we collect during the learning process as well as after it is completed. The goals are to make the learning process visible, to determine the depth of understanding, and to note the process the students undergo as they translate their knowledge of language arts into an art form or explore language arts ideas through the arts.

There are a variety of tools you can use to gather data to support your instructional decision-making:

■ **Ask questions to draw out, clarify, and probe students' thinking.** The questions in each strategy section will provide you with ideas on which you can elaborate. Use questioning to make on-the-spot adjustments to your plans as well as to identify learning moments as they are unfolding. This can be as simple as posing a new question or as complex as bringing a few students together for a mini-lesson.

■ **Walk around with a clipboard or notebook to capture students' comments and your own observations.** Too often we think we will remember students' words only to find ourselves unable to reproduce them at a later time. These annotations will allow you to note patterns within a student's remarks or among students' comments. They can suggest misconceptions that provide you with an entry to the next day's work. For example, you might share a comment such as, "Yesterday, some of you wondered whether a reader has to read nonfiction text in sequential order. Let's explore that today."

■ **Use the graphic organizers in the model lessons as support for the creative process.** Using these forms, have students brainstorm ideas for their artistic product and language arts connections. These organizers provide a snapshot of students' thinking at various points in the creative process and create opportunities for teachers to collect evidence of their learning from various perspectives (student planning, reflection and synthesis, peer review, and teacher observation) as well as documentation at different stages of the learning process (planning, implementation of ideas, review of work, revision, and so on).

■ **Use a camera to document student learning.** Each of the strategies leads to a creative product but not necessarily one that provides a tangible artifact or one that fits on a standard sheet of paper. Use a digital camera to take numerous pictures that can capture, for example, a piece of visual art at various stages of development or the gestures

How This Book Is Organized (cont.)

actors and storytellers use in their dramatic presentations. Similarly, use video to capture planning sessions, group discussions, and final presentations. In addition to documenting learning, collecting such evidence helps students reflect back on their learning. Consider developing a learning portfolio for students that they can review and add to over time.

- **Recognize that each strategy not only leads to a final creative product, but the creative processes leading to final work are laden with evidence of learning.** Comparisons can be made across products to note student growth.

- **Make students an integral part of the assessment process.** Provide students with opportunities to reflect on their work. For example, have students choose artifacts to include in their portfolio and explain the reasons for their choices. Have students reflect on their work as a class. Encourage discussion of artistic work to not only draw out what students have learned in their own creative process but also how and what they learned from the work of their peers. In this way students teach and learn from one another.

- **Design rubrics that help you organize your assessment data.** A well-crafted rubric can help you gather data more quickly as well as increase the likelihood that you are being equitable in your evaluation of assessment data. Select criteria to assess learning in language arts as well as in the art form, because arts integration supports equal rigor both in content and in the arts.

Arts integration deepens learning both in the content area being explored and in the art form being used. In a third-grade classroom at the Sumner School in Roslindale, Massachusetts, students were exploring character traits during a lesson about Amelia Earhart. First, students read a series of texts based on the life of this groundbreaking female pilot. Next, they were asked to consider text-to-self connections by creating a frozen sculpture with their bodies (the tableaux strategy), showing a character trait they felt represented some aspect of them. This generated a sense of the relevance of character traits and teased out a wide range of personalities and qualities. Students thought hard about what might represent their individual character traits and were thoroughly engrossed in sharing their own traits as well as considering the traits of their peers. Next, students formed small groups and brainstormed character traits of Amelia Earhart. They analyzed the texts for evidence of these traits, eagerly revisiting the text as they planned which scene they would create to demonstrate the trait in action. When set to the task, the room was abuzz with conversation about what scene would best bring to life the selected traits.

As students made choices about how to bring their ideas to life through images, the conversation moved between ideas about intangible concepts such as bravery and how these ideas could be translated into specific images. Each group created a tableau scene depicting a moment when the character trait was exemplified. The still images they created included vivid scenes from the text.

Soundscapes is another strategy to engage learners. Students in a third-grade classroom explored the concept of setting in *The Tin Forest* by Helen Ward. The teacher told students that she would be reading the text aloud without showing the pictures just yet, and she asked them to create mental images and imagine the sounds, smells, tastes, sensations, and memories that were triggered as they listened. Next, the teacher

How This Book Is Organized *(cont.)*

asked students to share some of their mental images and recall specific words from the text that allowed them to imagine the scene, such as strong verbs, snapshots (Lane 1992), thoughtshots (Lane 1992), similes, and metaphors.

Next, the teacher shared the rich and evocative illustrations by Chris Anderson, and students mined the images for details that deepened their comprehension. For the opening scene of the book, students shared a wide range of responses:

Sounds: beats of sad music; the sound of metal scraping; the sound of digging—a shovel against soil; the sounds of the old man's deep sighs

Tastes: taste of rust and smoke-filled air

Smells: heavy, slow-moving, smoke-filled air

Sensations: the feeling of cold, damp weather on skin; pinpricks of rain; wet soil; damp paper

Images: gray landscape filled with metal pieces of all sizes, wires, electronic devices; potato peelings, half-eaten food; a ramshackle shed; a hunched-over, wrinkled man of 101 years; images of corrugated tin rooftops

Following this exploration, students were asked to identify found objects with which to create a soundscape that would establish a sense of place in the story.

Students collected a wide range of materials: aluminum foil to be scrunched, a metal grater with a spoon for banging and scraping, rustling paper to make soft rain sounds, shoes to make footsteps, and a bucket of soil and a small spade to create the sound of digging. Also included in the soundscape was the sound of soft claps and vocal sounds that simulated the crackle of a fire.

Three groups created soundscapes to illuminate different moments in the story. Then, as the teacher read the text again, the students performed their soundscapes as their setting was introduced, while the rest of the class experienced the story and soundscape with eyes closed.

"I felt like I was there!" one student exclaimed at the end of the story. "The sounds totally made me feel the place," said another.

As there are so many aspects of this task to capture, a rubric can be quite helpful. A suggested rubric is provided in the Digital Resources (see page 260). Observation protocols help teachers document evidence of student learning, something all teachers must do. A variety of forms could be used, and it is not possible to include all areas that you might attend to in an interdisciplinary lesson. Two suggested forms are included in the Digital Resources (see page 260). For more guidance on assessment, see *Integrating the Arts Across the Curriculum, Second Edition*, by Lisa Donovan and Louise Pascale (2022).

Correlation to the Standards

Shell Education is committed to producing educational materials that are research and standards based. To support this effort, this resource is correlated to the academic standards of all 50 United States, the District of Columbia, the Department of Defense Dependent Schools, and the Canadian provinces. A correlation is also provided for key professional development organizations.

How to Find Standards Correlations

To print a customized correlation report for your state, visit our website at **www.tcmpub.com /administrators/correlations** and follow the online directions. If you require assistance in printing correlation reports, please contact the Customer Service Department at 1-800-858-7339.

Purpose and Intent of Standards

The Every Student Succeeds Act (ESSA) mandates that all states adopt challenging academic standards that help students meet the goal of college and career readiness. While many states already adopted academic standards prior to ESSA, the act continues to hold states accountable for detailed and comprehensive standards. Standards are designed to focus instruction and guide adoption of curricula. They define the knowledge, skills, and content students should acquire at each level. Standards also are used to develop standardized tests to evaluate students' academic progress. State standards are used in the development of our resources, so educators can be assured they meet state academic requirements.

College and Career Readiness

Today's college and career readiness (CCR) standards offer guidelines for preparing K–12 students with the knowledge and skills necessary to succeed in postsecondary job training and education. CCR standards include the Common Core State Standards as well as other state-adopted standards, such as the Texas Essential Knowledge and Skills. The standards listed on the lessons describe the content presented throughout the lessons.

Storytelling

Storytelling

Understanding Storytelling

Storytelling has been part of every culture since the beginning of time (Norfolk, Stenson, and Williams 2006). Stories have been used to educate, inspire, and entertain. There is the story itself, and then there is the telling of the tale by a skilled teller. Storytellers use language, gesture, eye contact, tone, and inflection as they share a story with an audience. A good storyteller can create a sense of instant community among listeners as well as a deep connection with the material being explored (Hamilton and Weiss 2005). Because the storyteller interacts with the audience as the story is told, listeners often feel they become part of the story world. Connections with characters are developed and empathy is established. Scharner (2019) notes, "We are wired for stories. It's how our brain prefers to receive information" (para. 2). If you've ever heard a good storyteller tell a compelling story, you know it can transport you to another time and place.

In the strategies that follow, students benefit both from listening to stories and from becoming storytellers themselves. As listeners, students are supported in their visualization of the stories, which makes a narrative easier to both imagine and remember (Donovan and Pascale 2022). As storytellers, students develop additional skills, including skilled use of voice, improved verbal and nonverbal communication skills, and sense of pacing. Once stories are developed, you also can ask students to write them down, further enhancing their literacy skills.

When students become storytellers, they fine-tune their communication skills. Oral fluency is developed as students explore vocal tone and inflection, pacing, sound effects, and the addition of rich sensory details to the telling. Listeners feel invited on a journey. Participating in the creation and telling of stories brings forward students' voices and their ideas.

Students find that stories provide vivid contexts that invite them into the world of the story. Characters are brought to life and interact with the audience through questions, eye contact, and the weaving of a believable tale.

"The benefits [of storytelling] are enormous. These can include increased enthusiasm for reading, focused engagement and improved listening skills, as well as the development of creative thinking and imagination" (Panckridge 2020, 44). As students create, tell, and retell stories, they also gain fluency in their communication skills, use of descriptive language, and persuasive abilities. They also expand their willingness to revisit, revise, and polish their work.

Elements of Storytelling

There are five key elements to storytelling (National Storytelling Network, n.d.). To learn more about these elements, visit **storynet.org/ what-is-storytelling/**.

- **Interaction:** The storyteller actively engages the audience and adapts based on the energy and response of the audience. As a result, every time the story is told it changes.

- **Words:** The storyteller uses words (spoken, signed, or manual) to create connections and invite listeners into the story world through sensory details.

- **Actions:** The story is activated through vocalization, physical movement, and small and large gestures.

- **Story:** The storyteller shares a narrative that has characters and action.

- **Imagination:** Storytellers encourage the active imagination of the listeners.

Storytelling (cont.)

Strategies for Storytelling

Personification

Some people describe assigning human qualities to inanimate objects or ideas as *personification* and assigning human qualities to animals as *anthropomorphism*. Other folks use these terms interchangeably. We will use *personification* to refer to all such assignments of human characteristics, as it is most familiar to teachers and students. However, you should feel free to use what best fits your curriculum. Personification is an ancient storytelling tool that continues today; think of both Aesop and the *Toy Story* movies (Cahill 2006). Stories that give animals and objects human traits allow listeners to think about their shortcomings in a safe way and invite us to think about moral or ethical values. When students personify elements of the natural world, such as the sun in a nonfiction narrative, they explore nonfiction concepts from multiple perspectives. These tales engage learners and allow us to consider different perspectives. Because animals and objects take on human characteristics, the strategy also lends itself to figurative language.

Exaggeration

It is human nature to exaggerate to make our stories more interesting. Often we hear someone's story and have the desire to top it with something bigger, better, or more grandiose from our own treasure trove of experiences. Storytellers use exaggeration to emphasize their points and pique the interest of their audiences. In fact, storyteller Jim Green identifies hyperbole as a tool in the storyteller's toolbox (Wohlberg 2012). Exaggeration also provides a way for students to explore unbelievable nonfiction facts.

In this strategy, exaggeration can be enhanced by the inclusion of incorrect language arts information, providing a vehicle for further developing students' understanding of language arts concepts. As in other techniques, embedding concepts related to language arts in a story gives students the opportunity to experience a context in which knowledge of language arts is useful.

> "I cannot emphasize enough the importance of a pause. Placed at strategic moments of the oral storytelling, a pause can enrapture the audience and make them eager to find out what happens next."
>
> —Srividhya Venkat (2020)

The Untold Story

In this strategy, students are asked to consider the fact that every story is told from a particular perspective. In foregrounding one vantage point, the viewpoints of others are minimized, marginalized, or even left out. Perspective taking is critical to students' social development, and "understanding the perspective of others is an important skill that benefits children in their complex reasoning abilities that are important in math problems, such as story problems" (Heagle and Rehfeldt 2006, 32). The untold story strategy asks students to consider whose perspective is prominent in a story and what voices or concepts are missing. Inviting students to begin to look for the missing voices or ideas can develop critical thinking skills and empathy.

Storytelling *(cont.)*

Retelling

Storytelling is an oral tradition that is grounded in telling and retelling stories. With each retelling, a story grows more polished and more dramatic, with clear high points and striking moments. Students become more responsive to working with listeners and more adept at using the storytelling process to spark the imagination of the audience. This revisiting of stories also strengthens students' writing skills, as stories get honed and more richly detailed with each retelling.

Students can use the plot of a story as a flexible frame, improvising as the story unfolds. This builds comprehension skills and gives students the opportunity to feel free to adapt the stories based on the response of listeners, dwelling longer on a particular moment or adding embellishment when needed. This responsiveness heightens awareness of the role of an audience, which translates into writing.

> "The storytelling listener's role is to actively create the vivid, multi-sensory images, actions, characters, and events—the reality—of the story in [their] mind, based on the performance by the teller and on the listener's own past experiences, beliefs, and understandings."
>
> —National Storytelling Network (n.d., para. 14)

Collaborative Storytelling

Collaborative storytelling often takes place in kids' play (Hourcade et al. 2004) and has long been part of the cultural traditions of many families and communities (Coulter, Michael, and Poynor 2007). Students work together to build a story by adding short segments in their oral telling. Stories can be sparked by graphics, character traits, or settings. The story can be "passed" back and forth, with each teller adding details and information before passing it on to the next teller. A natural part of the process is a

series of twists and turns that challenge students to maintain a shared story strand, keeping a clear logic so that the story remains together as it unfolds. This challenges them to listen attentively to the details and choices so that they can build on the unfolding events in meaningful and compelling ways by pivoting off given details, such as character traits, circumstances, and action. Students introduce obstacles and innovative solutions that take the characters on surprising journeys. Yew (2005) notes that constructing knowledge through the collective creation of narratives can provide more effective ways of learning in group settings than learning concepts individually.

Personification

Model Lesson: Nonfiction Literature

Overview

Students explore nonfiction literature that includes personification. They study the text as a model and retell the story through personification. As students explore the concept through storytelling, they deepen their understanding and view the concept through a different perspective. Students then choose a nonfiction concept and invent and tell stories of their own, using personification.

Materials

▸ nonfiction literature with personification

▸ *Character Development Planner* (page 30)

▸ *Elements of Storytelling* (page 23)

▸ *Storytelling Craft Tips* (page 31)

▸ craft supplies (paper and paint or markers) to create props *(optional)*

Standards

Grades K–2

▸ Uses key details from a text to support description of a character

▸ Demonstrates understanding of word relationships

▸ Uses voice and movement in a guided drama experience

Grades 3–5

▸ Explains a character by referring accurately to details and examples in the text

▸ Uses knowledge of language

▸ Investigates how movement and voice are incorporated in a drama work

Grades 6–8

▸ Cites textual evidence to support analysis of a character

▸ Interprets figures of speech

▸ Uses various character objectives in a drama work

Grades 9–12

▸ Cites strong textual evidence to support analysis of a character

▸ Interprets figures of speech

▸ Shapes character choices using given circumstances in a drama work

Personification (cont.)

Preparation

Decide how you will group students for this activity. Gather art supplies for students to use in creating props and books in which personification is used. Additional ideas are provided in the Specific Grade-Level Ideas.

Sample Literature

Living Sunlight: How Plants Bring the Earth to Life by Molly Bang and Penny Chisholm

Ocean Sunlight: How Tiny Plants Feed the Seas by Molly Bang and Penny Chisholm

We Are Water Protectors by Carole Lindstrom

Procedure

1. Select a text in which something—an object, a plant, a natural force—is personified. Read the text to the students for enjoyment. In this procedure, we point to *Ocean Sunlight: How Tiny Plants Feed the Seas* by Molly Bang and Penny Chisholm.

2. Ask students to notice how the author uses personification to help bring the text to life in a unique way that shares a different perspective. Point out how the "character" talks and shows personality, perspective, and voice. Add students' ideas to a class chart for them to reference throughout the lesson.

3. Tell students that they will tell the story again, this time becoming a personified object, plant, natural force, or whatnot to help bring the story to life. Introduce the *Elements of Storytelling* (page 23). Model how to think of gestures to depict the story. Provide examples for students. Talk about how the living or nonliving object in the book would talk, behave, and move with human qualities.

4. Ask students to choose a living or nonliving object, plant, or natural force from the book that they will personify. Invite students to create and tell a story of the "character" within the context of the book. Note that they can tell the story from the perspective of the personified object as the narrator, or they can create a narrator who becomes the character as the story unfolds. Distribute the *Character Development Planner* and direct students to use it to help plan how they will personify their character through voice, movement, descriptive words, and point of view as they tell the story.

5. Review the *Elements of Storytelling* (page 23) and *Storytelling Craft Tips* (page 31) with students.

6. Provide time for students to practice sharing aloud information about their characters. Once students feel comfortable, have them tell their stories to a group or to the class using the *Storytelling Craft Tips* for ideas. Use the Discussion Questions to debrief students. Encourage students to use descriptive detail, interactive moments, and voice to bring characters to life as the story is told.

7. Offer students time to write their stories as they create them or later during writer's workshop. Students find that writing down their stories during or after storytelling allows words and details to flow onto the page with purpose and in authentic ways.

> "The more I tell the story to different children, the better it becomes and the more I am able to embellish details. As my confidence grows, I am able to invite children to contribute and 'ad-lib' with the plot. Sometimes they completely alter the story, often with hysterical outcomes."
>
> —Jo Panckridge (2020, 44)

Personification *(cont.)*

Planning Questions

- What is personification?

- Have you ever read a nonfiction book that is written as a narrative or a story?

- How might you bring nonfiction texts to life through storytelling?

Discussion Questions

▸ What specific words helped you create a mental image?

▸ What descriptive language made for a compelling story?

▸ How did personification help you understand the nonfiction material?

▸ How did the pictures in the text provide additional information that added to the creation of your story?

▸ Describe the perspective of the character. What do you know about the character based on how the story is told?

▸ As you prepared to tell your story, what performance choices (voice, gesture, pacing, and so on) did you make to create suspense, engage your audience, and amplify the meaning of particular moments in the story?

▸ How did the storyteller bring the story to life through gesture, use of voice, and pacing?

▸ How did the process of storytelling engage listeners?

▸ How did description work in developing the story?

"The most important thing I would share about good storytelling is 'don't memorize, internalize.' Listening to someone struggle to remember the exact words of a story they have memorized is much less engaging than, say, hearing someone recount a dream they had last night. Nobody needs to write out their dream, then memorize what they wrote in order to share. In essence, they themselves have actually had the experience of the dream. The story you are telling should come from the same place. Not memorizing a text allows the story to evolve into richer, more nuanced language over time."

—Tom Lee, Storyteller (personal communication, April 12, 2021)

Personification *(cont.)*

Specific Grade-Level Ideas

Grades K–2

Explore the meaning of *personification.* Ask students, "Can the subject talk in real life? Why do you think the author has the subject tell the story?" As a class, create gestures, sounds, and movement for specific parts of the story. Reread excerpts to the class as they use these gestures, sounds, and movements in their own spaces at the same time.

Choose an object, place, or thing from the classroom and personify it through storytelling. For example, explore the object's role in the classroom, how and why it got there, and its possible feelings, opinions, wishes, and thoughts.

Grades 3–5

Students can incorporate the personification of more than one object or character into their storytelling. Ask students to consider how they can use their voice or simple gestures to depict different characters as they tell the story. Students also can personify elements in folklore such as myths, legends, folktales, and fairy tales. They can use the strategy of personification to retell the story from the point of view of an inanimate object in the tale. Students will enjoy inventing their own stories and telling them using personification.

Grades 6–8

Have students incorporate other forms of figurative language, including hyperbole, simile, and metaphor, into the oral telling of their story. Explain to students that using these techniques helps the story come alive for their audience. Students also can brainstorm a list of occurrences in nature and then use personification to invent a story that explains why it occurs (e.g., why the ocean has waves).

Grades 9–12

Invite students to conceive of, design, and implement an interactive storytelling experience for local community centers, rehabilitation facilities, nursing homes, daycare centers and more in which they model and teach the use of personification and the art of oral storytelling.

"Storytelling is powerful in ways that go beyond reading a story, and it benefits both the listener and the storyteller. Storytelling is powerful, because it is co-created and interactive."

—Lisa Donovan and Louise Pascale (2022)

Name: _____ Date: _____

Character Development Planner

Directions: Use this chart to plan how you will personify a nonfiction concept.

Character Traits
Voice
Gestures
Facial Expressions

   117848—Integrating the Arts in Language Arts   © Shell Education

Name: _____ Date: _____

Storytelling Craft Tips

How to Engage the Audience

- Ask a question: "And what do you suppose happened next?!"

- Before the story, choose a gesture or phrase for each character. When the character is mentioned, listeners use the gesture. For example, when the cat appears, students hunch down, curl their backs, and say, "Wheeeeeere's my milk?"

- Invite classmates along the journey with you. "Get out your binoculars and come along!"

- Repeat lines to increase audience awareness and add dramatic interest.

- Allow your voice to hold emotion, reflecting what is happening as the story unfolds.

- Use facial expressions and eye contact to help the audience feel connected to the story.

- Pace your speech and add pauses for dramatic effect. Slowing down and speeding up language can intensify the story as the audience follows along.

- Use descriptive details to help the audience picture the story as it is being told.

Exaggeration

Model Lesson: Captivate Your Listeners

Overview

Storytellers have always used exaggeration to make stories more interesting, and having students recognize these embellishments is a critical skill. In this strategy, students will revisit familiar stories (ones they have read or written). They will then select two moments in the stories during which exaggeration can be used to draw listeners in; emphasize a point; create surprise, curiosity, disbelief, emotion, and so on. As students tell their stories, their peers will try to identify the exaggerations.

Materials

▸ familiar stories (picture books, short stories, personal stories, etc.)

▸ *Captivate Your Listeners* (page 35)

▸ *Elements of Storytelling* (page 23)

▸ *Storytelling Craft Tips* (page 31)

Standards

Grades K–2

▸ Uses key details from a text to support description of a character

▸ Participates in a shared writing project

▸ Contributes to the adaptation of the plot

▸ Uses and adapts sounds and movements

Grades 3–5

▸ Explains a character by referring accurately to details and examples in the text

▸ Produces clear and coherent writing with purposeful exaggeration

▸ Revises and improves an improvised or scripted drama/theater work

▸ Investigates how movement and voice are incorporated into drama/theater work

Grades 6–8

▸ Cites textual evidence to support analysis of a character

▸ Produces clear and coherent writing with purposeful exaggeration

▸ Articulates and examines choices to refine a scripted drama/theater work

▸ Develops effective physical and vocal traits of characters in a scripted drama/theater work

Grades 9–12

▸ Cites strong textual evidence to support analysis of what the text says explicitly as well as inferences drawn from the text

▸ Produces writing in which the development, organization, and style are appropriate to task, purpose, and audience

▸ Practices and revises a drama work using theatrical staging conventions

▸ Explores physical, vocal, and physiological choices to develop a performance that is believable, authentic, and relevant

Exaggeration (cont.)

Preparation

Gather examples of exaggeration and videos of storytellers using moments of exaggeration in their storytelling. Decide how to group students for this activity. Additional ideas are provided in the Specific Grade-Level Ideas. You might get prepared to tell students about the commonly known icebreaker game called "Two Truths and a Lie." You might share the following texts by Ammi-Joan Paquette and Laurie Ann Thompson: *Two Truths and a Lie: It's Alive!, Two Truths and a Lie: Forces of Nature* or *Two Truths and a Lie: Histories and Mysteries.*

Procedure

1. Tell students that one way to captivate an audience is to find moments in a story when you can add a line of exaggeration. This might be about the setting (for example, how tall the trees are, how hard the wind blew); the intensity of the character's feelings (for example, how curious a character is), and so on. Share examples of statements of exaggeration and discuss. Show a video of a storyteller using moments of exaggeration in their storytelling.

2. Share a familiar story with the class and model using your judgment to decide one place in the story where exaggeration would draw in the listeners. Work together with the class to find one more spot in the story. Ask, "What should we exaggerate next, and why?" Suggest adding one spoken line, scene, or description of exaggeration, and create the line together as a class.

3. Distribute *Captivate your Listeners* (page 35). Tell students that they will work in partnerships or small groups to revisit a story and add moments of exaggeration.

4. Allow time for students to add moments of exaggeration, plan their performances, and rehearse their storytelling. Share *Storytelling Craft Tips* (page 31) with students to help them with their storytelling. Remind them of the importance of voice and gesture in the development of characters and how they can create compelling moments through timing and sound effects.

5. As partners or small groups tell their stories to the class, invite the class to try and identify which two moments are exaggerated. Discuss the impact of the choices students made.

Discussion Questions

▸ What was convincing about the ways others told their stories?

▸ What storytelling techniques were used to tell the stories?

▸ As an audience member, how did you determine which two moments were exaggerated?

▸ What choices did you make in your own storytelling? What did you emphasize through exaggeration?

Exaggeration *(cont.)*

Specific Grade-Level Ideas

Grades K–2

Focus on choosing three spots for exaggeration: one in the beginning, one in the middle, and one at the end of a familiar story. Brainstorm lines of exaggeration as a class. As you retell the familiar story, stop during the chosen moments and invite the class to chime in with the exaggerations. Model using familiar language in the stories that students can recognize from their own conversations, such as, "I ran so fast that I . . ." or, "I was so hungry I thought I would . . ."

Grades 3–5

Introduce the term *hyperbole*, and talk about how exaggeration can be used to create emphasis or effect in stories. Talk about the examples of hyperbole that have become common expressions in our casual speech, such as "a million times" or "I have a ton of homework."

Grades 6–8

Have students use exaggeration to explore storytelling with nonfiction and interesting facts. After researching facts about a topic of study, students can create their own exaggerations of one of the facts and write a short story that includes the exaggeration. Peers will try to guess which one is the exaggeration. Discuss how exaggeration affects the telling of a story in terms of detail and description, emotional quality of the telling, pacing and use of silence, vocal intensity of the voice, and use of gesture. As students tell their stories in convincing ways, ask audience members to listen carefully to identify the exaggerations.

Grades 9–12

In addition to the idea for Grades 6-8, as students work to decide which facts are exaggerated and which facts are not, focus on the skills of collaborative discussion in which they build on the ideas of others and persuade to make their point.

Name: _____ Date: _____

Captivate Your Listeners

Directions: Choose two places in the story to add a line or two of exaggeration. Consider, how will this captivate your audience?

Title of Story: _____

Exaggeration #1	Storytelling Craft Ideas
_____	
_____	
_____	
_____	
_____	
_____	
_____	

Exaggeration #2	Storytelling Craft Ideas
_____	
_____	
_____	
_____	
_____	
_____	
_____	

The Untold Story

Model Lesson: Seek and Tell

Overview

In this strategy, students explore how stories are focused on main characters and how the perspectives of other characters are often minimized or left out as a result. The students mine a text for the untold story—for a character whose story is not developed—and they craft that character's side of the story, bringing to light an untold perspective. Students discover that untold stories also exist in visual texts such as paintings and photographs (untold stories in characters and in scenes) in addition to multiple genres of written text including poems, historical fiction, nonfiction literature, and more.

Materials

▸ text of choice

▸ chart paper

▸ *The Untold Story of . . .* (page 39)

▸ *Elements of Storytelling* (page 23)

▸ *Storytelling Craft Tips* (page 31)

Standards

Grades K–2

▸ Identifies who is telling the story and acknowledges differences in points of view

▸ Recalls key details

▸ Identifies ways in which voice and sounds may be used to retell a story

Grades 3–5

▸ Compares and contrasts the point of view from which different stories are narrated

▸ Refers to explicit details and examples from the text when drawing inferences

▸ Imagines how a character's inner thoughts impact the story and given circumstances

Grades 6–8

▸ Analyzes how an author develops and contrasts points of view

▸ Cites strong textual evidence to support inferences

▸ Develops a character by articulating the character's inner thoughts, objectives, and motivations

Grades 9–12

▸ Analyzes particular points of view, what is directly stated, and what is really meant

▸ Cites strong and thorough textual evidence to support inferences

▸ Develops a character by articulating the character's inner thoughts, objectives, and motivations

The Untold Story *(cont.)*

Preparation

Choose a text that pairs well with a topic you are studying in class and presents a character whose story is not developed. If using a visual text, you might want to choose one that depicts a scene that exists in the background beyond the main scene. Additional ideas are provided in the Specific Grade-Level Ideas.

Procedure

1. Ask students to consider a familiar story and think about which character's point of view is left out. Depending on your grade level, you might begin with a text that you have previously read aloud to the class. Ask students to imagine what a different character from the story might think or feel.

2. Ask students, "How might exploring another character's untold story help us as readers? How might we better understand a story by thinking about the other sides of the story that remain untold?" Discuss why it is important to assume there are untold perspectives. Ask, "How can exploring another perspective help us understand a story, topic, or time in history more fully?"

3. Share the text you selected. If you've chosen a lengthy text, choose one key scene that features the character whose story will be brought to light. Then, during a second reading, ask students to think about important details they hear about the setting, characters, and events. Record students' ideas on chart paper.

4. Have students select a character from the text whose perspective is not directly shared (for example, the librarian or son in *Dreamers* by Yuyi Morales). Discuss as a class how that character's perspective might differ from the main character's point of view.

5. Distribute copies of *The Untold Story of . . .* Place students into pairs. Have students select a character from the text and discuss what they think their selected character's perspective and experience might be. Have students sketch ideas and talk out their character's story. Use the Planning Questions to support students as they work.

6. Invite students to review *Elements of Storytelling* (page 23) and *Storytelling Craft Tips* (page 31) as they practice their stories. If possible, record students using available technology. Debrief, using the Discussion Questions.

Planning Questions

▸ What details from the text are inspiring you to tell your character's story?

▸ How do we use voice, gestures, and sense of timing to convey a story?

▸ When we are storytelling, how does the reaction of our listeners change the way we tell the story?

Discussion Questions

▸ Which character's story did you tell and why?

▸ What details from the original text did you include? Why?

▸ What did you learn about this character?

▸ What did you learn about the relationship between this character and the main character?

▸ How did hearing the performance change your understanding of the story?

▸ In what ways might you feel connected to the story or the characters? What created this sense of connection?

The Untold Story (cont.)

Specific Grade-Level Ideas

Grades K–2

Using familiar fairy tales, folktales, or poems, choose a secondary character and create the character's untold story as a class. You might use the beloved poem "Bleezer's Ice Cream" by Jack Prelutsky (**poets.org/poem/bleezers-ice-cream**) and invite students to tell the story of a character who visits Bleezer's ice cream store and has to decide which flavor to sample and why.

Grades 3–5

Gather a group of texts about one topic and include different genres and modalities (for example, a poem, a painting, an excerpt from a historical fiction text, an oral history). Give each small group of students one of the texts. Have each small group mine their given text for untold stories and invite them to craft the missing perspective together as a group. Then, as a class, compare and contrast the sources and stories brought to life. Students also might explore the untold stories of endangered creatures and give them voice in a call to action. Use a text such as *Sea Bear: A Journey for Survival* by Lindsay Moore as a jumping-off point.

> "A good storyteller makes sure the characters, their motivations, desires, and obstacles are always clear to the listener. Provide just enough detail to allow the listeners to create their own unique visualizations."
>
> —Tom Lee, Storyteller (personal communication, April 12, 2021)

Grades 6–8

Share author Chimamanda Ngozi Adichie's TED Talk, "The Danger of the Single Story." Discuss how Adichie uses the "phrase 'single stories' to describe the overly simplistic and sometimes false perceptions we form about individuals, groups, or countries" (**www.facinghistory. org/chunk/countering-single-story**).

Grades 9–12

Share the slogan "Nothing about us without us," and ask students what this suggests about the importance of untold stories. Discuss with students the importance of having all people share their perspectives ("nothing about us") and have a voice ("without us").

Have students choose a topic around social action and calls to action. Invite them to mine for the untold stories and bring them to life with storytelling.

Have students research the recipients of the ORACLE Award from the National Storytelling Network. Ask students to investigate why the storytellers have received the awards (enriching the storytelling culture of a region, building bridges among countries, and other reasons).

Name: _____ Date: _____

The Untold Story of...

Directions: Think about the elements of storytelling and storytelling tips. Sketch or jot ideas for your story below.

Retelling

Model Lesson: Folktales and Rich Cultural Histories

Overview

In this strategy, students work in small groups to practice the valuable skill of retelling. They choose from a collection of folktales inspired by different cultures. Students determine the most important aspects of the story and retell those parts, adding their own interpretation, language, voice, and gestures.

Materials

▸ grade-level appropriate folktales or myths

▸ *Retelling Plan* (page 43)

▸ *Elements of Storytelling* (page 23)

▸ *Storytelling Craft Tips* (page 31)

Standards

Grades K–2

▸ Retells a story, including key details

▸ Demonstrates understanding of the central message or lesson

▸ Uses movement and gestures to communicate emotion

Grades 3–5

▸ Provides a summary of a text

▸ Determines a central message or theme

▸ Uses physical and vocal exploration for character development

Grades 6–8

▸ Provides an objective summary of the text

▸ Determines a central message or theme and how it is developed

▸ Identifies and develops effective physical and vocal traits of a character

Grades 9–12

▸ Determines a theme or central idea of a text, and analyzes in detail its development over the course of the text, including how it emerges and is shaped and refined by specific details

▸ Provides an objective summary of the text

▸ Explores physical, vocal, and physiological choices to develop a performance that is believable, authentic, and relevant to a drama/theater work

Retelling (cont.)

Preparation

Gather a collection of folktales from various cultures. Scan the texts or use the internet to find additional information about the cultures represented in the folktales. Decide how students will research the culture by either gathering grade-level appropriate research materials or bookmarking helpful websites. Additional ideas are provided in the Specific Grade-Level Ideas.

Procedure

1. Discuss with students how folktales have been told and retold over time and how stories have been passed orally from generation to generation. Ask students, "Do you think the details of the story stay the same each time they are retold, or do they change? Explain your answer."

2. Explain that stories are retold across cultures for a variety of reasons—for entertainment, for education, to preserve history, to share tradition, to question, and to explain phenomena. Note that today they are going to experience storytelling through the oral tradition. The basic elements of the story (plot, characters, setting, theme) will stay the same, but the details will evolve with each retelling. Students will explore the power of storytelling to engage an audience through rich details, use of voice, gestures, sound effects, interaction with the audience, and sense of timing.

3. Choose one of the tales from the collection of folktales you gathered and share it with students. Review the background of the culture represented by the folktale. Discuss what you know about the culture, and with students, talk about how the culture is reflected in the tale.

4. As a group, retell the folktale using *Storytelling Craft Tips* as a guide. Discuss the skill of retelling and the importance of choosing the most important aspects of the tale to include. Explain to students that retelling a story often means putting an individual spin on the tale. Remind students that old folktales were shared in previous generations through oral retelling. This retelling helps a story become more dramatic and polished.

5. Place students into small groups. Explain that each group will choose one folktale to retell. Distribute the *Retelling Plan* to groups and ask students to work together to reread the text and plan their retelling. Ask groups to consider what parts of the tale to include in retelling, what details to change or emphasize, what point of view to use, and how to interact with the audience.

6. Allow time for students to practice retelling their folktales. Remind them that it is OK to leave out some details in this type of retelling. The story is not fixed but shifts with each retelling. They should capture the essence of the story and use their own interpretation.

7. Have groups practice retelling with other small groups, and if appropriate, invite students to share with the whole class. Debrief, using the Discussion Questions.

Discussion Questions

▸ What happened to your story as you retold it again and again? What changed? What remained the same?

▸ What was most compelling as you listened and watched someone else retell a story?

▸ How did retelling your story several times affect you as a storyteller?

▸ What is the purpose of retelling stories orally?

▸ How might a folktale reveal aspects of the culture from which it came?

▸ What storytelling techniques did you use, and what was the effect on your audience?

Retelling *(cont.)*

Specific Grade-Level Ideas

Grades K–2

As a whole class or in small groups, have students work together to retell the folktale. Talk as a group about the parts of the tale that are most important to include in the retelling and what kinds of storytelling techniques could bring the narrative and characters to life.

Students can use a graphic organizer that helps them summarize the beginning, middle, and end of the tale. As they retell, they can refer to these sequential plot points to help keep them on track. Use technology to record the retellings.

Grades 3–5

Encourage students to try different leads and storytelling techniques as they retell their stories. For example, what would the effect be if they were to begin their oral retelling with a question or by describing the setting? Ask students to consider how sound effects could help create the sense of setting. Have students work with character voice to include emotion as well as reveal character traits. Oral storytelling can serve as a springboard for the writing process.

Visit the websites of the National Storytelling Network (**storynet.org**) and International Storytelling Center (**www.storytellingcenter.net**) to explore storytelling resources.

> "As amazing and magical as books are, there's something so pure and direct about oral storytelling. There's absolutely nothing between you and your audience. No pictures, printed words, props, or anything besides the sounds you weave together to make a story."
>
> —Bret Turner (2018)

Grades 6–8

Have students retell the main events of myth and work on honing their sense of timing and the use of silence, pauses, and tone to heighten the emotional quality. Offer students an opportunity to use technology to practice the retellings and consider the evolution of their storytelling skills and techniques over time.

Invite students to retell poems, such as the poems from two perspectives in *Echo Echo: Reverso Poems About Greek Myths* by Marilyn Singer.

Grades 9–12

Have students read across a text set of primary and secondary sources, evaluating each one, determining the central ideas, and integrating the information. Then choose one story from the body of information and use the storytelling tips to retell it. For example, students might visit **www.teachingwithtradebooks.com** and locate the text set called *Baseball Text Sets*, then find the padlet of *Woman in Baseball* to read through the texts of a variety of genres and modalities—primary source images, audio, video, and more.

Name: _____ Date: _____

Retelling Plan

Directions: Complete the chart to plan your retelling.

Folktale: _____	
What are the important parts of the story that we need to include in the retelling?	
What parts or details will we leave out?	
What details are worth developing further in our retelling?	
From what point of view will we tell the story?	
How will we interact with the audience?	
How will we introduce our story?	
What storytelling techniques can enhance the telling (use of voice, gestures, sound effects, timing)?	

Collaborative Storytelling

Model Lesson: The Story Unfolds

Overview

Students hear just the beginning of a picture book or chapter. Then, as a whole class, they work to invent and tell the rest of the story together. When it is their turn, they make up and tell the next part, keeping in mind the story elements of fiction (characters, problem, solution, setting, and theme) to move the story along in a meaningful way. Later they read the rest of the book to compare and contrast their invented story with the author's story. Instead of inventing a story in the moment, students also can retell an existing story together, each student telling one part of the whole story.

Materials

- story stick (a small prop or object)
- *The Plot Twister* (page 48) *(optional)*
- *My Story Plan* (page 49) *(optional)*
- *Elements of Storytelling* (page 23)
- *Storytelling Craft Tips* (page 31)
- art supplies (paper and paint or markers) for making props *(optional)*

Standards

Grades K–2

- Writes a narrative from another person's point of view, including descriptive details
- Participates in collaborative conversations
- Contributes ideas for dialogue and plot while collaborating on character development
- Uses voice, gesture, and movement to communicate emotions

Grades 3–5

- Writes a narrative from another person's point of view, including descriptive details
- Engages effectively in collaborative conversations with peers
- Collaborates to devise original ideas for a drama/theater work
- Makes physical choices to develop a character and create meaning

Grades 6–8

- Writes a narrative from another person's point of view, including descriptive details
- Engages effectively in collaborative conversations with peers
- Develops a character by considering inner thoughts and objectives
- Uses physical choices and character objectives in collaborative drama work

Grades 9–12

- Applies knowledge of language to make effective choices for meaning or style
- Engages effectively in collaborative conversations with peers
- Develops a character by considering inner thoughts and objectives
- Uses physical choices and character objectives in collaborative drama work

Collaborative Storytelling (cont.)

Preparation

Decide on a story starter. You might read the beginning of a picture book such as *The Lost Package* by Richard Ho (additional information on this book can be found at *The Classroom Bookshelf*). Locate a prop that can be used as a story stick to be passed around the circle to help with taking turns. You also might choose to gather art supplies for groups to use as they plan, practice, and tell their own stories. Additional ideas are provided in the Specific Grade-Level Ideas.

> Practice collaborative storytelling by using a compelling lead, such as, "Last Monday, I was folding my laundry when a tiny piece of paper fell out of my pocket. It was folded. As I picked it up, I saw that someone had scrawled the word *clue* on the outside. I knew I needed to know what was inside." Turn to the student next to you, and invite that student to continue the story by passing the chosen story stick.

Procedure

1. Review the main story elements of fiction with students: characters, problem, solution, setting, and theme.

2. Invite students to stand or sit in a circle. Tell them that they get to create a story together. Explain that you will begin the story by reading just the first part of your picture book or chapter of choice. Then they will create the rest of the story as a class by passing the telling on to the next person, using a story stick. Only the person holding the story stick may add to the story. When that person gets the story stick, they will add a little more to the story and then pass it along to the next person in the circle. Remind students that a good story has central characters and events that advance the plot in a way that makes sense.

3. When the story has made its way around the circle, ask students what worked and what did not work in the story and how they might make the story better if they were to revisit it. Ask students to use *Elements of Storytelling* and *Storytelling Craft Tips* to help bring the story to life and establish the characters. Share the author's original story and have students compare and contrast their invented story with the author's.

4. Explain to students that two or more people can invent a story by sharing ideas and taking turns. Tell students this is the kind of collaborative storytelling they are going to practice today.

5. As a class, discuss the role of a narrator in guiding the telling of a story and how members of the group can take turns being the narrator or acting out the characters as the narrator speaks.

6. Divide the class into small groups. Provide each group with a story starter of your choice (for example, assign just the beginning of a different story or have students invent a new middle and end to the story you worked on as a class).

7. Provide students with copies of the *The Plot Twister* and/or *My Story Plan* to aid them in planning their stories, if desired. These graphic organizers are not meant to be exact, but they can aid students in planning the big ideas of their stories.

8. Once groups have planned their stories, allow them time to practice retelling the stories using the same hand-off method as earlier in the lesson. The first student in the group kicks off the story with a short introduction and then "hands" the story to the next narrator to continue where the first student left off. Students continue the story

Collaborative Storytelling *(cont.)*

until it reaches a natural conclusion. This is noted when the narrator says, "The end."

9. If desired, invite students to write, revise, and illustrate their stories.

10. Discuss the process with students, using the Discussion Questions.

Discussion Questions

▸ Describe the story's characters, problem, solution, setting, and theme.

▸ How does each new storyteller add to the story in a way that builds the plot?

▸ What elements of storytelling were used, such as embellishment of details, sounds, voices, and gestures?

▸ What did you notice about your experience of the story as you listened?

▸ Describe your experience working with other students to create a story.

▸ As you listened to or told stories, what made the storytelling compelling?

"Humans are hardwired for narrative. We think in story, talk in story and connect with others through the power of story."

—Carmine Gallo (2019, para. 1)

Specific Grade-Level Ideas

Grades K–2

Create a story box filled with props. Have groups take turns pulling out a prop and telling their part of a collaborative story. Tell a story in the form of an oral letter ("Dear X"), and have each student add just one word to the sentences. Have them collaborate word-by-word. Retell a story that students are familiar with, stopping at different moments and inviting students to jump in and tell that section of the tale. Begin a new story in a predictable way ("Once upon a time . . ."). Invite students to add a couple of lines to the story by passing a prop or object to the next student. In this way the teacher can serve as the "story conductor," ensuring that each student gets an opportunity to participate in the storytelling. Identify the characters, setting, and main plot points in advance, and allow students time to spin a tale within the framework.

Grades 3–5

Invite students to use pantomime as they tell their parts of the story. For example, if the storyteller describes a character who is planting a garden, the storyteller might crouch down with an imaginary trowel and enact the motion of planting while the others in the circle pantomime the growing and changing vegetables, flowers, rich soil, wind, sun, and more.

Students also can use collaborative storytelling for retelling information they've heard in a nonfiction text. For example, they can share chronological facts that describe an important event, biography, or historical concept. Consider how the storytelling process can be woven together between tellers with a seamless quality.

Collaborative Storytelling (cont.)

Specific Grade-Level Ideas (cont.)

Grades 6–8

Have students add a new character to the story and see how this shifts scenes and circumstances. Students can use their understanding of a particular story to improvise the telling of "the rest of the story." Instead of using a prop, you might have students pass the storytelling from one another with a signal, gesture, or motion.

Have students work in small groups to collaboratively tell two versions of the same story using alternative perspectives or points of view. For example, they can tell a story from the point of view of the main character and then retell the story from the point of view of a minor character or the antagonist.

Grades 9–12

Give small groups a headline from a local newspaper article, such as: "Town Elections Next Week. Know the Issues to Vote On." Invite them to create a news story that could go with the headline. Then have them read the actual article. Small groups can work together to tell each version of the story (their invented story and the actual story) to the class. Each group member takes on a part or role in the telling of each story. Then have the class vote on which story actually appears in the newspaper.

> "What makes a good story? It evokes empathy. Listening genuinely. Engaging with the characters' dilemmas and desires. It's caring about what happens to the characters, as you might care about people you know. A desire for the heroine or hero to prevail."
>
> —Tom Lee, Storyteller (personal communication, April 12, 2021)

Name: _____ Date: _____

The Plot Twister

Directions: Record the events of your story in the graphic organizer. Make sure your events relate to each other to tell the story from start to finish.

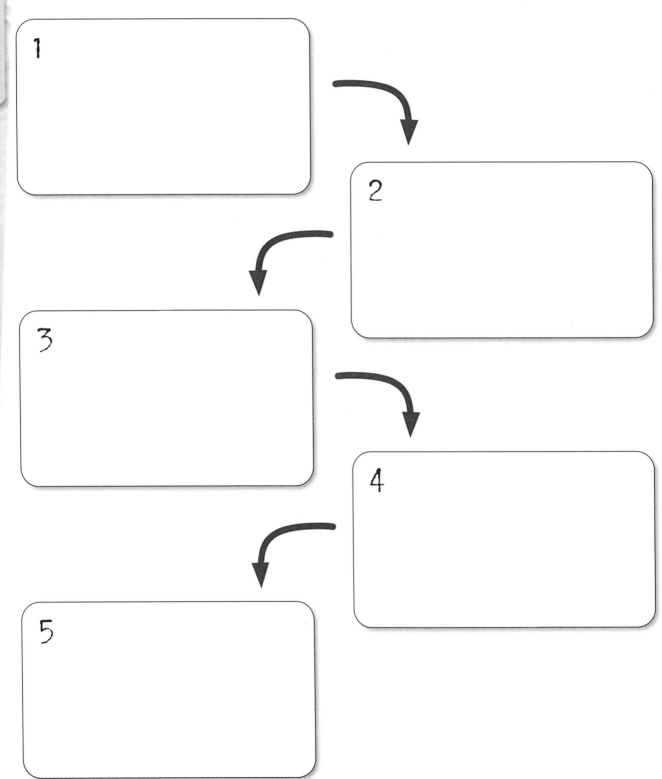

    © Shell Education

Name: _____ Date: _____

My Story Plan

Directions: Plan your collaborative story. Write the big ideas in each box.

Characters

Setting

Main Events

Drama

Drama

Understanding Drama

Integrating drama into the language arts classroom can deepen students' connection with language arts concepts and foster their ability to find relevance to their own lives and interests. Drama can provide engaging contexts for exploring language arts ideas. By enacting scenes that connect to a language arts concept or skill, students can apply their learning in real-world settings. Drama strategies work well outdoors, where students can take advantage of space and natural settings.

When we integrate drama into the language arts classroom, we invite our students to consider particular situations in which language arts ideas are embedded. As students explore these scenarios, they uncover and deepen their language arts thinking, make personal connections to language arts, and recognize its real-world relevance. Christopher Andersen (2004) notes that drama has the ability to re-create the essential elements in the world; as such, drama can place language arts in authentic situations that make sense to students.

When students explore language arts through the lens of a character, they are called upon to imagine themselves working through processes, events, and dilemmas. In their roles they must make choices, solve problems, translate concepts, and articulate ideas. This process requires students to explain, persuade, clarify, and negotiate their thinking (Elliott-Johns et al. 2012). As students investigate perspectives that are different from their own, they expand their worldviews and develop an awareness of their own. Such experiences help students clarify their thinking, understand different perspectives, and consider new strategies for solving problems.

Drama will provide students with contexts that can ground their language arts investigations. And of course, through dramatic explorations, students also learn and develop skills in drama.

Many of these strategies incorporate process drama, in which the teacher and students work together to explore a problem or situation without a script through improvisation (O'Neill 1995). This allows the drama to develop organically, with students' ideas and impulses leading the way. These drama strategies provide a rich context for language arts investigations where students imagine themselves in a variety of language arts situations. Exploring language arts ideas through dramatic scenarios creates motivation for students to participate eagerly in the exploration of ideas from multiple perspectives.

Elements of Drama

In the field of drama there are many different ideas about which elements are important in dramatic work. These definitions are adapted from a variety of sources, including the "Drama Handbook" (International School of Athens, n.d.), "The 12 Dramatic Elements" (Cash, n.d.), and "Elements of Drama" (Windmill Theatre Company, n.d.).

- **Roles**: The characters (people, animals, objects, ideas, and more) in a drama

- **Tension**: Dramatic friction or opposition that emerges from a conflict, struggle, or juxtaposition of ideas or motivations; dramatic tension drives action and generates interest

- **Time**: The pacing of how action moves as the drama unfolds

- **Dialogue**: The words spoken by characters in a drama

- **Situations**: The circumstances that frame the drama and identify what is happening and what the problem is

- **Space**: Where the drama unfolds or the use of the performance space; also the positioning of the body across levels in space (low, medium, and high)

Drama (cont.)

Strategies for Drama

Visualization

In this strategy, students imagine a moment as it unfolds by listening to a sensory description read aloud. Sometimes called mental movie, guided imagery, or guided tour, a dramatic visualization invites students into the world of a text, character, moment, or setting. Teachers use this strategy to "build background knowledge and experience, both factual and emotional, about an event and to build interest on a topic or story" (Neelands and Goode, n.d.). There are a variety of ways to use visualization. For example, you can read a text or tell a story using vivid details to portray a character who moves through a scene. Students use visualization to experience the character's perspective and explore the setting with the sights and sensory details as if moving through it themselves. "Ideally the text is in the second person ('you' form) and includes rich sensory detail to engage students more deeply in the situation or a dilemma" (Neelands and Goode, n.d.). This can serve as a prewriting or prereading activity to engage students more deeply with content.

Tableaux

Sometimes called image theater or human sculpture, *tableau* is a French word that means "frozen picture." It is a drama technique that gives students an opportunity to explore an idea without movement or speaking. In this strategy, students use their bodies individually or in small groups to create an image to tell a story, represent a concept literally, or create a tangible representation of an abstract concept. Working with physical stance (low, medium, high), suggested relationships (body placement and eye contact), and a sense of action frozen in time encourages students to explore ideas and provides a range of ways for students to share what they know about a concept. One person can create a frozen image or a group can work together. The process of creating group tableaux prompts discussion of the characteristics of

what is being portrayed. The learning occurs in the process of translating ideas to physical representation. Tableaux can also be used as a way to gain entry into a complex idea or bigger project (Walker, Tabone, and Weltsek 2011).

Enacting Scenes

The bread and butter of drama is the development and enactment of scenes. Students portray characters that find themselves in particular settings and influenced by specific circumstances. They make choices, solve problems, and react to relationships with other characters. We watch (or participate) as characters make choices and deal with implications. Scenes are valuable thinking frames and can be used flexibly across content and contexts. Studies suggest that learning through drama benefits comprehension, including increased confidence with speaking, fluency, and working with complex language (Brouillette and Jennings 2010). Drama integration supports writing skills in terms of focus, use of details, and the navigation of meaning through the consideration of multiple perspectives (Cremin et al. 2006). Students can enter a suggested scene or create their own in response to a particular context, need, dilemma, or topic. They find that a story is enacted through a series of scenes.

This process of acting out a text provides a meaningful opportunity for students to go back through the text and reread parts that were not clear, visualize elements in the story, and consider character choices, the role of context, circumstances, and character motivation. Students imagine the character coming to life, question what they are reading, and check for story elements in a natural, purposeful manner. This metacognition, or being aware of the reading strategies as they are used, leads students to a deeper understanding of the text.

Drama *(cont.)*

Monologue

A *monologue* is a dramatic scene performed by one person. In creating a monologue, students take on the perspective of a character in a story, real or imagined, and speak directly to the audience for one to three minutes. The character must be established without interacting with others (that would be a dialogue) and must speak in a way that engages the audience with this singular focus.

Often there are monologues in stories and plays that illuminate what a character is thinking. Most often, a monologue reveals a conflict of some kind that the character is wrestling with, a choice to be made, or a problem to be solved. Note that variations include soliloquy, in which a character speaks to themselves. The creation of a monologue provides the opportunity to investigate what Barry Lane calls a "thoughtshot" of a character's inner thinking (1992).

This strategy encourages students to "get into the head" of a particular character. Eventually the goal is for students to create their own monologues, but you may want to introduce the strategy by having students explore prepared ones in resources such as *Magnificent Monologues for Kids 2: More Kids' Monologues for Every Occasion* by Chambers Stevens and *Minute Monologues for Kids* by Ruth Mae Roddy.

Next students can develop characters and create and perform monologues for inanimate objects or forces, or they can portray specific characters (a historical figure; a character from a book, a newspaper article, or a painting; or an imagined character they have created). In order for a monologue to be dramatic, the character must have some tension or conflict that they are wrestling with. This conflict can be an internal or external dilemma. Its resolution or the exploration of this tension creates dramatic interest.

Improvisation

A foundation of drama, improvisation is when individuals create a scene or dramatization "in the moment," making it up as they go. This kind of drama unfolds in exciting and often unpredictable ways as circumstances and character motivation come together to influence how a scene progresses. Improvisation can develop divergent thinking, language use, and social skills while encouraging students to test ideas in a situation that is safe but feels real.

> "Drama is an invaluable tool for educators, since it supports every aspect of literacy development. Drama has been also recognized as a powerful learning medium because it creates a context for children to relate to their lived experience."
>
> —Anika Stojkovic (2017)

Visualization

Model Lesson: Imagine You Are...

Overview

The teacher reads a script with rich, sensory details that encourages students to become part of an imagined world within a curriculum area (experiencing it by imagining what they see, hear, feel, taste, and smell as the script is read). Students explore how descriptive words can create a sensory experience, deepening their interest and understanding of a topic.

Materials

- *Sample Scenario 1: The Life of Plankton* (page 59)
- *Sample Scenario 2: Flight of an Owl* (page 60)
- *Elements of Drama* (page 53)

Standards

Grades K–2

- Writes with detail to describe familiar persons, places, objects, or experiences
- Constructs mental images (visualization)
- Envisions and engages in a guided drama experience
- Applies skills and knowledge from other content areas in a guided drama experience

Grades 3–5

- Writes with precise language and sensory details to clarify and enhance ideas
- Constructs mental images (visualization)
- Articulates visual details of imagined worlds while engaging in a drama experience
- Applies skills and knowledge from other content areas in a guided drama experience

Grades 6–8

- Writes with precise vocabulary and figurative language to clarify and enhance ideas
- Constructs mental images (visualization)
- Articulates visual details of imagined worlds while engaging in a drama experience
- Applies skills and knowledge from other content areas in a guided drama experience

Grades 9–12

- Produces clear and coherent writing in which the development, organization, and style are appropriate to task, purpose, and audience
- Demonstrates understanding of figurative language, word relationships, and nuances in word meanings
- Constructs mental images (visualization)
- Identifies universal themes or common social issues and expresses them through a drama/theater work

Visualization *(cont.)*

Preparation

Review *Sample Scenario 1: The Life of Plankton* and *Sample Scenario 2: Flight of an Owl* and select one to use with students. Adapt the selected script as needed for students and area of focus. Play with the tone of your voice to communicate emotion and to set the stage for the visualization. Your willingness to be dramatic will intrigue students and help them feel comfortable in taking their own dramatic risks. Additional ideas are provided in the Specific Grade-Level Ideas.

> "Guided Imagery invites students to close their eyes to listen to a descriptive, narrative story and to imagine they are experiencing the events being described. Guided Imagery can be used to build background knowledge and experience, both factual and emotional, about an event and to build interest on a topic or story."
>
> —Jonothan Neelands and Tony Goode (n.d.)

Procedure

1. Introduce students to the idea of visualization. Explain that visualization is a drama strategy that uses voice and rich language to create a sensory scene through the imagination.

2. Invite students to find a comfortable place to relax and step into their imagination. They can close their eyes if it feels comfortable, or they can soften their gaze or lower their eyes, making it easier to focus inwardly.

3. Read one of the visualizations. Make your voice match the meaning to enhance the sensory experience. Encourage students to "look around in their mind's eye" and notice how imagination sparks their senses.

4. Invite students to share their experiences with visualization, noticing individual and sensory connections and insights. Discuss unique interpretations of the experience.

> "Students use words and images from the text to generate multisensory visualizations of text content, and in doing so they become prepared to use multisensory visualization to aid in their comprehension."
>
> —reDesign (n.d., para. 1)

5. Introduce and discuss the *Elements of Drama*. Choose an area of your curriculum and create a visualization together with input from students. For example, it could be based on a scene in a book and be written in the second person ("you") so that students focus on entering the world of the text. You could draw descriptive material out of a book, painting, dance, music, photograph, and so on to serve as a descriptive narration of what is unfolding. Encourage students to use imagination to include sensory detail.

6. Debrief, using the Discussion Questions.

Discussion Questions

▸ Tell us about your imagined experience.

▸ What did you notice as you imagined the text (see, feel, taste, hear, smell)?

▸ What emotions did you experience? What memories did it bring?

▸ What insights do you have as a result of this experience?

▸ What connections did you make to the text?

▸ How did the language evoke sensory connections?

Visualization (cont.)

Specific Grade-Level Ideas

Grades K–2

Before sharing a new read-aloud with the class, get students excited by reading a visualization that invites them to experience the setting of the story or a short scene in the story. For example, you might use the provided visualization called *Sample Scenario 1: Flight of an Owl* before reading *Owl Moon* by Jane Yolen. When writing your own visualization as a hook for your readers, be sure to include rich sensory images to draw them in. Students also can illustrate what they imagine as they hear the visualization unfolding.

Grades 3–5

Invite students to write visualizations to be used as riddles, challenging others to guess the subject of the piece. Using audio editing software or apps, have them create a soundscape to play as they read their visualization.

Grades 6–8

In addition to the suggestions for grades 3–5, focus on the process of revision. Have students create a visualization and then test-drive it with their peers. After reading it to a listener, have them reflect on what it was like to read their visualization by asking themselves: "Were there any spots where the reading felt clunky due to word choices? Or due to repeated words? Or due to shifting out of second-person

Grades 6–8 (cont.)

point of view? Or maybe due to the order of words in a sentence?" Have students revise after considering the answers to these questions, as needed.

Tell students to ask their listeners the following: "What moments in the visualization really worked for you or challenged you to imagine with clarity? Were there any spots that were difficult to imagine or moments in which you were pulled out of the visualization?" Invite writers to revise their work based on feedback from their listeners.

Grades 9–12

Use the provided visualization titled *Sample Scenario 1: The Life of Plankton* to spark a research project on environmental issues. After reading a text set of information about plankton and the impact of plastics in the ocean (including images, newspaper articles, research papers, interviews, news reports, educational videos, and more), invite groups to research additional environmental issues and challenges of today and to explore environmental advocacy. Have each group write a visualization collaboratively, and share it with the class and community.

Encourage the use of figurative language and scientific vocabulary in the creation of their visualizations.

Sample Scenario 1: The Life of Plankton

Imagine you are floating in the ocean

The water surrounds you

Bubbles churn and tumble around you

Pushing you gently

Drawn this way and that way in the foam.

The water is soothing, it holds you and a million others like you

You are tiny

Microscopic

A single cell organism

drifting, drifting, drifting

Along with the current

You are plant

Your structure...spikes and curves...

distribute your weight and prevent you from sinking

You are buoyant

Notice the sunlight piercing though the top layer of the sea

Moving through the transparent panes of your body

Activating your green factory

Your chloroplasts pump pump

and respond to the demands of the light bright rays

Shimmering down through the water

As you float you absorb

carbon dioxide from tiny pockets of air

Synthesize and release

Sending oxygen bubbles up up up to the surface

You watch as these break

Sharing resources with the air

You continue to drift

Moving to and fro

Up and down

You replicate

Again and again

Doubling, quadrupling,

You are exponential

Strength in numbers

And all the while your ranks feed the sea

You see others nibbled

Eaten whole

You continue

To produce

Until you are taken in

Into the body of a fish

swallowed whole and transformed

Fueling the energy of the sea

Sources for the facts in this scenario:

Bang, Molly and Penny Chisholm. 2012. *Ocean Sunlight: How Tiny Plants Feed the Seas.* New York: Scholastic.

Thys, Tierney and Christian Sardet. 2012. "The Secret Life of Plankton." www.youtube.com/watch?v=xFQ_fO2D7f0/.

National Geographic. 2019. "Plankton." *National Geographic Resource Library.* www.nationalgeographic.org/encyclopedia/plankton/.

Woods Hole Oceanographic Institution. n.d. "Plankton." Accessed October 1, 2021. www.whoi.edu/science/B/people/kamaral/plankton.html

Sample Scenario 2: Flight of an Owl

Imagine you are gliding through the woods on buoyant wings. The wind slides through your feathers silently. The angle of your wing bends slightly as you bank a turn. You study the landscape of your home as you soar. Trees are silhouetted against the snow below you. The white, bright moon creates long, silver shadows.

You fly over the frozen pond. All is still as you move toward a favorite perch. Your legs unfurl in slow motion as you approach. You pump your wings back to slow your flight and stop for a moment midair, then gently catch the branch, your talons wrapping tightly around as you steady your weight.

Your beak opens and closes, tasting the night air. No wind. You watch. Your eyes are wide, blinking slowly. You begin a slow rotation of your head to scan the landscape, moving all the way left then all the way right. You can turn your gaze to scan all that is before you and all that is in back. Slowly, slowly. In the distance you see two shapes cut through the night at the edge of your woods.

You listen. They are far from you, but you can detect the crunch of the snow as they walk, their breath, a muffled sound. They turn toward each other. You watch until they are no longer visible.

You hear an animal yelping in the meadow beyond the woods. You hear a long, low wail from the tracks beyond the farm.

A familiar call comes to you from across the woods. You feel the urge to respond rise in your throat. You call back in a raspy, clear voice. *Whooo whooo whoo whoo*. You listen. Call again.

Time goes by. You sense the movement and listen until you're sure. A tiny scratching, scraping beneath the snow. You drop from the branch silently, stealthily. In an instant you hit the snow, talons grasping. Patience is rewarded.

You pump your wings, rising up to the sky with your prize, against the early light of dawn.

Sources for Facts in This Visualization

Yolen, Jane. 1987. *Owl Moon*. New York: Philomel Books.
Ogden, Lesley Evans. 2017. "The Silent Flight of Owls, Explained." *Audubon*. www.audubon.org/news/the-silent-flight-owls-explained.

Owl facts found in the above source:
"Owls have large wings relative to their body mass, which let them fly unusually slowly."
"The structure of their feathers serves as a silencer. Comb-like serrations on the leading edge of wing feathers break up the turbulent air that typically creates a swooshing sound."
"Those smaller streams of air are further dampened by a velvety texture unique to owl feathers and by a soft fringe on a wing's trailing edge."

Tableaux

Model Lesson: Inferring Theme

Overview

Students create *tableaux*, or frozen statues, without moving or speaking to explore the theme of a text. Students locate evidence in the text to infer a theme (such as belonging, friendship, survival) and use their bodies to create a tangible representation of the theme. Working with the placement of one's body on different levels (low, medium, high), relationships (body placement and eye contact), and action frozen in time enables students to explore ideas and provides ways for them to share what they know about a theme.

Materials

▸ any text or set of texts (can be related to a unit of study)

▸ *Tableaux Tips* (page 66)

▸ *Tableaux Brainstorming Guide* (page 67)

▸ *Gallery Walk Observation* (page 68)

▸ *Elements of Drama* (page 53)

Standards

Grades K–2

▸ Identifies the theme of a story

▸ Recalls key details

▸ Expresses ideas inspired from the text through movement

▸ Creates body shapes at low, middle, and high levels

Grades 3–5

▸ Determines multiple themes found in a text

▸ Refers to details and examples from the text to support inferences

▸ Develops movement that expresses and communicates an idea inspired from a text

▸ Creates body shapes at low, middle, and high levels

Grades 6–8

▸ Determines multiple themes found in a text and their development

▸ Cites strong evidence to support inferences

▸ Develops movement that connects and communicates ideas inspired from a text

▸ Creates body shapes at low, middle, and high levels

Grades 9–12

▸ Determines a theme of a text and analyzes how it emerges and is shaped by specific details

▸ Demonstrates understanding of figurative language, word relationships, and nuances in word meanings

▸ Examines and justifies original ideas and artistic choices in a drama work

▸ Cooperates as a creative team to make interpretive choices for a drama work

Tableaux *(cont.)*

Preparation

Search online for images of tableaux. Select some appropriate images to share with students. Additional ideas are provided in the Specific Grade-Level Ideas.

Procedure

1. Introduce *tableau* as a French word that means "frozen picture" using the examples of tableaux you selected.

2. After viewing several examples, invite students to consider *Elements of Drama* and what makes an interesting tableau (suggested action, interesting composition, contrasting visual ideas, interesting use of space, and so on).

3. Ask students to create a still image with their bodies that depicts an emotion such as surprise. Identify the choices they make, such as facial expressions (wide eyes), gestures (hands in the air), and levels (stepping back and leaning to one side). Note that there are many ways to show a single emotion.

4. Share the information found in the *Tableaux Tips* with students. Model each term for students to help them understand its meaning.

5. Place students into groups of two to four. Have groups select a text (they can all choose the same text, or they can choose different texts) to use to explore the themes within it.

6. Distribute copies of the *Tableaux Brainstorming Guide* and have students work in their groups to locate evidence in the text that supports the themes they infer. Groups also should brainstorm ideas of frozen images they could create to model the themes.

7. Invite students to create a group tableau with a theme from their brainstorming guide that they will then present to the larger group. They can make their images more dramatic by doing one of the following:

   ‣ exploring the placement of their bodies on different levels, adding visual interest (for example, low-level crawling on the ground, mid-level sitting on a chair, or high-level reaching into the air on tiptoes)

   ‣ including a sense of frozen action

   ‣ using space to enhance the composition

   Have ready the *Tableaux Tips* for creating a compelling image so you can coach students as they're making artistic choices (side-coaching).

8. Invite students to participate in a "gallery walk." Each group prepares to share their tableau in a particular location in the room or outside. Introduce the presentations by saying, "Imagine we are in an art gallery. We'll walk around and look at the sculptures. At each stop on our gallery walk, we will talk about what we notice and brainstorm what words come to mind as well as what makes a compelling tableau." If desired, have students stand in a neutral position and then "bring the image to life" at a clap or agreed-upon signal (for example, say, "Curtains up!"). Groups present their tableaux one at a time for the rest of the class.

Tableaux *(cont.)*

9. Gather students around one of the tableaux. Ask them to "read" the image quietly first using the *Gallery Walk Observation Sheet*. Then have students say aloud what they notice in the tableau and brainstorm ideas for the theme represented. Continue to move through the gallery walk until all images have been shared. Use the Discussion Questions to guide student thinking.

10. As you move around during the gallery walk, keep a record of the words used to describe the tableaux. You will end up with a rich list of adjectives, synonyms, and metaphors that will help students identify the themes represented in new ways. Add to the list as each group describes their process of creating their tableau. This is often where ideas are translated and the richest realizations occur. Documenting students' language will reveal the connections they have made in understanding the vocabulary words and the use of tableaux to create meaning.

Tableaux vivant was a popular genre from 1830–1920. It was often used as a parlor game in Victorian England "to amuse guests and engage them in a deeper appreciation of art." Characters portrayed scenes from life, history, art, and books. The focus was on "staging, pose, costume, make-up, lighting, and the facial expression of the models. Sometimes a poem or music accompanied the scene, and often a large wooden frame outlined the perimeter of the stage, so as to reference the frame of a painted canvas."

—Shannon Murphy (2012, para. 2, 3)

Discussion Questions

For the viewers:

‣ What concept do you think is being represented?

‣ What words come to mind as you view the tableau?

‣ What do you see in the frozen image that suggests the theme?

‣ What action is suggested?

‣ What is most compelling about how the image is composed?

‣ What similarities and differences were there across tableaux?

‣ How does viewing a frozen image reveal the meaning of a theme?

For the participants:

‣ Describe your artistic process for creating an image of the theme.

‣ How does translating a theme into a frozen picture enhance your understanding of the theme?

‣ Which themes were most engaging to depict? Most challenging?

‣ What did you notice about the process of collaboration?

‣ How did tableau help you to connect to the ideas being portrayed?

Tableaux *(cont.)*

Specific Grade-Level Ideas

Grades K–2

Have the whole class explore a theme together using a text such as *Love* by Matt de la Peña, *Here and Now* by Julia Denos, or *Joy* by Corrinne Averiss.

Invite students to work in small groups to create a tableau for the same theme and see how each group represents the word differently. Words such as *family* can generate rich discussion of the many forms a family can have.

Choose a setting such as a grocery store, farm, or beach. Ask students to help you create a scene that might take place in this setting. Guide up to five or six volunteers, one at a time, to enter a frozen picture of the scene. Ask, "What else belongs in the scene?" as they join. Coach students to experiment with different motions by suggesting ideas from the *Tableau Tips*. Students show activities they might be engaged in as they "step into" the image.

Grades 3–5

Have students work in small groups. One or two group members go to the center of the space and begin the sculpture with a pose. The rest of the participants "add on" one by one to create a group sculpture until all group members are involved.

In addition to theme, use tableaux to explore vocabulary found in informational texts. For example, through tableaux, have students explore vocabulary terms in a nonfiction narrative such as *The Wolves Are Back* by Jean Craighead George. Potential terms include *wilderness, silenced, tranquil, peace, yearned, marveled*, and *frightened*. These concepts will yield a wide range of rich descriptions that have strong connections to the words as students describe what they see in the tableaux.

"Exploring ideas in drama can provide students with an outlet for their thoughts and emotions – which is important in a world of constant change."

—Keith West (2011)

Tableaux (cont.)

Specific Grade-Level Ideas (cont.)

Grades 6–8

Additional topics for students to explore can relate to social or environmental justice.

Students might explore the plotline of a story, moments of a character's life, the progression of a sequence of events, or a step-by-step process. Consider having students add an image depicting the moment before a story begins or after a story ends. Invite students to use a "slideshow" method of tableau in which they create multiple tableaux to show a progression. Students present frozen images one right after the other. The viewers can share their thinking about what they noticed after the slideshow. The presenters can say, "Curtain down!" and "Curtain up!" between frozen images, indicating that the viewers should close their eyes in between slides so that they see only the still images and not the movement as images are formed.

Grades 9–12

Invite students to take a side in a debate and create a frozen image that shows their argument. Instead of looking at a single image, choose an issue and have groups create different sides of the issue through frozen pictures, such as issues of activism or social justice.

Use the "Real-to-Ideal Image Theater" way of working through tableaux. To do this, engage students in investigating an issue by creating an image that depicts the issue ("Real"; for example, loneliness) and then creating an image that shows what the world would be like if the problem were solved or nonexistent ("Ideal"; for example, inclusivity/belonging). Ask students to move between the two images in five counts (this can be clapped out, signaling students to move their bodies to an image of change that will ultimately lead to the ideal image). These evolving images visually reveal the incremental changes that would need to be made to resolve the issue—the small changes that need to happen to move from the real to the ideal (Boal 2002).

Name: _____ Date: _____

Tableaux Tips

As you create your tableau, consider using focus, action, space, and levels to create a compelling and dramatic image.

Focus: As you create your image, identify where you want the viewers' eyes to go. Create/compose your tableau in a way that creates a sense of focus to help the viewers notice what is most important first.

Action: Your image is still, but you want to create a sense of an active moment captured in time. Think of your tableau as an active moment that was paused right in the middle of the action.

Space: Your tableau is a frozen sculpture. Harness the power of a three-dimensional image by using space intentionally.

Levels: Arranging people's bodies on different levels makes the tableau more interesting. See the following suggestions.

Using Levels in Drama

Levels	Frozen Movements
low-level	crawling, crouching, rolling, crab walking
mid-level	bending, walking hunched over, skipping, skating, sliding, swimming through the air
high-level	reaching, jumping, walking on tiptoes

Source: Monica Prendergast. Used with permission.

Name: _____ Date: _____

Tableaux Brainstorming Guide

Directions: Record themes from your selected text. Provide text evidence of the themes. Then brainstorm frozen images you could create to show the themes.

Theme	Text Evidence	Frozen Image Ideas

Name: _____ Date: _____

Gallery Walk Observation

Directions: As you observe each tableau, record your observations in the chart.

Observation Notes	Tableau 1	Tableau 2	Tableau 3
Words to describe the tableau			
Notes from the creators about their artistic choices			
The theme represented			
What we've learned about the theme			

Tableaux

Enacting Scenes

Model Lesson: Using Reading Strategies

Overview

In this strategy, cooperative groups work together to act out one scene from a text of any genre. Students take on the roles of specific characters, ideas, or environmental elements. They act out the scene by exploring characters' needs, wants, and motivations as they navigate conflicts that bring to life the drama. Through this process, students use reading strategies such as rereading and scanning for clarification as they plan their enactment.

Materials

▸ supplies to use as props

▸ text of any genre for enacting (folktale, mystery, nonfiction narrative)

▸ *Drama Planner* (pages 72–73)

▸ *Elements of Drama* (page 53)

Standards

Grades K–2

▸ Utilizes comprehension strategies such as rereading and visualization while reading

▸ Describes characters, settings, and major events in a story

▸ Contributes ideas for dialogue and plot while collaborating on a short scene

▸ Uses voice, gesture, and movement to communicate emotions

Grades 3–5

▸ Utilizes comprehension strategies such as rereading and visualization while reading

▸ Describes theme, characters, settings, and major events in a story

▸ Collaborates to devise original ideas for a drama/theater work

▸ Makes physical choices to develop a character and create meaning

Grades 6–8

▸ Utilizes comprehension strategies such as rereading and visualization while reading

▸ Analyzes theme, characters, settings, and major events in a story

▸ Develops a character by considering inner thoughts and objectives

▸ Uses various physical choices and character objectives in a collaborative drama work

Grades 9–12

▸ Utilizes comprehension strategies such as rereading and visualization while reading

▸ Analyzes how characters develop, interact with other characters, and advance the plot or develop the theme

▸ Identifies text information that influences character choices in a drama work

▸ Uses experiences to develop a character that is believable and authentic in a drama work

Enacting Scenes *(cont.)*

Preparation

Gather props or supplies from which students can make props. Choose a text that can be enacted by students, preferably one with characters, ideas, and events that are easy to work on in small groups. Also, decide whether you would like each group to enact a different text or different scenes from the same text. Additional ideas are provided in the Specific Grade-Level Ideas.

Procedure

1. Tell students that they will be creating and enacting scenes from a story. Divide the class into small groups and assign a text, or have them choose their own. Discuss *Elements of Drama.*

2. Explain to students that enacting a scene from a story will require close attention to detail in the text. Discuss the reading strategies that students will find themselves using as they prepare to enact their scene: rereading the text, scanning the text for important information, identifying actions that move the story forward, visualizing the characters and details of the setting, determining the author's message, considering story elements, visualizing scenes as they create a beginning and an end, and using any prior knowledge about the story they may have.

3. Introduce the *Drama Planner* and distribute a copy to each group. Provide time for students to work in small groups to read and reread the text. Monitor groups and point out reading strategies as you observe them being used or hear them being discussed. Are students rereading the text? Scanning for important information? Visualizing the characters? Considering story elements? Visualizing scenes as they create a beginning and an end?

4. Have students rehearse their scenes, improvising action and dialogue from what they remember about the story. Use the Planning Questions to guide students.

5. Have each group enact their scene for the class. After performing, have students write up their scenes in their writer's notebooks. Debrief with students about the process, using the Discussion Questions. Highlight how their knowledge of the text (because of reading strategies that helped aid comprehension) contributed to a successful enactment.

Planning Questions

▸ How will you begin and end your scene?

▸ What props might you need to help dramatize the scene?

▸ What interesting action might take place as the plot unfolds?

▸ Besides the identified characters in the story, are there other objects or forces in the story that can be created as characters?

▸ What choices will you use in depicting your character (voice, movement, costume)?

▸ How will you show what your character wants in the scene and the obstacles in the way?

Discussion Questions

▸ What reading strategies did you use to draw information from the text in planning your scenes?

▸ What other endings to your scene can you imagine?

▸ In what ways did enacting scenes affect your understanding of the text?

▸ What choices did you make in deciding how to enact your scene?

Enacting Scenes (cont.)

Specific Grade-Level Ideas

Grades K–2

Talk with students about the folktale "The Little Red Hen." If desired, read the book *Interrupting Chicken* by David Ezra Stein and discuss how Little Red Hen changes the endings to the stories to save each character from an unfavorable outcome. Or discuss with students how they could change the original story in an unexpected way. Work with students to read and reread the story before enacting original beginnings and endings.

Share a wordless picture book with the whole class, discussing the sequence of events as they unfold. Point out how the illustrator uses body language and facial expressions to communicate the characters' thoughts and feelings. Choose a meaningful scene and have groups bring it to life.

Grades 3–5

In addition to the K–2 Specific Grade-Level Ideas, have groups create a scene that does not exist in the text but could. Have students improvise these scenes first and then write them in their journals and explain why these invented scenes would be meaningful to the text. You will find that, because they acted out the scenes, their writing is more richly detailed and free flowing. Provide students with a digital camera to take pictures of particular moments. Students can print and tape these photographs into their writer's notebooks and write about the moment.

Grades 3–5 (cont.)

Gather a collection of wordless books and provide small groups with a few books such as *Imagine!* by Raúl Colón. Have them discuss these questions as they browse the books: "Why do you think some authors choose to tell their stories through pictures instead of words? What information about the characters, settings, and story are revealed through illustrations? Are some events highlighted more than others? How? How do the authors reveal how the characters feel? How do the authors reveal the characters' traits?" Invite groups to choose a scene from one of the books and enact it.

Grades 6–8

Have students choose a chapter from a book they are reading or a stanza from a poem. Invite them to change the scene that happened before the chapter and after the chapter. Have students enact those scenes for the class.

Ask students to consider how they could change the outcome of the story if they were the author, and then have them dramatize their new version.

Invite students to create and enact a scene that mirrors themes from their lives.

Grades 9–12

Invite students to enact a scene from a newspaper and discuss how the story changes based on the perspective of the writer.

Name: _____ Date: _____

Drama Planner

Directions: Work with your group members to plan the scene you will be enacting.

Story moment to be enacted:

_____

_____

Characters involved in the scene:

_____

_____

What does your character want in the scene? What obstacles are in the way?

_____

_____

Action in the scene:

_____

_____

Point of tension or conflict that triggers action in the scene:

_____

_____

Name: _____ Date: _____

Drama Planner *(cont.)*

Directions: What reading strategies did you use to help you understand the story and plan your scene? Check off strategies from the list:

❑ I reread to remember or answer a question I had.

❑ I scanned for important information.

❑ I visualized the characters coming to life and details of the setting.

❑ I thought about the problem and solution.

❑ I determined the author's message.

❑ I used what I already knew about stories to understand my scene better.

❑ Other: _____

Monologue

Model Lesson: Meet the Character

Overview

In this lesson, students use monologue to deeply understand a significant person or character. They read a variety of texts from a collection of books and primary sources (letters and quotations) and draw from various modalities (print, audio, photographs, and artifacts). Using information from a variety of sources, students write and perform monologues in which they take on the perspective of a historical figure.

Materials

▸ collection of texts about an individual or subject

▸ *My Notes* (page 81)

▸ *Georgia O'Keeffe Monologue Sample 1 and Sample 2* (pages 78-79)

▸ *Monologue Planner* (page 82)

▸ *Elements of Drama* (page 53)

▸ *Georgia O'Keeffe Sample Text Set and Photo* (page 80) *(optional)*

Standards

Grades K–2

▸ Describes a person fully, using information from multiple texts

▸ Writes a narrative from another person's point of view, including descriptive details

▸ Contributes ideas for dialogue and plot while collaborating on character development

▸ Uses voice, gesture, and movement to communicate emotions

Grades 3–5

▸ Describes a person in depth, using information from multiple texts

▸ Writes a narrative monologue from another person's point of view, including descriptive details

▸ Collaborates to devise original ideas for a drama/theater work

▸ Makes physical choices to develop a character and create meaning

Grades 6–8

▸ Describes interactions and events in a person's life, using information from texts

▸ Writes a narrative monologue from another person's point of view, including descriptive details

▸ Develops a character by considering inner thoughts and objectives

▸ Uses various physical choices and character objectives in collaborative drama/theatre work

Grades 9–12

▸ Analyzes accounts of a subject in different mediums (e.g. print and multimedia), determining which details are emphasized

▸ Produces clear writing in which the development, organization, and style are appropriate to the task

▸ Integrates cultural and historical contexts with personal experiences to create a character that is believable and authentic

▸ Identifies text information, research, and the director's concept that influence in a drama work

Monologue *(cont.)*

Preparation

Gather a collection of texts that focus on the same person but are written by different authors. The collection might include biographies, historical fiction, poetry, articles, or primary sources. Draw from various modalities, including print, audio, photographs, and artifacts. Subjects could include artists (Georgia O'Keeffe, Pablo Picasso, Diego Rivera), historical figures (Rosa Parks, Thomas Jefferson, Marie Curie), animal activists (Jane Goodall), and conservationists (Rachel Carson). See Recommended Resources (page 15–16) for ideas.

Read over *Georgia O'Keeffe Monologue Sample 1* and *Georgia O'Keeffe Monologue Sample 2* so that you can decide which is appropriate for students. Present it to students with dramatic interest. You can share the *Georgia O'Keeffe Sample Text Set and Photo.* You also may select an example of a monologue from literature to share with students. Additional ideas are provided in the Specific Grade-Level Ideas.

Procedure

1. Display the collection of texts and sources about your chosen individual or subject. Explain to students that when they look for texts about one subject, they often will come across different types of books— informational books and fictional books that sometimes include facts. They also may find poetry, articles, and primary sources such as letters and quotations. Talk to students about the importance of learning from those who have studied the individual or subject, such as authors, and, in the case of individuals, from the subjects themselves.

2. Introduce *My Notes* to students and explain that they will be working in groups to read and analyze books about the same topic. Place students into groups and distribute *My Notes* to each group. Circulate and facilitate group work as needed.

3. Once students have gathered notes on their topics, tell them that they will present the information they learned through a monologue. Share *Georgia O'Keeffe Monologue Sample 1* or *Georgia O'Keeffe Monologue Sample 2* with students as a sample monologue. Talk with students about how a monologue is different from a dialogue. Introduce *Elements of Drama.*

4. Direct students to work in their groups, using the same books as reference material in planning a monologue. Distribute the *Monologue Planner* to groups and have students work together to answer the questions and discuss possible ideas for a monologue.

5. Provide time for students to develop individual monologues in class. They should use their group notes and the texts as reference material. Then have students present their monologues. Debrief the monologues using the Discussion Questions.

Discussion Questions

▸ What insights did you gain into the character by creating a monologue?

▸ What emotions did you feel as you experienced the monologue?

▸ What was your character's dilemma?

▸ How did using different types of texts and sources influence the way you created your monologue? How do you think it might have been different if you had only used one text?

▸ What did you notice about the dramatic choices of your peers?

Monologue *(cont.)*

Specific Grade-Level Ideas

Grades K–2

Use the *Georgia O'Keeffe Monologue Sample 1* with younger students. Students may find more success with this strategy when they are given a specific context—it helps them consider how their character would react in that situation. For example, ask them to imagine that they are entering a party where nobody knows their assigned character. How would they introduce themselves? What is important about their lives to share with others? Because conflict is the core of drama, ask students to focus on a dilemma that the character is trying to figure out. This can be a decision the character has to make, a problem the character has, or a turning point in the character's life.

Monologue also can be used to teach students about an author's purpose for writing and the genre they chose. Have students read different kinds of texts and create short monologues that explain why an author wrote a text in a certain way and what opinions that author holds about the topic.

Grades 3–5

Some students may choose to perform their monologues for others in the school or local community. Provide students with multiple opportunities to practice their monologues with a peer so that they internalize what they want to say rather than memorizing it. Explain that the details of the monologue might be a bit different every time they act it out, but the gist will be there each time. Once students become deeply familiar with a character through rehearsing their monologue, they will be able to accurately improvise the piece. Having index cards available may help the performers relax as they share their work with the class.

Students can explore point of view, perspective, and motivation through the use of monologue. Have students read texts and then discuss them from various perspectives. For example, a fictitious historical account about the Revolutionary War can be discussed further by having students create opposing monologues—one from the point of view of a Revolutionary soldier and one from the point of view of a Loyalist colonist.

"Characters in real life and in fiction, face moral choices. The exploration of those choices is undertaken in a safe environment. Here, actions and consequences can be examined, discussed and experienced without the dangers and pitfalls that this type of experimentation would lead to in a real-life situation."

—Keith West (2011)

Monologue *(cont.)*

Specific Grade-Level Ideas *(cont.)*

Grades 6–8

Have students create monologues from the points of view of other people and things in their character's life (for example, Abraham Lincoln's pen, a flower in Edith Wharton's gardens, or the space shuttle *Endeavour* carrying Mae Jemison). Have them explore people from the same period in history or the same profession, and invite students to write a monologue from their points of view. Compare the character traits of these people through monologue. Explore the missing voices in a particular story or historical moment.

Students also can explore the way in which a monologue can fit into a longer dramatic performance. Students can consider and identify appropriate times for one character to speak in a scene that fits together with a multifaceted story.

Grades 9–12

Encourage students to develop their research skills to create their monologue by practicing the skill of determining the usefulness of resources in relation to their task of presenting a moment of conflict or decision making through monologue. Which sources are most helpful, and why? Also, challenge students to find a place in their monologue to include something they directly state is different from what is actually meant, drawing on satire, sarcasm, irony, or understatement.

"As is true any time we wonder about other people's lives, our monologues are only guesses, at times marred by stereotype. But the very act of considering, 'How might this person experience this situation?' develops an important 'habit of the mind' and draws us closer together. We write the monologues along with our students and can testify to the startling insights and compassion that can arise."

—Bill Bigelow and Linda Christensen (2001, 29).

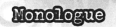
Georgia O'Keeffe Monologue Sample 1

Grades K–2

My approach to painting is different from what everyone else is doing. Moving against the crowd is hard! But I persist. I continue on because I have things in my head that are not like what anyone taught me—shapes and ideas so near to me, so natural to my way of being and thinking. I cannot just walk by a flower without looking! Have you ever truly looked at a flower? I mean really looked at it? Come closer. Hold it in your hand. Now look. Look at the center. The way the lines branch out and create striking patterns. Notice the way the color is light in some places and dark in others . . . the way the contrast of light and dark make you want to look and look and look. If you take a flower in your hand and really look at it, it's your world for a moment. Do you have things in your life that speak to you like this?

Grades 3–5

I always knew I was an artist. I remember walking the hills of Sun Prairie in the 1890s as a child and feeling drawn to rocks and plants in the beautiful Wisconsin landscapes. Even bones fascinated me. As I walked, something would capture my attention and I'd pick it up. I was drawn to it. Later, I'd sketch it. My parents and siblings were always telling me nature belongs outside and made me move my piles of treasures outside. I loved exploring the shape and color of a thing through color and line.

I took art lessons at home and drawing lessons from my grammar teacher. And my teachers in school encouraged me. But after high school, I realized I wasn't good enough to make a career of painting realistically. I had attended the Art Students League in New York City in 1907, and I grew frustrated with my abilities. I felt for a time that I wasn't successful. I guess we all question ourselves along the way. I didn't want to work in traditional ways. And so, I stopped painting. I walked away from it. I destroyed every piece completed there. I was done with painting. I couldn't communicate in the traditional methods being used. I felt...stifled...like I couldn't breathe.

So, I felt lost for a time. I found other things to do, of course, instead of painting, and life went on. I was a commercial artist for a while; I taught art in an elementary school. And then...one summer I took a course in art for teachers. And...everything changed. I connected with a professor who opened the world for me. Professor Arthur Wesley Dow was his name, and he showed me that my art could be about feeling. About what was inside me. He encouraged me to work with light and dark color and line. It was a moment for me...a turning point that seemed to snap things into focus in my life. I revisited my passion for nature. I believe the natural world has a deep power. The power of life in a flower, or a skull whitened by the sun is equal to the strength of a NYC skyline. Truly. It is.

I had found my true work.

Georgia O'Keeffe Monologue Sample 2

Grades 6–12

(Georgia O'Keeffe has a letter in her hand. She turns it over and reads the sender's address. She smiles slightly.)

The great photographer Alfred Stieglitz. Hmm, I wonder...

(Carefully she opens the letter and reads.)

Well, I'll be. One brief visit and he's reaching out. Good. My work has sparked his attention.

(She reads a quote from the letter.) "I can't stop thinking about your drawings and paintings. Your poppies, sunflowers, and jimsonweed. The blue Texas sky and lavender dawns. Ms. O'Keeffe, you intrigue me. You see the world in a way that is unique—through shape, color, and abstraction..."

(She laughs.) Too true, and I've been reprimanded for it all my life. How is it that you recognize my vision so quickly, so fully?

(She reads on.) "You must exhibit in New York. Won't you come? *(pausing)* Please consider it. I will raise the funding you need to paint full-time. Your work should be allowed to flourish. There's a whole new world for you here."

A whole new world. *(She looks out the window.)* Perhaps a whole new world is what's needed. I am well aware, Mr. Stieglitz, that I live in a time when society does not deem it proper for women to become artists. I've heard again and again that teaching art is not the proper place for a woman. "Women aren't meant to be artists!" Ridiculous! I have never followed the mainstream. But you see me. You understand my work.

I remember my first prize for an early painting I called *Dead Rabbit with Copper Pot*. I could feel the excitement coursing through my veins—the sense that this was my life unfolding. I have the same feeling now. My fingers are trembling. Alfred Stieglitz, he intrigues me. His style is distinctive. He's a pioneer, as I am. Though it's easier for a man these days to pursue his vision, he recognizes my view of the world.

All right, Stieglitz, I accept your invitation. *(She sighs with anticipation and looks into the distance.)* Georgia O'Keeffe in New York City.

Tonight, I'll sleep under the stars on the roof. Under the Texas sky I love so much. It will be hard to leave. The spirit of the land here inspires my work. The wind, the sky—there's no other place I feel so at home. Nature is my true company. But this Alfred Stieglitz. There is something about him.

(She gathers her things and strides confidently out of the room.)

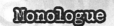

Georgia O'Keeffe Sample Text Set and Photo

This is a sample text set for a monologue on Georgia O'Keeffe that includes picture books, biographies, primary source photographs, letters, visual art, and more.

Websites

The Library of Congress Digital Collection
Georgia O'Keeffe and Alfred Stieglitz Correspondence
www.loc.gov/collections/georgia-okeeffe-and-alfred-stieglitz-correspondence/about-this-collection/

The Georgia O'Keeffe Museum Collections Online
collections.okeeffemuseum.org/

Books

Georgia's Bones by Jen Bryant
Georgia Rises: A Day in the Life of Georgia O'Keeffe by Kathryn Lasky
Georgia in Hawaii: When Georgia O'Keeffe Painted What She Pleased by Amy Novesky
Georgia O'Keeffe: The Artist in the Desert by Britta Benke
Through Georgia's Eyes by Rachel Rodriguez
Getting to Know the World's Greatest Artists: Georgia O'Keeffe by Mike Venezia
My Name is Georgia: A Portrait by Jeanette Winter

Alfred Stieglitz. *Georgia O'Keeffe*, 1918. Alfred Stieglitz Collection.
The Art Institute of Chicago

Name: _____ Date: _____

My Notes

Directions: Brainstorm and develop ideas using a set of texts.

Subject/individual being studied	
General background information	
Significant events (and feelings about these times)	
Conflicting information found in the texts	
Information learned from illustrations or photographs	
Other interesting facts (hopes, dreams, concerns)	

Name: _____ Date: _____

Monologue Planner

Directions: Answer the questions to help plan your monologue.

My character's name:	What has influenced the character?
Where does the character live?	What does the character value?
What is the character known for?	What character traits does the character show? How?
What challenge, decision, or dilemma does the character have?	What does the character want in this monologue?

Improvisation

Model Lesson: Characters Come to Life

Overview

In this strategy, students explore a character's reactions, responses, and traits. Using evidence from a text, they dramatize a moment that does not exist but could. The character is given a problem or situation, and students invent how the character might react in the moment. In this lesson, students are assigned a specific set of circumstances and take on a character who spontaneously enacts how they might behave, speak, and act in that situation.

Materials

▸ chart paper

▸ construction paper (one sheet per student)

▸ collection of wordless books with strong characterization

▸ *Getting Ready for Improvisation* (page 88)

▸ *Elements of Drama* (page 53)

Standards

Grades K–2

▸ Describes characters in a story, using key details

▸ Predicts how characters might behave based on identified character traits

▸ Contributes ideas for dialogue and plot while collaborating on character development

▸ Uses voice, gesture, and movement to communicate emotions

Grades 3–5

▸ Describes a character in depth, drawing on specific details in the text

▸ Predicts how characters might behave based on identified character traits and feelings

▸ Collaborates to devise original ideas for a drama/theater work

▸ Makes physical choices to develop a character and create meaning

Grades 6–8

▸ Describes how characters respond or change, citing text evidence

▸ Predicts how characters might behave based on analysis of their traits and feelings

▸ Develops an improvised character, expressing their inner thoughts, objectives, and motivations

▸ Uses physical choices and character objectives in drama

Grades 9–12

▸ Describes how characters respond or change, citing text evidence

▸ Predicts how characters might behave based on analysis of character traits and feelings

▸ Develops an improvised character, expressing their inner thoughts, objectives, and motivations

▸ Uses physical choices and character objectives in drama

Improvisation (cont.)

Preparation

Select a set of wordless books with strong characterization. Additional ideas are provided in the Specific Grade-Level Ideas.

Procedure

1. Share a wordless book with the whole class, discussing the sequence of events as they unfold. Point out how the author uses body language and facial expression to communicate the characters' thoughts and feelings. Tell them that when reading a wordless book, readers make inferences about the characters. These ideas are not revealed in words, so readers must make inferences based on the information provided in the pictures. Discuss the theme of the text: What is the message that the author wants us to know?

2. Explain to students that they are going to do an improvisation. They will select a character from one of the wordless books and then role-play that character in a scenario/event from the book. Tell students: "All action should be motivated by what you already know about the characters and situation and by what is brought forth as you improvise" (Cougar Dramatics, n.d., 8).

   Example: In the wordless book *Flotsam* by David Wiesner, a boy finds an old-fashioned camera that washes up onto the shore. The camera holds images of fantastic and magical creatures from the sea engaged in astounding activities. Note that the character can be any gender and any age. Invite students to identify clues about the character and the character's personality, interests, and background using the "Role on the Wall" strategy.

3. To do this, create the outline of a head and torso on the board. On the outside of the outline, record clues the students notice about the character from an external perspective. The character . . .

   ‣ is on vacation at the ocean

   ‣ is curious

   ‣ loves to explore

   ‣ is with their family

   On the inside of the outline, record ideas about what might be going through the character's head:

   ‣ "I wonder . . ."

   ‣ "I'm bored"

   ‣ "There's no one to play with"

> Role on the Wall "invites students to infer meaning about a character and to visually map the relationship between characteristics (emotions) and actions (behaviors) onto a simple outline of a human figure."
>
> —Jonothan Neelands and Tony Goode (2021, para. 1)

4. Have a group of students play out the scene through improvisation. They will follow the story structure but will create dialogue and actions in the moment, responding to each other's actions and words along the way. Ask students to move into the improvisation by imagining what conversations would take place as the action moves forward.

   Example: One student can portray the character on the beach as first curious; then bored; then swimming, being tossed by the waves; and then finding the camera. Other students can portray other characters on the beach, such as the lifeguard, curious kids coming over to look, bystanders, and so on. Each character can react in different ways to the unfolding action and dialogue. Perhaps the group of kids try and convince the main character to give up the camera, or maybe the lifeguard says that the camera is junk and should be thrown out.

Improvisation *(cont.)*

5. If desired, the improvised scene can be played out, discussed, and played again with different choices. Take time to debrief about choices made in dialogue, choices about the characters, and how the frame of the scene provided a frame for exploring character choice and language.

6. Now show students the collection of wordless books. Give them time to browse the books and then encourage them to think about the following questions:

   ▸ Why do you think some authors choose to tell their stories through pictures instead of words?

   ▸ What information about the characters, settings, and story are revealed through the illustrations?

   ▸ Are some events highlighted more than others? How?

   ▸ How do the authors reveal how the characters feel?

   ▸ How do the authors reveal the characters' traits?

7. Distribute *Getting Ready for Improvisation.* Have students work in pairs to choose one wordless book from the collection, respond to the questions, and preplan their improvisation. Use the Planning Questions to stimulate students' thinking.

8. As additional preparation for their improvisation, have students create a "Role on the Wall." To do this, give each student a large sheet of construction paper and have them draw the silhouette of the character they selected. Have students brainstorm what they know about the internal aspects of their character (emotions, character traits, needs, and desires) on the interior of the silhouette. Then have them brainstorm external aspects that affect the character (observed behavior, assumptions from others) on the outside of the silhouette.

9. Once students have planned their improvisations, invite partners to share them with the whole class. Discuss the improvisations, using the Discussion Questions.

Planning Questions

▸ What is happening in the scene?

▸ What can you infer about the characters from the information offered in the illustrations?

▸ What might the character be saying?

▸ What else do you know about the characters based on other things depicted in the story?

▸ How might you bring the scene to life through words and movement?

▸ How might you create your scene with a clear beginning, middle, and end?

▸ What is motivating the characters in the scene?

Discussion Questions

▸ What choices were made that brought the story to life?

▸ What character traits were demonstrated through the improvisation?

▸ How did improvisation help you better understand the characters and how they respond to problems, setting, and plot?

▸ What did the improvisation tell you about the story and its characters that the book did not?

▸ How do the different motivations of characters drive the choices they make?

Drama

Improvisation *(cont.)*

Specific Grade-Level Ideas

Grades K–2

Introduce students to improvisation with short theater games such as the transformation game "This Is Not a Stick." Put a stick or other object, such as a scarf, in the middle of a circle. Tell students that it can be anything other than what it is and that they will show us what it is using pantomime (acting without words). Students enter the circle one by one, pick up the object, and "show us" what it is through acting. For example, the stick could become a toothbrush, a jump rope, or a puppy depending on how students act it out. The rest of the students name what they think is being performed. When the item is guessed correctly, the next student can enter the circle and bring another idea to life through pantomime. This exercise builds the skill of creating something in the moment, which helps set the stage for improvised scenes.

"Improvisational activities help students tremendously. Every year I have had students tell me how much fun they had and I observe them change before my eyes. They are not as apprehensive about participating in class, whether it is reading aloud or doing presentations. These activities do not take up a lot of class time, yet the benefits are both social and academic."

—Joellen Maples (2007, 275)

Grades 3–5

Set up short scenes. Invite students to pantomime actions in the scene without using words. In character, they will respond to each other in the moment.

Or, you might also isolate a frozen moment or "freeze frame" in which one actor strikes a pose. Then, another actor enters the scene, poses to complete the image, and adds one line of dialogue to bring the scene to life. The frozen actor responds with one line. For example:

Actor 1: Creates a still image by leaning forward, looking at the ground

Actor 2: Enters the image (kneels down and looks) What do you see?

Actor 1: The most extraordinary parade of ants

Actor 1 leaves the image

Actor 2: Remains in the former position kneeling down looking down

Actor 3 Enters and creates a new image by reaching for Actor 2's hand

Actor 3: Here! I found your keys!

Actor 2: Thank you!

Actor 2 Leaves the image

Find additional theatre games for improvisation at Drama Resource (**dramaresource.com/category/drama-games/improvisation/**)

    © Shell Education

Improvisation *(cont.)*

Specific Grade-Level Ideas *(cont.)*

"The structure built into all improv games allows students to lend their own unique ideas and perspectives to shape the performance. Learning to open up and give of one's self while simultaneously learning to accept the ideas of others who differ from us develops the kind of open-minded mindset that teachers seek to develop in their students."

—Mary DeMichele (2019, para. 14)

Grades 6–8

Invite students to choose a character from a text and give the character different motivations. Have them change certain circumstances in the text to see how the plot could unfold differently. This subtle shift requires students to remain true to their portrayal of a character, but what fuels character choices will have dramatic implications on how the scene unfolds. You also could give students slips of paper with different genres and ask them to perform the scene in the style of different genres (for example, moving from comedy to tragedy).

Students also could use other art mediums as inspiration for their improvisations, such as a painting, photograph, or primary source image.

Grades 9–12

Have students use improvisation to create a situation in which characters have two opposing stances on an issue. Create a persuasive oral argument or a debate scenario between two or more characters. Provide students with questions or controversial statements, and then ask them to improvise two or more "position statements" in character to support or defend one side of the argument or the other.

Students also could use other art mediums as inspiration for their improvisations, such as a painting, photograph, or primary source image.

Visit **www.brainworks.mcla.edu** for improv games for virtual and in-person learning environments.

Name: _____ Date: _____

Getting Ready for Improvisation

Directions: Work with a partner to choose one of the following options. Take notes about ideas for action or dialogue for your characters.

Choose one scene from the book that you plan to act out. Write about or map the action that takes place in the scene.

Write words that come to mind as you think about what the character wants, what the character is thinking, and, as a result, how the character feels and behaves.

Poetry

Poetry

Understanding Poetry

Poetry engages students in writing, reading, speaking, and listening. Creating poems can capture the essence of an idea. As stated by Polly Collins, "when students create poems about topics of study, they enhance their comprehension through the connections they have made between the topic and their own lives, the topic and the world around them, and the poetry and the content texts they have read" (2008, 83). Developing understanding of language arts through the creation of poems challenges students to consider concepts related to language arts in new ways and to share their understanding through language and metaphor. Often, students enjoy creating poems but are not sure how to begin. The strategies provide guidance that will help students identify and work with rich language to explore the intricacies of language arts. Students use mentor poems to discover craft such as rhythm and beat, line breaks, and vivid verbs. They find that poems do not have to include end rhyme. "We are more interested in 'surprising images' or words that have a special sound pattern. They empower students to be 'word-gatherers'" (McKim and Steinbergh 1992). Students are invited to put words together in fresh new ways, drawing on evocative language and the playful juxtaposition of ideas, and create images through words as they write poems about concepts in language arts. This active engagement changes students' relationships with language arts as they find their own language to describe what they know.

By working with poetic language, symbolism, and metaphors, students can deepen their understanding of ideas and develop their abilities to express. Dr. Janette Hughes notes, "Poetry encourages an economy and precision in language that transfers to other types of oral and written communication" (2007).

Using poetry to explore language arts builds conceptual understanding. When students become poets, they fine-tune their writing and explore the use of patterns, rhythm, and metaphor. Writing poems challenges students to use language in fresh ways and develop a deeper understanding of language arts.

> "Poetry personalizes information. . . . It's a way for kids to internalize information. . . . It's the doorway into literacy for a lot of kids."
>
> —Georgia Heard (as cited in Borris 2016, para. 5, 12)

Elements of Poetry

The following list of terms related to poetry is informed by the Academy of American Poets (n.d.), and the work of Kwame Alexander (2019), Georgia Heard (1999), and Mary Oliver (1994).

- **Sound:** The creation of meaning with sound, often through the use of onomatopoeia, assonance, consonance, alliteration, and more.

- **Rhythm:** The beat of the poem, created through pattern, repetition, rhyme, syllables, and more.

- **Imagery:** Precise word choices and figurative language create an image in the reader's mind by evoking the senses and imagination.

- **Structure:** The organization of ideas. Some poems are free verse, others follow a specific form. Intentional line breaks and use of space on the page create meaning.

- **Density:** What is said (or can be said) in the space; density distinguishes poetry from regular speech and prose.

- **Audience:** Poets write with their audience in mind, revealing tone or attitude toward the message, subject, and more.

Poetry *(cont.)*

Strategies for Poetry

Poem for Two Voices

Compare-and-contrast is one of the most effective instructional strategies that teachers can use (Marzano 2007). A poem for two voices encourages students to explore two different perspectives on a topic. This form of poetry works well with opposite but related concepts or perspectives. Similarities and differences between concepts can be explored, providing the rhythm and feel of a dialogue. The poem is constructed by two writers, encouraging conversation about the content being explored and the ways to best translate ideas into poetic form. This collaborative work enables students to share what they know with their peers and to deepen learning. These poems also prompt students to better differentiate between two concepts being learned at the same time.

Spoken Word Poetry

Spoken word poetry has gained popularity in the last few decades, providing students with opportunities to share their writing and ideas in compelling new ways. Writing and performing their own poetry gives students the opportunity to explore a wide range of topics and issues from their own perspective as they "build their vocabulary of feeling, train their emotional intelligence, and prepare themselves to speak more accurately and confidently about any piece of writing or work of art" (Poetry Out Loud, n.d., 20). "Characterized by rhyme, repetition, improvisation, and word play, spoken word poems frequently refer to issues of social justice, politics, race, and community" (Poetry Foundation, n.d.).

> Poetry is "the bones and the skeleton of the language. It teaches you, if nothing else, how to choose your words."
>
> —Former US poet laureate Rita Dove (as cited in Umansky 2020, para. 2)

Found Poetry

This strategy prompts students to find and collect words or phrases from a variety of sources and encourages experimentation with the placement and juxtaposition of ideas to reveal fresh language, insights, relationships, and content connections. "Found poetry refashions a nonpoetic text (newspaper article, instruction manual, dictionary entry, etc.) into poetry through lineation, excision, and collage practices" (Poetry Foundation 2015, para. 1).

McKim and Steinbergh write about the juxtaposition of words noting, "The very fact of manipulating the words, discarding some, trading others, adding what one needs for sense, can teach us something about selection and choice in making poems. Joining two or three words that normally do not appear together can make fresh images, charging them with new energy and excitement" (1992). "Writing found poems is a structured way to have students review material and synthesize their learning" as students select language that resonates with them organizing around a particular topic (Facing History and Ourselves, n.d., para. 1).

> "Because writing found poetry is a personal process, students will approach their work in various ways. Some students will use pencil and paper. Others will cut out words and phrases from the printed source document and physically arrange them on a desktop or blank sheet of paper" (Library of Congress, n.d.).

Poetry (cont.)

"I Am From" Poems

This biographical strategy gives students the opportunity to investigate traditions, attitudes, environmental influences, and commonly held perceptions about a particular idea or within a particular era. Inspired by George Ella Lyon (2010), "I Am From" poems follow a pattern using the phrase *I am from* and can be created through student responses to prompts (Kuta 2003). Using the senses to reflect on what has been seen, heard, smelled, touched, and tasted, students become aware of how they (or characters, fictional or real) have been shaped by their unique experiences. The observations and reflections help students become aware of how time and place can influence one's perspectives. When written about characters, students consider how context and background influence the development of a character's frame of reference.

Ekphrastic Poetry

Ekphrastic poetry invites students to translate a work of art into a poem. "Through the imaginative act of narrating and reflecting on the "action of" the art form engaged with, "the poet may amplify and expand its meaning" (Kurzawski 2011). Responding to works of art through poetry encourages literacy learning for all levels. Students can "invent dialogue, create a story, ask questions, or reflect on what details in the painting mean." This can "often lead the poet to new insights and surprising discoveries" (Craven 2018, para. 4, 24). Hollander (2014) writes that ekphrastic poetry shares how the poet is interacting with the art piece by "addressing the image, making it speak, speaking of it interpretively, meditating upon the moment of viewing it, and so forth." While ekphrastic poetry is most often associated with visual art, it works well with other art forms such as music, dance, and theater.

> "When poetry is woven into the fabric of the everyday life of the classroom, it opens a window into a world outside of the classroom; it leads students to see the magic of the everyday, ordinary worlds all around them. Students begin to think in poetry, to speak poetry, and to read and write poetry naturally."
>
> —Georgia Heard (as cited in Ferlazzo 2020b)

Poem for Two Voices

Model Lesson: Compare and Contrast

Overview

Students explore poems for two voices that are constructed in a variety of ways (for example, some are conversations back and forth, while others compare and contrast). Students work in groups to create their own poems for two voices. As they do so, they gain a deeper understanding of perspective and point of view. Students also explore the interweaving of voices around a common issue or idea. These poems can prompt students to play with the back-and-forth nature of conversation and ideas. As the mentor poem "Something Has to Change" illustrates, poems for two voices can provide opportunities for the close reading of primary sources and documents.

Materials

▸ *Sample Poem for Two Voices* (pages 98–99)

▸ *Poem for Two Voices Plan* (page 101)

▸ *Tips for Performing Poetry* (page 102)

▸ *Elements of Poetry* (page 91)

▸ *Poetry Craft Tips* (page 100)

Standards

Grades K–2

▸ Identifies who is telling the story and acknowledges differences in points of view

▸ Writes poetic narrative in which they recount events

▸ Collaborates with peers in a guided drama experience

Grades 3–5

▸ Compares and contrasts the point of view from which different stories are narrated

▸ Produces clear and coherent writing appropriate to poetic form

▸ Collaborates with peers to revise and improve a dramatic work

Grades 6–8

▸ Analyzes how an author develops and contrasts points of view

▸ Produces clear and coherent writing appropriate to poetic form

▸ Revises and refines choices in a dramatic work

Grades 9–12

▸ Analyzes particular points of view, what is directly stated, and what is really meant

▸ Produces clear and coherent writing appropriate to poetic form

▸ Practices and revises a dramatic work

Poem for Two Voices *(cont.)*

Preparation

Explore a variety of poems for two voices, and try writing one of your own. Select some sample poems to share with students. If appropriate, select the *Sample Poem for Two Voices* or use other resources, such as the poems on Amy Ludwig VanDerwater's website called *The Poem Farm* or the book *Joyful Noise: Poems for Two Voices*, by Paul Fleischman, to use with your class during the lesson. Additional ideas are provided in the Specific Grade-Level Ideas.

Procedure

1. Display the selected poems for two voices with students. Explain that poems for two voices are constructed in a variety of ways. Sometimes they reveal different perspectives. Other times they consist of a playful back-and-forth between characters. At times there are shared lines located in the middle that show what the voices have in common. These shared lines are read together.

2. Select student volunteers to read/perform the selected poems with you in front of the class to help the class understand how the poems work.

3. Ask students questions, such as:
   ‣ What do you notice about how these poems are formed?
   ‣ What do you learn about each perspective?
   ‣ How do the poems reveal contrasting ideas?
   ‣ What do you notice about the lines read by both voices together?
   ‣ How does linking two voices in this poetic form create interest for the reader?

4. In pairs, instruct students to select a topic they would like to explore. Use the Planning Questions to guide discussion. Introduce *Poetry Craft Tips*.

5. Offer the *Poem for Two Voices Plan* to students and provide them time to plan and create their poems. Partnerships might choose to jot or sketch ideas into the planner while talking out their parts. Encourage them to act out their poems with their partners.

6. Provide students time to practice performing their poems aloud in two voices. As needed, help students in preparation for presenting their poems using the information in the *Tips for Performing Poetry* guide.

7. Have each pair present their poem to the rest of the class. Use the Discussion Questions to guide discussion. If desired, students can record their performances, listen to them, and discuss afterward. You also can share these poems on a class blog or as audio recordings.

> "Anyone lucky enough to have been read poetry as a child carries certain lines forever, and anyone who has found poetry as an adult knows to hang on as if to a wild horse. For poems wake us up, keep us company, remind us that our world is big and small.
>
> —Amy Ludwig VanDerwater (2018, XII)

Planning Questions

‣ What feelings are associated with each point of view?

‣ What words or phrases are associated with each idea?

‣ How might you reveal the differences and similarities of each point of view?

‣ What shared ideas or central lines could you write for the voices to read together?

Poem for Two Voices *(cont.)*

Discussion Questions

▸ What differences did you identify between the points of view?

▸ What did you learn by creating your poems?

▸ What did you learn by listening to poems read in two voices?

▸ What could you add to a poem you heard?

▸ How did the poetic form bring ideas to life?

Specific Grade-Level Ideas

Grades K–2

To provide students with other examples of poems for two voices, gather several of the books in Mary Ann Hoberman's *You Read to Me, I'll Read to You* collection and explore the poems included.

As a class, act out the characters in a familiar read-aloud before creating a collaborative poem for two voices. For example, using the book *Fireflies!* by Julie Brinckloe, you might have students infer and act out the points of view of the fireflies and of the boy who catches them. Create a poem as a class.

Additionally, students might compare and contrast topics of study, such as two different living things in an ecosystem, animal habitats, weather events, the main characters from two versions of the same fairy tale or folktale, or the jobs and roles of two different community members. Students learning their letter sounds might compare and contrast two letters and their sounds. For example, one voice might be things that start with the *b* sound (birds, box, bubbles, beach) while the other voice might be things that begin with the *s* sound (star, spider, sand, sock).

Poem for Two Voices *(cont.)*

Specific Grade-Level Ideas *(cont.)*

Grades 3–5

Share informational texts with the compare-and-contrast structure, such as *Is My Dog a Wolf? How Your Pet Compares to Its Wild Cousin* by Jenni Bidner. Have students demonstrate their understanding of the similarities and differences between different yet related topics by writing a poem for two voices.

With students, brainstorm a list of topics that you are exploring in the classroom. Invite students to create poems for two voices to compare and contrast concepts. Topics may include two planets in the solar system, two historical figures, two inaugural poets, two types of insects from an informational text, and more.

Grades 6–8

Have pairs of students find two different perspectives from a newspaper article or primary source. Invite pairs to take on the different perspectives, and have them go back and forth, creating a poem for two voices in the moment as they respond to one another. After creating lines that explore the issue and rehearsing the poem orally, have students revise and record their poems in written form or using technology.

Grades 9–12

Have students research and use evidence in texts to create poems around current issues and how they are portrayed in relation to point of view, assumptions, and biases. To do so, have students review different media (newspapers, advertisements, political cartoons, news broadcasts, social media postings, and more) to inform the development of their poems. Students will investigate how point of view can shape the way that information is conveyed.

Students also can explore historical contexts and the voices that have been marginalized or are dominant over time. Consider listening to oral histories to inform the perspectives of the poem. Poems for two voices can use quotations or exact words and phrases drawn from primary sources and can be performed in ways that include vocal tone and dramatic tension for heightened impact. These poems are powerful vehicles for activism and exploration of social and environmental justice issues.

Learn more about using primary sources with poetry by viewing *Teaching with Primary Sources*, a short video guide at the Academy of American Poets website (**poets.org**). This video features a discussion between Education Ambassador, Richard Blanco, and Educator-in-Residence, Dr. Madeleine Holzer.

Sample Poem for Two Voices

Reading Across a Text Set for "Something Has to Change"

Photographers were hired by the Works Progress Administration through the Farm Security Administration during the 1930s to help document the Great Depression's effect on American life. Photographer Dorothea Lange came upon a pea crop that had been ruined by freezing rain during her travels in March 1936. Lange snapped several photographs that day of a migrant worker and her children. One of those images was immediately published and became an icon of the Depression.

Ben Phelan (2014) writes of the photograph known as "Migrant Mother": "There are few images as deeply ingrained in the national consciousness as Migrant Mother. Yet for decades, no one knew what had become of this woman and her family. No one even knew her name: Lange never asked, and by the time the photo appeared in a local newspaper, the woman and her family had moved on to the next town."

Lange contacted the editor of the *San Francisco News*, telling him that "migrant workers were slowly starving to death in Nipomo, California. The story the *News* ran about them featured Lange's pictures; UPI picked it up, and within days the federal government supplied the workers with twenty thousand pounds of food. By that time, however, the woman and her family, desperate to find work, had moved on" (*Smithsonian Magazine* 2002, para. 3).

This poem for two voices infers two different perspectives of a momentary meeting between photographer Dorothea Lange and migrant worker Florence Owens Thompson in the Great Depression.

Text Set Used to Create This Poem

Listed beneath each source are direct quotations, particular words and phrases, and facts used in the poem.

Dunn, Geoffrey. 2003. "Photographic License." *New Times*. www.newtimesslo.com/archive/2003-12-03/archives/cov_stories_2002/cov_01172002.html.
Words or phrases paraphrased: seven hungry children; destitute

Lange, Dorothea. "The Assignment I'll Never Forget: Migrant Mother." *Popular Photography*, February 1960, 42–43.
Directly Quoted: "[She] seemed to know that my pictures might help her and so she helped me."
Words or phrases paraphrased: living on frozen vegetables from the surrounding fields

Library of Congress Research Guides. n.d. "Dorothea Lange's 'Migrant Mother' Photographs in the Farm Security Administration Collection." Accessed August 9, 2021. guides.loc.gov/migrant-mother/introduction.

Phelan, Ben. 2014. "The Story of the 'Migrant Mother.' *Antiques Roadshow*, April 14, 2014. www.pbs.org/wgbh/roadshow/stories/articles/2014/4/14/migrant-mother-dorothealange/.
Words or phrases paraphrased: Thompson wanted to spare her children the embarrassment

Smithsonian Magazine. 2002. "Migrant Madonna." www.smithsonianmag.com/arts-culture/migrant-madonna-60096830/.
Directly Quoted: "I did not ask her name or her history."
Directly Quoted: "She said she wouldn't sell the pictures. She said she'd send me a copy. She never did."
Words or phrases paraphrased: a sign that said "Pea-Pickers Camp"; the woman and her family, desperate to find work, had moved on
Fact gleaned: 20,000 pounds of food

Sample Poem for Two Voices (cont.)

Something Has to Change

Something has to change.	Something has to change.
	I was a photographer hired to document the impact of the Depression on America
I was a migrant worker struggling to feed and clothe my children	
	I drove by a sign for the pea-pickers camp
We were living off the vegetables that had frozen in the fields	
	I walked through mud toward a mother surrounded by seven hungry children huddled in a tent
She approached me to document the needs of migrant workers in a photograph	
	I took a handful of photographs of a family in poverty to tell the story
She said she wouldn't sell the pictures. She said she'd send me a copy. She never did.	
	[She] seemed to know that my pictures might help her and so she helped me. ...I called my editor, sharing the news that migrant workers were slowly starving in Nipomo…
I didn't want to embarrass my children	
	He published one of the images The photograph created change, and twenty thousand pounds of food were delivered within days . . . food for the destitute migrant workers
Desperate to find work, we had moved on	
	I did not ask her name or her history.

*See *Reading Across a Text Set for "Something Has to Change"* for sources that inspired this work.

117848—Integrating the Arts in Language Arts

Name: _____ Date: _____

Poetry Craft Tips

Directions: Read the tips below and choose one or more to try out in your poem.

- Help readers make a mental image in their mind by choosing **precise words**.
  Example: *periwinkle* instead of *blue*

- Use words that show one or more of the **five senses.**

- The decision of where to use **line breaks** impacts meaning.
  Example: Set a word or phrase on a line all by itself for impact.

- Use **alliteration** with purpose.
  Example: To show the mood or to create pacing (how quickly or slowly the reader reads a section of your poem)

- Try a **circular ending**. Begin and end your poem by repeating a word, phrase, or idea.

- **Vary the length of your stanzas.** Follow a long stanza with a short stanza (or the reverse) to show a change in events, a change within a character, the passing of time, and more.

- Repeat words or phrases to create rhythm and beat.

- Repeat words or phrases to show that an idea is important.

- Convey feelings, motivations, and action with **strong verbs.**
  Example: *dip into the water* is different from *cannonball into the water*

- Use a **metaphor** or **simile** to compare, enhancing meaning and imagination.

Source: Adapted from "Writing Strategies Used in Poetry" (pages 48–49) of *Writing Is Magic, or Is It? Using Mentor Texts to Develop the Writer's Craft* by Jennifer M. Bogard and Mary C. McMackin (2015).

Name: _____ Date: _____

Poem for Two Voices Plan

Directions: Brainstorm ideas for your poem before you begin writing. Use this planner to organize your ideas.

Summary of Event: _____

Poem Title: _____

Voice 1: _____

Voice 2: _____

Thoughts and Ideas

Shared Thoughts and Ideas

Thoughts and Ideas

Name: _____   Date: _____

Tips for Performing Poetry

Directions: Consider these helpful tips as you play around with different ways to recite a poem.

Tips to Consider

- Think about how you want your audience to feel as you recite your poem.

- Find parts that might be spoken loudly, quietly, quickly, or slowly.

- Find a place in which you can pause for added effect.

- Use facial expressions to match meaning.

- Match the tone of your voice to the meaning of the lines.

- Find places for big or small movements.

Spoken Word Poetry

Model Lesson: Performing Poetry

Overview

Considering one's audience is at the heart of this strategy. The goal is for students to affect an audience with the power of their words as they perform a poem orally. They learn about spoken word poetry by viewing videos of a variety of spoken word poets and jotting a list of what the poets do to create an impact. Students then choose a poem that they connect with and feel passionate about (an existing poem or one they wrote). They think about who needs to hear this message (audience) and how they will perform the poem to have an effect on the particular audience.

Materials

- video clips of spoken word performances to share with students

- texts of choice (see the *Recommended Resources* on pages 15–16 for ideas on where to find diverse texts)

- *Gathering Ideas for Performing Poetry* (page 108)

- *Tips for Performing Poetry* (page 102)

- *Marking the Meaning* (page 109) *(optional)*

- *Elements of Poetry* (page 91)

- *Poetry Craft Tips* (page 100)

Standards

Grades K–2

- Describes how words or phrases suggest feelings or supply meaning

- Demonstrates understanding of word relationships and rhyme in writing

- Contributes to group guided drama experiences and informally shares with peers

Grades 3–5

- Demonstrates understanding of figurative language

- Uses knowledge of language and rhyme in writing

- Presents drama/theater work informally to an audience

Grades 6–8

- Demonstrates understanding of figurative language

- Demonstrates understanding of language, word relationships, and rhyme in writing

- Performs a rehearsed drama/theater work for an audience

Grades 9–12

- Determines the meaning of words and phrases as they are used in the text, including figurative and connotative meanings

- Demonstrates understanding of figurative language, word relationships, and nuances in word meanings

- Performs a scripted drama/work for a specific audience

Spoken Word Poetry *(cont.)*

Preparation

Locate video clips of spoken word performances that are appropriate for your grade level from resources such as Poetry Out Loud (**poetryoutloud.org**), the Poetry Foundation, Brave New Voices, or Facing History and Ourselves. Locate a video of inaugural poet Amanda Gorman's performance of "The Hill We Climb." See the Recommended Resources (pages 15–16) for additional poetry websites. Additional ideas are provided in the Specific Grade-Level Ideas.

> Performance poetry "involves creating poetry that doesn't just want to sit on paper, that something about it demands it be heard out loud or witnessed in person."
>
> —Spoken word artist Sarah Kay (2011)

Procedure

1. Distribute copies of *Gathering Ideas for Performing Poetry*. Introduce the idea of spoken word poetry by sharing videos and examples of spoken word artists performing poems. For example, we suggest inaugural poet Amanda Gorman's performance of "The Hill We Climb." Explain to students that they can use their activity sheets to write things they notice in the videos while they watch.

2. Ask students, individually or as a group, to create a list of specific choices the performers make to bring the poem to life using their bodies, voices, and emotions (for example, pacing, intonation, inflection, sense of emotion, volume, speed). Students can reference their notes from *Gathering Ideas for Performing Poetry* to share ideas.

3. Explain to students that they are going to perform a poem of their choice (an existing poem or one they write on their own). If it is helpful, invite students to use the *Marking the Meaning* graphic organizer to

look for patterns and interesting moments in their chosen or original poem. Some students may choose to improvise a poem in the moment.

4. Model working with a poem. Review *Elements of Poetry*. Consider the story or message being communicated, the emotions and tone explored, and the use of poetic devices appropriate for students. Demonstrate for students how to identify opportunities to amplify meaning by adding performative elements such as voice intonation, the integration of pauses, gestures, and facial expression. This can include emphasizing key words and phrases and highlighting shifts in emotion and sensory descriptions.

5. Display or distribute copies of *Tips for Performing Poetry* and discuss the suggested tips.

6. Ask students to think about the meaning of their poems and how they wish to express the message for a specific audience. Invite them to bring their poems to life by employing ideas from their list of effective strategies for performance (step 2) as well as the *Tips for Performing Poetry*.

7. Place students into small groups and have them rehearse their poems.

8. Provide opportunities for students to rehearse the poems several times, integrating feedback from self-reflection and peer reviews to strengthen their performance. If desired, have students record their poems so they can reflect on their performances and make adjustments.

Spoken Word Poetry *(cont.)*

9. Give students an opportunity to perform their poems for an audience (large or small). Use the Discussion Questions to debrief students.

10. **Extension idea:** After students have explored a variety of spoken word examples and texts, invite them to create their own. This can be linked to a topic of study, or you can give students the choice to select an idea based on a theme. This even can be details or topics from their own lives. Offer *Poetry Craft Tips* as a resource for students.

"Poetry provides many opportunities for authentic oral practice. When students rehearse their reading of a poem, they repeatedly read the text aloud for a real purpose—to prepare to perform it expressively and meaningfully for an audience."

—Timothy Rasinski (2014, 32)

Discussion Questions

▶ How were messages communicated through the spoken word performance?

▶ What do you notice about performance choices in the use of voice (pacing, intonation, inflection, sense of emotion, volume, speed)?

▶ How do the performance choices bring the meaning of the poem to life?

▶ Why do you think some poets insist that poems are meant to be heard?

Spoken Word Poetry *(cont.)*

Specific Grade-Level Ideas

Grades K–2

Discuss with students how poems can announce, tell the news, complain, entertain, and more. Provide students with poems that are fun to share—poems that are relatable; full of rhythm and beat, silly words, or rhymes; and based on their interest. For example, check out "Bleezer's Ice Cream" by Jack Prelutsky and the list called *Poems Kids Like* at **www.poets.org**.

Invite students to use spoken word poetry to share their own opinions (favorite book, pet, season) or to share a problem in their world that they want to fix. Model and help them practice techniques from the *Tips for Performing Poetry* on page 102.

Explore nature through spoken word poetry. For example, have students view and follow a live animal webcam or a migration journey. Then write a class poem with students that tells the news of the latest happenings. Have students perform the poem as a class to tell others the news. Visit Journey North (**www.journeynorth.org**) for migration journeys. Include books about nature such as *Bloom Bloom!* by April Pulley Sayre, and invite students to perform the poem and even add an original line or two to the books they choose.

Grades 3–5

In addition to implementing ideas for K–2, students can choose a moment in their lives that has somehow shaped who they are. Have them tell the story of that moment through a spoken word poem and bring the audience into the moment using techniques from *Tips for Performing Poetry* on page 102. Spark students' thinking by playing and discussing Krista Tippett's interview with Naomi Shihab Nye. You can find the interview online at **onbeing.org/programs/naomi-shihab-nye-your-life-is-a-poem-mar2018/**.

To encourage students to think about what is meaningful to them, invite them to create a heart map and explore what is in their hearts. Students also can create a spoken word poem with the purpose of persuading others to take action or to make changes. This might be organized around a question they pose to encourage their audience to think in new ways. You might spark ideas by reading a picture book that encourages calls to action such as *All the Water in the World* by George Ella Lyon and *We Are Water Protectors* by Carole Lindstrom.

> "Poetry is a tool for disruption and creation and is necessary for generations of humans to know who they are and who they are becoming in the wave map of history. Without poetry, we lose our way."
>
> —Joy Harjo (2019)

Spoken Word Poetry *(cont.)*

Specific Grade-Level Ideas *(cont.)*

Grades 6–8

Share the work of poet and spoken word artist Elizabeth Acevedo. See the book *The Poet X* (2019) and her performance of her poetry (2018) about life in middle school.

Invite students to read *The Undefeated* by Kwame Alexander and experience Alexander's performance of the poem online. Offer small groups an opportunity to perform the poem. Pose the question, "How might the class perform the poem together?"

Discuss with students how poems can address social and personal roles. Show students how spoken word poetry can be a vehicle for activism. Visit the Poetry Foundation's website to explore a collection of poems called *Poems of Protest, Resistance, and Empowerment: Why Poetry Is Necessary and Sought After During Crises:* **www.poetryfoundation. org/collections/101581/poems-of-protest-resistance-and-empowerment**.

Have students choose an issue they are passionate about and create a spoken word poem to help make a change, increase awareness, promote dialogue, and spark a call to action. Challenge them to write or find a "power line" that will anchor and launch their poem. Have them improvise from the jumping-off point of the power line.

Grades 9–12

In addition to the ideas for grades 6–8, share National Youth Poet Laureate and inaugural poet Amanda Gorman's TED-Ed Student Talk "Using Your Voice Is a Political Choice" (2016). Ask students to create poems that demonstrate a stance inspired by Gorman's claim that "poetry has never been the language of barriers, it's always been the language of bridges."

Show students examples of the Climate Museum's poetry slam at the Apollo Theater in Harlem (Lindwall, 2019). Have students identify techniques (gestures, pauses, methods for emphasis) they could imitate in their own work.

"Emotions are to poetry as improvisation is to jazz. It's a key element. Without it, you don't have the thing. We can feel emotions from reading words on the written page but sharing them when we recite a poem means using our voice, body language, and gestures along with our facial expressions."

—Kwame Alexander (2019, 128)

Name: _____ Date: _____

Gathering Ideas for Performing Poetry

Directions: Listen to a spoken word poem. Write what you notice.

Title of poem: _____

What body movements and hand gestures are used?	
How are facial expressions used?	
How does the speaking volume and speed change?	
How are pauses used?	
What other actions do you notice?	

Name: _____ Date: _____

Marking the Meaning

Directions: Choose a poem and write about it.

Title of poem: _____

Name of poet: _____

What patterns do you notice in the poem?	
What catches your attention or surprises you in the poem?	
What is the poem about? What specific choices will you make in your performance to share the poem's meaning?	
What phrases are most striking or important?	

Found Poetry

Model Lesson: A Word Bank

Overview

This lesson starts with a shared sensory event, such as a rainstorm, or a weather event experienced virtually. Students drop what they are doing and observe with their senses. As a class, they use their senses to brainstorm a list of words and phrases that come to mind in the moment, and the teacher records the ideas. This creates a bank of rich, sensory words and might include onomatopoeia, strong verbs, repeated words for rhythm (*drip, drip*), and more. Once the word bank is created, students pluck their favorite words and phrases right from the bank and arrange them into found poems by playing with rhythm and beat and repetition, setting a word on a line of its own, using circular endings, and more.

Materials

▸ *Sample Found Poems* (page 114)

▸ chart paper

▸ *Elements of Poetry* (page 91)

▸ *Poetry Craft Tips* (page 100)

"There is no single strategy for creating a found poem. Select words and phrases and use them creatively in any way that moves you." (Library of Congress, n.d.)

Standards

Grades K–2

▸ Demonstrates understanding of word relationships and rhyme in writing

▸ Links events in a poetic narrative

▸ Collaborates with peers in a guided drama experience

Grades 3–5

▸ Uses knowledge of language and rhyme in writing

▸ Organizes clear and coherent writing appropriate to poetic form

▸ Collaborates with peers to revise and improve a dramatic work

Grades 6–8

▸ Demonstrates understanding of language, word relationships, and rhyme in writing

▸ Organizes clear and coherent writing appropriate to poetic form

▸ Revises and refines choices in a dramatic work

Grades 9–12

▸ Demonstrates understanding of figurative language, word relationships, and nuances in word meanings

▸ Produces clear and coherent writing in which the development, organization, and style are appropriate to task, purpose, and audience

▸ Cooperates as a creative team to make interpretive choices for a dramatic work

Found Poetry (cont.)

Preparation

This lesson is meant to react to a spontaneous shared event with the class. Although it is written as the reaction to a live thunderstorm, any shared sensory-rich experiences will work, such as the hatching of class butterflies or chicks, a current event/breaking news story students watch or experience, or a reflection on a class trip or school assembly. You also could play a video of an experience in nature, such as the ocean waves crashing or a tornado moving through an area, to foster a sensory experience. Additional ideas are provided in the Specific Grade-Level Ideas.

Procedure

1. When it begins to storm outside, have students drop everything they're doing, gather around the windows, and observe the rain and thunder. Alternatively, show a video experience of a natural event such as a storm or crashing waves. Make sure the volume is turned up so that students can experience the sounds of the event. See the preparation notes for other sensory experience ideas.

2. Ask students to share words and phrases that come to mind while they are experiencing the moment in real time. Record the phrases on chart paper, creating a bank of words. Accept all ideas and offer some sound words, verbs, short phrases, and repeated words.

3. Model the act of choosing words from the bank, and show students how to play with the words to create a found poem. Play with the order, play with the line breaks, and trade a few words or phrases with other words. Experiment with repeating a word to create a rhythm and a beat. Try a circular ending in which you begin and end the poem with the same word or line. Keep the process fluent and flexible.

4. Invite students to create one or two of their own found poems using the same bank of words. They'll likely ask you if they can add a word or phrase that is not in the bank. Yes! This shows they are engaged and generating words on the spot, and you can even have them add words to the bank as they continue to generate ideas.

Students can brainstorm words and phrases or create their found poems in a digital environment such as Jamboard, Google Slides, or another digital interactive whiteboard app.

5. As students work, look for opportunities to point out any examples of line breaks, alliteration, metaphor, simile, or onomatopoeia that are included in their poems. Challenge them to consider *Poetry Craft Tips* as they work.

6. Invite students to speak the words aloud as they put them together, listening for rhythms they like and playing with pauses.

7. After students explore, begin an ongoing discussion about the craft of line breaks and how poets break lines in a certain places for impact (setting a word on a line of its own, for example). Invite them to think about how the line breaks impact the meaning; the way in which the poem is read, and the visual appeal of the poem. You might visit Amy Ludwig VanDerwater's website called *The Poem Farm* to read her thoughts about line breaks and white space, and to share her collection of poems that model the technique of intentional line breaks.

8. Provide students time to share their poems with the class. Use the Discussion Questions to reflect on the process.

Found Poetry *(cont.)*

Discussion Questions

- What craft strategies were you excited to try out (repeating a word or phrase, setting a word or phrase on a line of its own, using a strong verb or precise word)?

- How did you play with the arrangement of the words?

- What did you learn from listening to other students' poems?

- What did you learn about intentional line breaks?

Specific Grade-Level Ideas

Grades K–2

Create word bowls full of words (cut from sources such as magazines, content-area texts, words you write on strips of paper, and so on). Students choose words and phrases from the bowl and arrange them in found poems. You also might have students cut their own words from magazines or newspapers and create their own word bowls.

Share poems from Georgia Heard's *The Arrow Finds Its Mark: A Book of Found Poems* and choose one as a mentor poem for writing a found poem with the class.

Share the poem "Rhyme" by Elizabeth Coatsworth to explore rhythm and beat.

Grades 3–5

Students can use found poetry as a way to summarize an article from a magazine or a short text passage. They can choose words and phrases that summarize the main idea of the article and present the main idea through a found poem.

Students also might create poems using existing words and phrases they find in texts such as recipes, magazines, newspapers, song lyrics, clothing catalogs, letters, or their writer's notebooks. They should choose words or phrases that speak to them—words that create mental images or spark interest. Have students experiment with line breaks to create meaning and explore how the poem looks and sounds. They also can experiment with a variety of ways to juxtapose the words and may add others as needed.

Have students use a mentor text for found poetry such as *The ABCs of Plum Island, Massachusetts* by Jenn Bogard to capture the history, nature, and industry of a special place. Students can find words in local newspaper articles, blogs, maps, signs, books, videos, displays in the community, and more. Have them experience the excitement of researching primary sources at their local library archival center (in person or online). Invite a local librarian to demonstrate how to cite the sources they use in their found poems.

"A poetic line break is the deliberately placed threshold where a line of poetry ends and the next one begins."

—Hannah Huff (2018, para. 4)

Found Poetry *(cont.)*

Specific Grade-Level Ideas *(cont.)*

Grades 6–8

In addition to the specific grade 3–5 ideas, invite students to research the history of inaugural poetry and find out which poets have read poems at US presidential inaugurations (Robert Frost, Maya Angelou, Miller Williams, Elizabeth Alexander, Richard Blanco, Amanda Gorman). Show students videos of the readings and invite them to jot words and phrases that strike them while listening. Have students use these found words to create their own found poems that capture the inspiring themes of the inaugural poems such as hope, valuing perspectives, and coming together.

Invite students to try out blackout poetry with a book such as *Make Blackout Poetry: Turn These Pages into Poems* by John Carroll. Blackout poetry—also called erasure poetry—is a form of found poetry in which the writer blacks out words on a poem (or any type of text) to call attention to other words/phrases or create new meaning from the words/phrases that remain visible on the page. For a digital tool for creating blackout poetry, students might visit the website Blackout Poetry Maker at **blackoutpoetry.glitch.me/**.

"When students have selected their words and phrases, they combine, arrange, and rearrange them, considering not only the content and meaning of the emerging poem but also its rhythm and line breaks." (Library of Congress, n.d.)

Grades 9–12

Invite students to collect words and phrases from primary source texts such as letters or newspaper articles about a historical movement or time period. You might introduce them to Tracy K. Smith, the 22nd US poet laureate from 2017–2019, and her work with erasure poetry, which is a type of found poetry.

Invite students to keep a list to capture words and phrases as they read a complex text, watch videos, and read articles. Students may find it helpful to summarize the key ideas of a text and cement learning through found poetry.

Organize students in small groups to share and pool their words. Put the word collections in bags or bowls and have groups swap word collections with one another. Students then can create a group poem of found words with their new set of words as a way to distill highlights of a unit.

Sample Found Poems

This word bank was created by students during a thunderstorm. Then the students created the poems shown below.

Word Bank

angels bowling	daytime	inside recess	pouring
birds hiding	drip	it's over	puddles
boom	drop	leaves holding on for life	raincoats
boots	eerie	light	tap tap tap tap
chilly	flash	lightning	trees
cold	flicker	nighttime	trees bend
crash	goose bumps	pour	trees sway
dark	gray		wet

Found Poems

Tap tap tap tap.
Flicker
Boom
Boom

Tap tap tap tap.
Flicker
Daytime
Flicker
Nighttime

Tap tap tap tap.
Boom!

Flash

Flash

Flashes of light

Angels bowling

Boom!

Inside Recess

While the trees

Bend and sway
Bend and sway

Inside recess
while the

Sky flicker flickers

It's pouring rain.

Inside Recess

"I Am From" Poems

Model Lesson: Character Context

Overview

Students write an "I Am From" poem from the point of view of a character in a story, magazine article, nonfiction literature, newspaper, movie, plays, and so on. "I Am From" poems were developed by teacher and writer George Ella Lyon (2010). She suggests a simple writing prompt for exploring personal histories and influences. Students begin each line with the phrase *I am from* and then introduce specific details of the character's life, such as special people, places, objects, influences, cultural traditions, foods, and sayings. This reflective process provides students with the opportunity to understand a character.

Materials

▸ collection of texts about the same subject

▸ *Sample "I Am From" Poems* (pages 119–120)

▸ *"I Am From" Planner* (page 121)

▸ *Elements of Poetry* (page 91)

▸ *Poetry Craft Tips* (page 100)

Standards

Grades K–2

▸ Describes characters in a story and how they respond to events and challenges

▸ Recalls key details

▸ Collaborates with peers in a guided drama experience

Grades 3–5

▸ Describes a character's feelings and motivations

▸ Refers to explicit details and examples from the text when drawing inferences

▸ Collaborates with peers to revise and improve a dramatic work

Grades 6–8

▸ Analyzes how aspects of a character are revealed

▸ Cites strong textual evidence to support inferences

▸ Revises and refines choices in a dramatic work

Grades 9–12

▸ Analyzes how complex characters are developed

▸ Cites strong and thorough textual evidence to support inferences

▸ Practices and revises a dramatic work

"I Am From" Poems (cont.)

Preparation

Read *Sample "I Am From" Poems* to become familiar with how the format can be used to write about a literary character. Select one sample poem to share with students, or select a different "I Am From" poem from a search online or that you write yourself. Additional ideas are provided in the Specific Grade-Level Ideas.

Procedure

1. Explain to students that they get to choose a character from any piece of text and write about their life story through the character's point of view. Read aloud the sample poem you selected. Have students discuss the ways in which the writer describes the character's experiences from the character's point of view.

2. Distribute the *"I Am From" Planner* and have students discuss the various categories and possible responses. Consider adding additional prompts based on specific characters you are studying. You may wish to review the poem(s) you read in relation to the *"I Am From" Planner*. Use the Planning Questions to facilitate discussion.

3. After this overview, allow time for students to talk, reflect, and record words, phrases, or sentences about their literary characters.

4. Invite students to use their brainstormed words and phrases to create their own "I Am From" poems. Make sure students understand that they do not have to include all the topics or words they brainstormed.

5. Provide time for partners to revise and confer about their poems. Encourage students to talk with others who know the character through text, movies, or plays. Invite students to revise using ideas from Poetry Craft Tips.

6. Invite students to practice presenting their poems orally, providing opportunities to rehearse reading a few times alone or with a partner.

7. Offer students a chance to share and discuss their poems. Use the Discussion Questions to lead the discussion about the poems.

Planning Questions

▸ Who are the people who influenced your literary character? Why? How?

▸ What are the places or settings that influenced your character? Why? How?

▸ What are the objects that influenced your character? Why? How?

▸ What cultural traditions might the character have grown up with?

▸ What sayings might the character have heard or said?

▸ What interests or passions does the character have?

▸ What poetic devices can you use (repetition, metaphor, alliteration)?

Discussion Questions

▸ What did you learn about the character?

▸ What are some ways your poems are different? The same?

▸ What are some examples of words or phrases that reveal where the character is from (places, experiences, people, objects)?

▸ As you listened to the poems presented, what struck you about the characters' backgrounds and influences?

"I Am From" Poems (cont.)

Specific Grade-Level Ideas

Grades K–2

Develop interview questions with your students and have them interview their caregivers to find out some of their favorite things from when they were babies and toddlers. For example, favorite book, blanket, toys, food, first word, and more. Work with students to create "I Am From" poems using these ideas.

Show students how to use "I am" statements to form the poem in present tense. Read aloud and discuss the text *I Am Every Good Thing* by Derrick Barnes, written in the present tense with celebrations and affirmations through "I am" statements. (Note: This is also a powerful text to use for spoken word poetry.)

Work with students to write a class poem with content from your curriculum. For example, create an "I Am From" poem from the perspective of a community helper, a favorite author or illustrator, an earthworm, the character in a favorite class song or book, a hibernating bear, a seedling, or the school principal. You also can read aloud a text such as *A Place to Start a Family: Poems About Creatures That Build* by David L. Harrison to model how to write from the perspective of an animal that builds a shelter for itself by reading a text.

Grades 3–5

Invite students into a meaningful discussion to explore identity and what makes up one's identity (Is it the notion of "place"? How is it more than the physical "place"?) by reading aloud *Where Are You From?* by Yamile Saied Méndez. Visit the *School Library Journal's* blog *The Classroom Bookshelf* and find the entry called "Complicating and Celebrating Identity: Where Are You From?" to guide you in your discussion with students.

Invite students to create an "I Am From" poem for advocacy and environmental justice. You can spark their ideas with a text such as *Sea Bear: A Journey for Survival* by Lindsay Moore and model how to write from the perspective of the polar bear. Visit the *School Library Journal's* blog *The Classroom Bookshelf* and read the entry called "A Subtle Call to Action for Planet Earth in Debut Picture Book *Sea Bear: A Journey for Survival*" to learn more about this book.

Students also can interview each other "in character" using the *"I Am From" Planner*. Invite students to write poems from the point of view of characters in a text and have them introduce themselves in character as they read their poems.

"I Am From" Poems *(cont.)*

Specific Grade-Level Ideas *(cont.)*

Grades 6–8

Invite students to read and discuss *Where I'm From* by George Ella Lyon and use it as a mentor text.

Invite students to give voice to marginalized perspectives (people, animals, sea life, the environment) through an "I Am From" poem. For example, have students research Joy Harjo, a US poet laureate and member of the Muscogee/Creek Nation, by watching her interviews online, reading her biographical content, and reading a collection of her poems (found at **poets.org**). After hearing Joy Harjo talk about her life and her art, and reading a body of her work, have students write an "I Am From" poem using evidence from the multimodal texts to imagine and write from her perspective. How does she give voice to Indigenous peoples?

Students might also research and write from the perspective of a Young People's Poet Laureate, such as Naomi Shihab Nye, Margarita Engle, Jacqueline Woodson, Kenn Nesbitt, J. Patrick Lewis, Mary Ann Hoberman, or Jack Prelutsky.

Grades 9–12

In addition to the grade 6–8 suggestions, students can use "I Am From" poetry to explore the perspectives within scientific concepts, including chemical processes, elements of the periodic table, their everyday occurrences, and more.

"My sense of place—I have—it's not quite a theory, but the way I've been thinking about it lately as an engineer—that everything has a physical landscape, an emotional landscape, and a natural landscape. And I think the way those three things combine form our sense of place and belonging and connection."

—Richard Blanco (2020)

Sample "I Am From" Poems

One Day
by Ann Piper

I am Omar.
I am from lost memories of Somalia,
Where my parents, my brother Hassan, and I lived,
Peacefully,
Lovingly.

Until the men with guns came.

I am from running,
With my brother, always searching.
Searching.
Searching.
Hopeful for my mother's smile.

I am from Dadaab Refugee Camp in Kenya, Africa,
Where "Everything can change
Or nothing can change"
For Fifteen Years
Until

I am from America,
Flying in a big metal bird.
"Those who are lost look to the stars to lead them home"
Still hopeful for my mother's smile.
One day.

Inspired by: *When Stars are Scattered* by Victoria Jamieson and Omar Mohamed (2020)

Sample "I Am From" Poems (cont.)

Plankton

I am from blue water oceans
Tiny plants that float in your seas
Countless shapes, sizes, colors and ornamentation
a billion of us drift
in the top layer of the ocean

I am from grazing
across an invisible pasture of sea light
Feeding on nutrients
Multiplying every day

I am from food chains
eaten by fish, animals and zooplankton
I jumpstart the chain of life

I am from photosynthesis
carbon dioxide + sunlight = sugar + energy
Pumping out oxygen from my tiny body
Half of the oxygen you breathe is from our work!

I am from making life with light
I hold nitrogen, phosphorus and iron
all living things require these for their metabolism
Everything is connected

This poem was created from language in *Ocean Sunlight: How Tiny Plants Feed the Seas* by Molly Bang and Penny Chisholm (2012).

Name: _____ Date: _____

"I Am From" Planner

Directions: Complete the chart by brainstorming ideas for an "I Am From" poem about a literary character. Then, on a separate sheet of paper, write your poem, beginning a line with "I am from" and developing the idea over one or more lines. Then, start fresh with "I am from" and add more ideas.

Who or what is important to the character? What is in the character's heart?	Important moments in the character's life:
The character's wishes, wants, or needs:	Places or objects that are special to the character:
Quotations from the character:	The character's traditions or beliefs:

Ekphrastic Poetry

Model Lesson: Art Inspires Art

Overview

In this lesson, students immerse themselves in examples of poems inspired by art. They visit a museum (virtually or in person) and choose a work of visual art (painting, drawing, sculpture) that sparks their interest. They engage by viewing the artwork closely and translating it into poetry. When creating their original poems, students might take the perspective of a subject or inanimate object within the art; speak directly to something or someone in the art; respond to colors or shapes that strike them; focus on a detail or a piece of the scene; and more, depending on their interest.

Materials

‣ a museum trip (virtual trip or in person)

‣ *Ekphrastic Poetry Sample 1* (pages 125–128) *(optional)*

‣ *Ekphrastic Poetry Sample 2* (pages 129–132) *(optional)*

‣ *Ekphrastic Poetry Sample 3* (pages 133–134) *(optional)*

‣ *World Make Way: New Poems Inspired by Art from the Metropolitan Museum of Art*, edited by Lee Bennett Hopkins *(optional)*

‣ *Elements of Poetry* (page 91)

‣ *Poetry Craft Tips* (page 100)

Standards

Grades K–2

‣ Describes the overall structure of a poetic text

‣ Writes a poetic narrative

‣ Collaborates with peers in a guided drama experience

Grades 3–5

‣ Explains and refers to the structural elements of poems

‣ Produces clear and coherent writing appropriate to poetic form

‣ Collaborates with peers to revise and improve a dramatic work

Grades 6–8

‣ Analyzes how a poem's form or structure contributes to its meaning

‣ Produces clear and coherent writing appropriate to poetic form

‣ Revises and refines choices in a dramatic work

Grades 9–12

‣ Demonstrates understanding of figurative language, word relationships, and nuances in word meanings.

‣ Produces clear and coherent writing in which the development, organization, and style are appropriate to task, purpose, and audience

‣ Refines a dramatic concept to demonstrate a critical understanding of historical and cultural influences of original ideas applied to a dramatic work

Ekphrastic Poetry *(cont.)*

Preparation

Using a text such as *World Make Way: New Poems Inspired by Art from the Metropolitan Museum of Art*, edited by Lee Bennett Hopkins (2018), or the samples provided on pages 125–134, get to know the concept of Ekphrastic poetry, which is poetry created about art. Locate examples to share with students from books or websites such as **randomnoodling.blogspot. com**. Additional ideas are provided in the Specific Grade-Level Ideas.

Procedure

1. Share examples of Ekphrastic poems and their corresponding paintings, and lead a discussion with students about the poems. What do they notice? Enjoy? Wonder?

2. Have students visit collections of art from a museum or gallery website; outdoor murals, sculptures, or installations; or a museum in person.

3. Instruct students to choose a piece of visual art that speaks to them.

4. Allow students time to observe the art closely. In preparation for writing their own poems, they should create a list of their experiences with the art. Ask them the following questions:
   ▸ What did you notice about the elements of visual art used in the work (items in the painting or parts of the photograph)?
   ▸ How do the elements work together to communicate or share a message?
   ▸ How has the art affected you personally (emotions, memories, connections)?

5. Revisit the elements of poetry and encourage students to intentionally integrate these into their writing. Remind students that not all poems have to rhyme.

6. Have students respond to the visual art by writing a poem as they are looking at it.

7. Invite students to share their poems with each other to celebrate how one form of art can be turned into another form of art.

> To find inspiring art, consider the website of your local or regional museum or gallery, a famous museum such as the Metropolitan Museum of Art or the Louvre, or a website such as Google Arts and Culture or the Library of Congress. Also, consider outdoor art installations, murals, and sculptures in your local area.

8. If desired, challenge students to revise their poems using one or more ideas from *Poetry Craft Tips*. You might also discuss the elements of visual art/design (line, shape, color, form, texture, value, space). (See the *Elements of Visual Art* page 171 for more explanation about these terms.)

9. Discuss students' poems using the Discussion Questions.

Discussion Questions

▸ What part of the artwork strikes you?

▸ What does the artwork make you think of or remind you of?

▸ Will you write a free verse poem or a poem with a specific format?

▸ What craft strategies could you try? (Consider one of the following: repeating a word or phrase, alliteration, metaphor, strong verb, intentional line breaks, precise word choices, simile.)

▸ What do you notice about the poetic choices of others?

Ekphrastic Poetry *(cont.)*

Specific Grade-Level Ideas

Grades K–2

View a piece of visual artwork as a class. Guide students to brainstorm words and phrases they think of when they view the artwork. Create a word bank from those words and phrases. Next, have students take turns choosing words and phrases from the word bank and work as a class to arrange the words into a class found poem. You also might write words or poem lines on sentence strips and have small groups play with the order and arrangement.

Grades 3–5

Explore the book *Paint Me a Poem: Poems Inspired by Masterpieces of Art* by Justine Rowden. Identify an existing Ekphrastic poem and the related piece of visual artwork and share them with students. Then have students add a line or a stanza to the poem.

Have students create poems from the artwork of classmates.

> "Students need to become friends with poetry. They need to know that poems can comfort them, make them laugh, help them remember, and nurture them to know and understand themselves, others, and the world around them more completely."
>
> —Georgia Heard (as cited in Ferlazzo 2020b)

Grades 6–8

Use the Visual Thinking Strategy approach for close observation of an image by asking the following questions: "What do you see? What makes you say that? What else can you find?" (Learn more about this approach at **vtshome.org.**). Record observations and wonderings on chart paper as a jumping-off point for writing poems.

Select two paintings that represent two perspectives of the same event or time period (for example, photographs of New York City, one in the 1900s and another present day). Invite students to focus on the vantage point of a particular character or object in one painting and write a poem featuring that perspective. Next ask students to choose a different character or object in the painting that portrays the other perspective. Discuss the similarities and differences and how they were covered in the painting and in the poems.

Grades 9–12

Invite students to perform their poems and speak them aloud. Have them spend some time in small groups to mine for tips on reciting poetry using the resource called "Tips on Reciting" (2012) on the Poetry Out Loud website at: (**www.poetryoutloud.org/competing/tips-on-reciting**).

Have students decide whether to show the visual art during or after the performance.

Ekphrastic Poetry Sample 1

The Grandmother by Honore Daumier, Rosenwald Collection, courtesy of the National Gallery of Art, Washington, DC.

Ekphrastic Poetry Sample 1 *(cont.)*

Acorn
by Christina DeFilipp

of all the trees swaying in the
windy woods
that grand matriarch with knurled
fingers
and limbs that carry a rooted story
deeply beneath the forested floor
that one of sturdy trunk and
weathered bark
with branches reaching to the
limitless sky
and green kisses that flutter to the
wind
that tree is a shelter during
every storm
a solemn refuge for the wayward
and weary
she is shade for babies and home
to the birds
this seated grandmother of oak
and ash
holding new life up to the
heavens like
some acorn of hope to the
dying forest

The Grandmother
by Nancy McDonnell Joyce

Grammy, Grandma, Granny,
You are perfected practice and
patience
My teacher and friend.

Abuela's understanding lap,
Love that is strong, pure,
and unconditional,
My Babushka, my Bubbie,
my Oma.

Mimi's gifts of wisdom and grace,
Sharing hugs while the
cookies bake,
My Memaw, my Nana, my Nonna.

Grandmother's caring warmth
and security,
Kindness and sweet memories,
Generations of gentle humanity,
Grandmothers.

Poems inspired by *The Grandmother* by Honore Daumier

Ekphrastic Poetry Sample 1 (cont.)

Legacy
by Tara Mason

Leave something
Grasp something
Be something

This is the way the ladies ride:
Clippity Clop Clippity Clop

Eyes of joy look into eyes of joy

Joy for a life well lived
Joy for a life beginning

This is the way the gentlemen ride:
Clippity Clop Clippity Clop

Generations come and go

This one will leave a path
That one will take it over
Adhering and veering

This is the way the farmer rides:
Clippity Clop Clippity Clop

Leave pleasant memories
Grasp beautiful matter
Be the connection

Poem inspired by *The Grandmother* by Honore Daumier. Italicized text taken from the nursery rhyme, "This Is the Way the Ladies Ride," originally published in *Boys' and Girls' Bookshelf Volume 1* (1912).

Ekphrastic Poetry Sample 1 (cont.)

Grandmother's Love
by Alyssa Mewer

If you only knew
Just how much I love you

A love so profound
Only in your heart can it be found

A bond so deep
I'll send you whispers in your sleep

I'll hold you in my heart
Even when we are apart

If you only knew
Just how much I love you

look into my eyes
by Joe Metz

look	look
into my	into my
ancient eyes	newborn eyes
what do you see	what do you see
opportunity to grow	curiosity as to why
and know oh	your eyes seem
so much	so familiar

Poems inspired by *The Grandmother* by Honore Daumier

Ekphrastic Poetry Sample 2

Dancer by Honore Daumier, Rosenwald Collection, courtesy of the National Gallery of Art, Washington, DC.

Ekphrastic Poetry Sample 2 *(cont.)*

Dancer
by Claudia Carpenter

I gather my skirts, fan them, they sweep
I feel the strength up my legs as I leap.

I bend, I bow, I dip down
No easy feat in my corseted gown

And come up for a quick breath.
Will suffocation be the cause of my death?

Like a fish taken out of water
I do sometimes wonder why I bother.

Always, I feel the judgment in their gaze.
And yet, the Gentlemen and the Ladies watch in a smoky haze.

How tantalizing I must be
Though in Church, they vehemently disagree.

But, like clockwork they appear
The bourgeoisie simply a veneer.

The curve of my shoulder
The smirks of my beholder.

So, I twirl faster now, back and away.
After all, we each have our own part to play.

Poem inspired by *The Dancer* by Honore Daumier

Ekphrastic Poetry Sample 2 *(cont.)*

The Dancer
by Ruth M. Sallade

My dream was not to grow up and become a dancer
My dream was that I was a dancer
    in my soul

The house finally empty
Music on the record player
    or in my head.
I had no preference how it arrived
    in my soul

Empowered by the solitude
    and music
I felt the movement come alive
    in my soul

An elegant, graceful dancer
A gifted, far reaching to the stars dancer
Standing on my tippy toes with my outreached hand
    in my soul

My audience was me
The dancer was me
    born of mutual admiration of each other
I didn't need or want anyone else
    in my soul

It was our alone
    stepping
    in our soul
    time.

Poem inspired by *The Dancer* by Honore Daumier

Ekphrastic Poetry Sample 2 *(cont.)*

Outgrown
by Christina DeFilipp

the glass slippers didn't fit
her calloused feet any longer
so she took them off lovingly
and smashed them into pieces
pulverizing glass back into sand
and when the crushing ended
she scooped up the remnants
and walked barefoot to the castle
where she sprinkled her freedom
all around the fortress walls
and she danced unapologetically
waltzing right over that fairytale
to her own happily ever after

Untitled
by Jacklyn Mingo

moving freely to the melody
music takes over the body
and mind
let past mistakes and troubles blur
    away like objects out of focus
focus here
    in the moment
    in the present
    Be Free

Poems inspired by *The Dancer* by Honore Daumier

Ekphrastic Poetry Sample 3

Monet's Winter Boulevard
by Ariel Dwyer

The sun shivers in the cold,
winter clouds
His weak rays of light
bouncing off
Glittering, white flakes

Drifting

In flurries

Down to the Earth

Already cloaked in white.

Sparkling snow settles on
shoulders
Sending shivers
Down spines of folks walking

Waiting . . .

Wishing . . .

For this long, hard winter to end.

Monet's Garden Path
by Jessica Bonifas

On this rustic pathway.
Sweet smells float through
the air.
Surrounded by the sound of
diligent workers buzzing.
Their little plump bodies
weaving in and out of the
prismatic pathway.
Birds conversing on the tree
canopies overhead.
Encased in a blanket
of vibrancy.
The mind and body at ease.
Listening to the symphony of
the garden.

Inspired by *Garden Path at Giverny* by Claude Monet, 1902

Inspired by *Boulevard Saint-Denis, Argenteuil, in Winter* by Claude Monet, 1875

Ekphrastic Poetry Sample 3 *(cont.)*

Head from a Statue of King Amenhotep I
by Christina DeFilipp

Fragment

where do you go to find
the part of yourself
that broke years ago

what rock do you lift
what hill do you climb
to help you search

for that missing piece
that accidentally chipped
and was taken by time

Inspired by *Head from a Statue of King Amenhotep I*, ca. 1525–1504 B.C.

Saint Rémy
by Emma Shea

Rolling, curving, swaying
Hills smelling of honeysuckle
Clouds drift on currents
Of warm air
Cypress branches reach

Blanket laid in the grass
The perfect spot
Willow branch basket
Filled with delights

Laying back
Breathing deep and slow
Eyes closing
Sunlight warms the faces

Of two friends
Escaping time,
Escaping everyone

Inspired by *Wheat Field with Cypresses* by Vincent van Gogh, 1889

Music

Understanding Music

Strategies for Music

Found Sounds

Soundscapes

Chants

Songwriting

Music and Memories

Music

Understanding Music

Music has played a significant role in every culture since the beginning of time. Our favorite tunes are readily available to us given our ever-present smartphones, and music has become even more prevalent in our lives. But the question is, how can music be easily and effectively integrated into the curriculum? For some students, connecting with rhythm, beat, and melody provides individual access to learning. Any teacher who has created a cleanup song knows music can motivate children and help them make transitions from one activity to another. Recently, attention has been given to the benefits of integrating music in academic performance. It has been suggested that early music training develops language skills, spatial relations, and memory (Perret and Fox 2006). Current research even provides evidence showing the power music has to engage children in learning early literacy skills, such as reading comprehension and verbal memory, listening skills, vocabulary development, phonemic awareness, and writing and print awareness. (Kindermusik International, n.d). Paquette and Rieg also note that incorporating music into the early childhood classroom is particularly beneficial to English language learners' literacy development (2008).

In the strategies described in this section, language arts ideas are explored alongside the basic elements of music. Students engage in singing, playing, and composing music; exploring found sounds; and, most important, learning the skills of good listening. Asking students to "listen up" is common in every classroom, but teaching students how to listen and what it means to really listen is often overlooked. The musical strategies provided here will focus on deepening knowledge of listening—which is a fundamental musical skill—as well as deepening knowledge of and skills in language arts. By implementing these musical strategies, students also will develop a deeper understanding of and skills in creating music. No previous musical training is needed for you or your students.

Integrating music into the language arts curriculum engages and motivates students. As students identify, apply, and generalize ideas to real-world situations, language arts becomes meaningful and purposeful. Abstract ideas are connected to concrete models, and students' representational fluency deepens. The more avenues we provide for students to experience language arts, the more likely we are to connect with the variable ways in which students learn.

Elements of Music

The most basic accepted definition of *music* is "organized/intentional sound and silence."

According to Jacobsen (1992) and Estrella (2019), the basic elements of music from a Western perspective include the following:

- **Pitch:** The highness and lowness on a musical scale

- **Harmony:** Notes of different pitches played at the same time

- **Melody:** How notes are put together in a sequence

- **Dynamics:** The loudness and quietness of composition (musical piece) and transitions between the two

- **Rhythm:** How time is controlled in music (beat, meter, tempo)

- **Timbre/Tone Color:** The sound quality of a note

- **Texture:** The number of layers in a composition (musical piece)

Music *(cont.)*

Strategies for Music

Found Sounds

Sounds are all around us; they are found when we attend to them or manipulate them. Think about the sound of light rain, the rustle of leaves, the wind in the trees, or the squeals of delight you hear near a playground. There is rhythm in these sounds. Composer R. Murray Schafer thinks about the world as a musical composition. He notes, "We must learn how to listen. It seems to be a habit we have forgotten. We must sensitize the ear to the miraculous world around us" (1992). What makes a sound musical rather than sounding like noise may depend on the listener, but it also is related to pitch, rhythm, tempo, and tone color or timbre. When students collect found sounds, they gain a new appreciation for what music is and develop careful listening skills. They also can better understand the environment from which sounds come. Students can put sounds together in interesting compositions, exploring environments and contexts from where stories unfold, as well as the power of onomatopoeia as language mirrors sounds. Louise Pascale notes, "Often, we describe things visually rather than auditorily. Students can describe the sounds they hear in a more vivid way (a loud sound can become an ear-piercing sound, brassy, shattering, etc.). This can build language" (2012, personal communication). This strategy is an excellent way to prepare students for the soundscape strategy.

Soundscapes

In this strategy, students have the opportunity to understand a particular environment, habitat, or historical setting purely through sound. Students analyze a particular event, place, or situation by experimenting and then, as accurately as possible, re-create it by making accurate sounds. The audience will feel as if they are immersed in the soundscape, whether it be a particular habitat such as the rainforest, a desert oasis, a moment in history such as the California Gold Rush, or even a moment in time from a chapter book.

The challenge for the performers is to carefully select just the essential sounds—ideally found sounds and not prerecorded sounds—and place them sequentially in such a way that produces an accurate reproduction of the sound environment. (Refer back to the found sound strategy.) Being mindful of basic elements of music such as dynamics, tempo, rhythm, pitch, texture, tone color, and so on, can ensure the soundscape is more accurate. An effective soundscape is typically only three to four minutes in length, can give the listener a true sense of "being there," and can provide a deep and long-lasting understanding of the subject (Donovan and Pascale 2022). The performers also can produce an "orchestral score," providing notation of what sounds are performed and when, which provides them with a "map or guide" of their performance. The format for the score is determined by the performers.

Chants

Chants involve the rhythmic repetition of sounds or words without a melody. Similar to rap, they are spoken to a variety of rhythms, pitches, and tempos. By combining varying dynamics (ranging from soft to loud), pitch (variations from high to low), tempos (speed), and even movement, students can create engaging chants that help them learn and remember information more easily. Chants can be created about any content topic, such as parts of speech, the steps in a life cycle, or the names of the continents. Chants also can be constructed by layering lines on top of each other that are then spoken simultaneously. An essential component of using chants as a musical strategy is to have the students add a movement to support each statement or phrase. This reinforces the lyrics by having students not only verbalize the lyrics but transfer the understanding of the words into their bodies.

Music *(cont.)*

Many chants are available online and are effective to use as examples, but it is critical that students create chants themselves. If they create the lyrics and the movements, they'll own the chant as "theirs," and they are much more likely to remember it.

> "Chants are useful because they draw on the power of rhymes and rhythm. They can help students make content material more engaging, informative, and memorable because once students become more engaged, they also learn at a much deeper level."
>
> —Lisa Ciecierski and William Bintz (2012)

Songwriting

When students sing, they create a deep connection with the melody, rhythm, and lyrics of a song. What's more, creating and making music deepens the development of language arts skills by increasing vocabulary and using musical strategies for expressing mood, creating metaphors, telling stories, or describing a person, place, or time. Although students might have the opportunity to sing in school, far less attention is given to challenging them to create their own songs as a strategy for directly connecting to and enhancing a particular content area. Songwriting invites students to become lyricists, and as they do, they become familiar not only with the importance of tone, rhythm, and tempo but with the power of rhythmic language to convey meaning. Songwriting connects directly to elements of creative writing such as symbolism, allegory, and figurative language, as well as rhyme and meter. The real value of songwriting is that it gives students an opportunity to use all their language skills to say something that is uniquely theirs. Students can begin by creating new lyrics to a familiar melody. Song lyrics, put to a rhythm and/or melody, help

the brain remember information far beyond simply stating facts. And creating original lyrics prompts students to discuss, synthesize, and categorize curricular concepts. As they get more comfortable, students may choose to create original melodies and even score their written compositions.

Music and Memories

Music plays a powerful role in defining culture for both individuals and groups of people. Whether we are aware of it or not, music provides a powerful sense of identity for all of us. Through this strategy students discover their own musical culture by putting together a "playlist" of songs they feel describes who they are and perhaps how their musical story has changed over time. Additionally, students can interview someone from an older generation from their own family, the community, or their neighborhood to learn interesting stories about the role music has played in someone else's life. This interview process gives students the opportunity to then reflect and compare their own musical culture to that of the person they interviewed, noticing similarities and differences and honoring both musical cultural experiences.

> "Language arts and music are closely related in several ways. Each contains the elements of rhythm, pitch, and accent; convey direct and implied meanings; create imagery and affect the emotions; convey important cultural information; integrate both time and sound; tell stories—with words, or more abstractly in sound, or combine to tell a story in a riveting manner."
>
> —Patricia Shehan Campbell, Carol Scott-Kassner, and Kirk Kassner, as cited in Ferlazzo (2020a).

Found Sounds

Model Lesson: Sounds Around Us

Overview

In this lesson, students take a listening walk and explore the act of careful listening. During the walk, they note the sounds they hear. After the walk, students come up with categories to sort the sounds (such as natural, plastic, metal, pleasant, unpleasant, and so on). Finally, students create visual or narrative displays (lists, poems, etc.) to represent the sounds they heard along the walk.

Materials

▸ a collection of books and poems that feature onomatopoeia (see preparation for text ideas)

▸ *Our Sound Words* (page 144)

▸ chart paper (*optional*)

▸ *Elements of Music* (page 137)

Standards

Grades K–2

▸ Identifies how words appeal to the senses

▸ Describes how words or phrases suggest feelings or supply meaning

▸ Demonstrates and explains reasons for personal choices of musical ideas

▸ Presents a final version of personal musical ideas

Grades 3–5

▸ Determines the meaning and nuances of words and phrases

▸ Demonstrates understanding of figurative language

▸ Explains selected and organized musical ideas

▸ Describes connection of personally created music to expressive intent

Grades 6–8

▸ Determines the figurative and connotative meaning of words and phrases

▸ Demonstrates understanding of figurative language

▸ Explains how knowledge relates to personal choices and intent when creating and performing music

▸ Demonstrates the relationship between music and another discipline

Grades 9–12

▸ Determines the figurative and connotative meaning of words and phrases

▸ Analyzes the impact of word choices on meaning and tone

▸ Demonstrates how sounds and musical ideas can represent concepts or texts

Found Sounds *(cont.)*

Preparation

Gather texts that feature the writing craft of onomatopoeia. Consider using *Snow Sounds: An Onomatopoeic Story* by David A. Johnson, *Hush! A Thai Lullaby* by Minfong Ho and Holly Meade, *The Rain Stomper* by Addie Boswell, or *Over and Under the Pond* by Kate Messner. Additional ideas can be found in the Specific Grade-Level Ideas.

Procedure

1. Tell students that writers use sound words to convey meaning. Share a collection of texts in which the authors use onomatopoeia and invite students to hunt for sound words in small groups.

2. Distribute *Our Sound Words* to students. Take students on a *listening walk* around the school or outside to observe and write about the sounds they hear in the second column of *Our Sound Words*. Interesting sounds can be found anywhere. Invite students to walk silently without talking. The only task is to listen—to every sound, including the ones they might be making themselves (heartbeat, jacket rubbing against a pant leg, footsteps, coughing, breathing, and so on).

3. After the walk, have students make a class list of the sounds they heard. Have them describe the sounds they heard and notice how different the responses may be—everyone went on the same walk, but not everyone heard the same things.

4. Have students name possible categories that sounds fall into, such as natural, plastic, metal, shaker, percussive, pleasant, or unpleasant. Note that most sounds fall into more than one category. Have students categorize the class list of found sounds and ask them to explain their thinking.

5. Give students time to finish the remaining columns of *Our Sound Words*, exploring the sounds through their senses, precise words, and possible onomatopoeia choices.

6. Show students the examples on page 143. Have students discuss: "How are sounds represented in words or images? What do you prefer? Why?" Invite students to capture the sounds from the listening walk in a narrative or visual display.

7. **Extension:** Have students look through their own writing pieces and locate at least one place where they can add a sound word for impact.

> A listening walk engages students in listening to the sounds of their environment. Invite students to note what they hear in a journal.
>
> —Lisa Donovan and Louise Pascale (2012, 66)

Discussion Questions

▸ How do sounds impact your experience of the story?

▸ How and why might you use onomatopoeia or sound words in your own writing?

▸ How can found sounds be used as sound effects to enhance a story?

▸ How did you represent your sounds (a poem, list, sound map, image, or other)?

▸ What artistic choices did you make when you captured your sounds as words or images?

> "Students can record sounds they hear in a particular place and time by creating a 'sound journal.' They can record their findings with a list of words, a visual, or a narrative. They could even photograph their sounds. Students can also invent their own 'onomatopoetic' language."
>
> —R. Murray Schafer (1992)

Found Sounds *(cont.)*

Specific Grade-Level Ideas

Grades K–2

Invite students to bring a bag on their listening walk and pantomime collecting sounds and putting them in their bag. (Donovan and Pascale 2022).

Ask students to choose one sound they heard, draw what made that sound, and draw an abstract sketch of what the sound might look like.

Provide a variety of household items that produce sound (shoes that squeak, utensils to rub together, plastic or paper bags, bubble wrap, and so on) and invite students to use the found objects to recreate the sounds they heard.

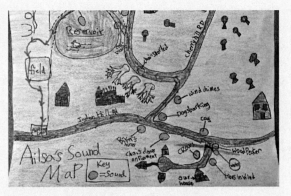

A. Carmisciano, 4th grade, 2020
This sound map illustrates where sounds were heard.

Grades 3–5

Invite students to collect objects. Then ask them to find two ways to play their selected object to make two different sounds. For example, they can blow on the top of a bottle, scrape the side of it, tap the top, or roll it.

Have students share different sounds for each object. As each student shares, instruct the rest of the students to listen with their eyes closed (if comfortable) and speak out when an idea occurs to them for what the sound reminds them of (a shaking water bottle sounds like a babbling brook, a piece of tissue paper being crumpled sounds like a light rain, short scrapes across a cheese grater sound like a cricket, air blown into a bottle sounds like a foghorn, and the popping of tiny bubble wrap sounds like a crackling fire). Provide time for students to experiment with their found sounds ("instruments") and explore different ways they can be used to make sounds.

Grades 6–8

Working in groups, have students use their found sounds to create a soundscape to bolster the setting of a scene from a myth, drama, poem, or chapter they are reading. Ask them to collect items to use as found sounds that will enhance the meaning of an excerpt from the text. To create the composition (soundscape), have students determine who will play which found sound and in what order. Will they play all at once or take turns? Will the found sounds overlap? Have students perform their soundscape while an excerpt from the myth, drama, poem, or chapter is read aloud.

Grades 9–12

Have students create a sound journal to document and describe the sounds they hear. Instruct everyone to stop for three minutes a day and write what they hear. Students must date the entry and note the location. The entries can be a list, narrative, poem, or visual depiction of the sounds they hear. See the following examples of each.

Found Sounds *(cont.)*

Narrative

Tuesday, 4/7/20

It sounds productive

The refrigerator is singing, doing its job, keeping the food cold

The scented oil diffuser is humidifying the dry air with patchouli

The washing machine is on its final spin cycle, cleaning clothes

The office clock is ticking, reminding us how time is passing

The wood stove is ablaze with fire, heating and lighting the room

The keyboard is clicking, my fingers striking letters like a piano composing a song
(C. DeFilipp, 2020)

Visual Representation

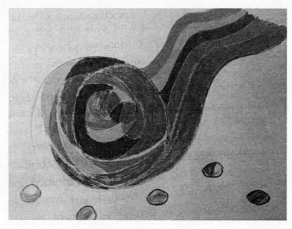

Monday, Apr. 20, 2020
Pine Point Beach, Scarborough, ME
Low tide
I hear calm ocean, quiet, crunch of shells under feet, then smooth sand.
(N. Joyce, 2020)

List

Tuesday, 3/31/20

- Humidifier
- Cat meowing
- Text being sent with a swish

(C. DeFilipp, 2020)

Poem

Tuesday, 4/27/20

What does Hope sound like?

The question was posed, "What does Hope sound like?"

Well, I read an article today about how the stars are finally able to shine over Delhi, India
Because of the reduction in toxic smog

How stargazers in Southern England are seeing the most beautiful skies lately
Because there are less emissions from cars

So I looked up at the Maine sky myself and while it's not very blue on this day . . .
I can hear all the quiet streets for a million miles

I hear the clouds silently pass over closed factories,
I hear the birds happily reclaim their domain
And our fearful lungs breathe in a little more deeply

Hopeful, that while this silent warfare continues

So too does Mother Nature, quite happy with herself

For making humanity notice the heavens again.

(C. DeFilipp, 2020)

Name: _____ Date: _____

Our Sound Words

Directions: Use the chart below to note and explore sounds you hear along the listening walk.

Found Sound	What caused the sound and where	Use your senses to describe the sound with precise words.	Possible onomatopoeia word to capture the sound (examples: *splash, click, pop*)
1.			
2.			
3.			
4.			
5.			

Soundscapes

Model Lesson: Exploring Setting

Overview

In this strategy, students explore ways to create a soundscape. A *soundscape*, defined by Murray Schafer (1977), is an acoustic environment consisting of events heard, rather than objects seen. A soundscape provides details of a setting through an auditory sense. Students work together to determine the specific characteristics of settings within a text. The goal is to create an accurate "scene" or setting using only sounds. This process involves careful analysis, revising, critical thinking, and problem-solving skills. By engaging in this sound exercise, students deepen their understanding of a written text of any format and genre (an excerpt of a book of any genre, a letter, a monologue, a poem, a painting, and so on) and any modality (visual, audio).

Materials

▸ text with evocative settings

▸ *The Sounds of a Setting* (page 149)

▸ paintings or primary source photographs *(optional)*

▸ percussion instruments *(optional)*

▸ *Elements of Music* (page 137)

Standards

Grades K–2

▸ Demonstrates understanding of key details and setting

▸ Describes how words or phrases suggest feelings or supply meaning

▸ Demonstrates and explains reasons for personal choices of musical ideas

▸ Conveys expressive intent for a specific purpose

Grades 3–5

▸ Describes setting, drawing on specific details

▸ Demonstrates understanding of figurative language

▸ Explains selected and organized musical ideas

▸ Presents music and conveys connection to expressive intent

Grades 6–8

▸ Describes how setting informs the plot

▸ Demonstrates understanding of figurative language

▸ Explains how knowledge relates to personal choices and expressive intent when creating and performing music

Grades 9–12

▸ Analyzes the impact of the author's choices regarding how to develop and relate the setting of a story

▸ Determines figurative and connotative meanings

▸ Demonstrates how sounds and musical ideas can represent concepts or texts

Soundscapes *(cont.)*

Preparation

Select a text to share with students that has multiple or evocative settings, such as *The Tin Forest* by Helen Ward or *Bringing the Rain to Kapiti Plain* by Verna Aardema. Note that other works such as paintings and poetry provide rich sensory contexts for soundscapes. Consider visiting the website of your local museum or the Library of Congress for images that will add depth to your curriculum.

Students can use found sounds or percussion instruments, such as triangles or drums, to create music. They also can vocalize and create sounds using their voices. If using instruments, gather those ahead of time. Additional suggestions are provided in the Specific Grade-Level Ideas.

Procedure

1. Share the story, excerpt, or other text that you have chosen. Share it first for enjoyment. Ask students questions that focus on setting, such as "What are some specific sensory images in the text that communicate the setting?"

2. Ask students to help you locate specific sensory images that describe the setting. Review with students how sensory images help readers see, hear, feel, touch, smell, and taste images that are described in a text. Discuss the qualities of each unique setting.

3. Introduce the concept of a soundscape. Explain to students that a soundscape is a layering of sound effects that will help them re-create a place or event. It is a technique students can use to bring a text to life using sound alone. Tell students that they will re-create and give life to a particular setting from the text they have heard or read. Introduce *Elements of Music*.

4. Place students into groups. Have groups complete *The Sounds of a Setting*. Explain to students that this chart will help them plan their soundscapes. Students will work together in groups to identify the ways the setting is presented. Encourage discussion of sensory images and sounds that can be used to re-create this place or time period. If prompting is needed, ask questions such as:
    ‣ What would we hear in this setting?
    ‣ How can we re-create those sounds accurately?
    ‣ Do the sounds overlap?
    ‣ Are some sounds soft? Loud?
    ‣ Do some sounds move?
    ‣ What role does silence play in the setting?

5. Have groups use percussion instruments, found sounds, and/or their voices to practice playing sounds that reflect the setting. The challenge becomes how to bring the setting to life by overlapping sounds to create a sound landscape or soundscape that represents one or more sounds in the setting. Use the Planning Questions to stimulate students' thinking.

6. Have groups share their soundscapes with the class. Read the story aloud or show the text as the soundscapes are shared. Using the Discussion Questions, explore how the sense of setting deepens the message of the text and how music helps students understand the setting.

7. **Variation:** If groups explore different settings within one text, all groups can come together to form one ensemble. Explain that you will read the story, and as each setting unfolds, the group assigned to that setting will perform their soundscape as a backdrop to the text. This is most

Soundscapes *(cont.)*

effective if the listeners close their eyes so they can focus only on listening and are not distracted by how the sounds are reproduced.

8. **Extension:** After composing a soundscape of a particular setting, have students write an orchestral score that indicates the different parts and when to play them. Creating a score for a soundscape is simply providing the performers a roadmap of their composition. The score, similar to a real orchestral score, can be as detailed as the performers prefer. It can be color-coded to identify specific parts, and dynamics (loud/ soft) can be indicated with light and dark lines. One person in the soundscape group can be designated as the "conductor."

Sample Soundscape Score

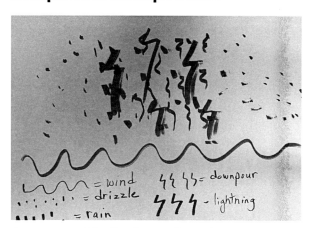

Score created by Dr. Louise Pascale

Planning Questions

▸ How might you bring this sensory aspect of a scene to life through a soundscape?

▸ How could you use sounds to introduce the theme of the text?

▸ As you listen to the story, what sounds and images do you imagine?

▸ What other sound ideas could fit within the setting?

▸ How do you connect to each setting? What does it make you remember or feel in your own life?

▸ How might you use the elements of music to compose your soundscape?

▸ How might a soundscape enhance the reading of a text?

▸ What will ensure accuracy?

▸ In what ways was reading the story together with the sounds like a musical composition in which sounds are played together?

Discussion Questions

▸ In what ways did the soundscapes help you understand each setting in the story?

▸ In what ways did the soundscapes help you understand how the settings changed?

▸ What sensory images from the book helped you create the soundscape?

▸ How did the creation of a soundscape bring each distinct setting to life?

▸ Using the elements of music, describe the artistic choices you made in creating your soundscape.

▸ As you tried different choices in your soundscape, what results did you get in creating a composition that captured the setting?

▸ What struck you about the soundscape presentations of other groups?

Soundscapes *(cont.)*

Specific Grade-Level Ideas

Grades K–2

Explore how one picture book can feature different settings. Using *The Tin Forest* by Helen Ward, discuss how the different settings make the students feel and the mood they give them. Work with the class to create an ensemble (with a conductor) for one or more of the settings in this book.

Grades 3–5

Invite students to locate sensory images that describe the setting in the books they are reading. In addition to the ideas for grades K–2, small groups can use *The Tin Forest* by Helen Ward to create an ensemble with a conductor to explore how settings are similar and different. This particular text also gives students an opportunity to carefully examine how writers can hook their readers by creating a lead about the setting. In the case of *The Tin Forest*, a circular ending (in which the ending circles back to the beginning) features the setting. In addition to the setting lead, writers also show (not tell) through alliteration, strong verbs, sensory images, repeated lines, personification, and snapshots.

Share music from popular movies such as composer John Williams's compositions for *Star Wars* and discuss how sound can set a scene, create mood, and even evoke a character. Challenge students to use soundscapes to create different effects.

Grades 6–8

Small groups can create an ensemble with a conductor and experiment with conducting cues such as tempo (speed) and dynamics (volume) in relation to the setting, characters, and progression of story events.

Students can explore the differences among settings of different genres.

Students can view an orchestra and conductor in progress and create a story with settings inspired by the music. Have students write a composer's statement that explains the choices they made to create a mood or setting.

Grades 9–12

In addition to the ideas for grades 6–8, students can use soundscape to communicate, through sound, the mood and meaning of one scene from a play by William Shakespeare. Have students analyze how the mood impacts the listener and enhances meaning. Students might use a combination of found sounds, instruments, and voice.

"Students use sound to 'read' the text and set the tone of the scene; soundscapes become student-centered instruments for enhancing and revealing the meaning of a story."

—Gina DeBlase (2005)

Name: _____ Date: _____

The Sounds of a Setting

Directions: Use the chart to take notes from the text and plan your soundscape.

Setting	
Sensory images in the text	
What do you see, hear, feel, taste, and smell?	
What sounds can be put together to create a sense of setting?	
What instruments and found sounds can you use?	
How you will use the elements of music (dynamics, texture, tempo, pitch, rhythm) to create your soundscape?	
Where will you insert sounds to match the text?	

Chants

Model Lesson: Main Idea in Nonfiction Narratives

Overview

Students read a narrative nonfiction text and explore the main idea by writing and performing chants with six to eight lines. Through this process, students go back to the text and reread to find specific words and phrases that show the main idea and supporting details. They decide when to include specific words or phrases from the book in their chants and when to put ideas into their own words.

Materials

- narrative nonfiction text
- *Sample Chants* (page 154)
- *Planning for Chant* (page 155)
- *Elements of Music* (page 137)

Standards

Grades K–2

- Retells stories, including key details
- Uses key details from a text to support description of the story
- Demonstrates knowledge of music concepts and contrasts
- Demonstrates and describes music's expressive qualities

Grades 3–5

- Summarizes a text
- Refers accurately to details and examples in a text
- Demonstrates understanding of structure and elements of music
- Demonstrates and describes how intent is conveyed through expressive qualities of music

Grades 6–8

- Provides an objective summary of the text
- Cites textual evidence to support analysis
- Demonstrates and describes how intent is conveyed through expressive qualities of music
- Demonstrates the relationship between music and another discipline

Grades 9–12

- Determines theme of a text and analyzes its development, including how it is shaped
- Cites evidence to support an analysis of what a text says explicitly and inferentially
- Demonstrates and describes how intent is conveyed through expressive qualities of music
- Demonstrates the relationship between music and another discipline

Chants (cont.)

Preparation

Locate a narrative nonfiction text such as *The Wolves Are Back* or *The Buffalo Are Back* by Jean Craighead George. Review *Sample Chants* and *Planning for Chant*. Additional ideas are provided in the Specific Grade-Level Ideas.

Procedure

1. Share a narrative nonfiction text with students. When you are finished reading the text, discuss the main idea. Model how to scan back through the text to find specific evidence for the main idea. Record students' ideas so they can reference them throughout the lesson as they list words or phrases that describe the main idea. Discuss the supporting details and work together as a class to locate evidence in the text. Pull out these details and record them for students to reference.

2. Explain to students that one way to further explore the main idea and supporting details of a text is through chants. Explain that in a chant, each line is sung or spoken by a group in a particular rhythmic pattern and pitch (high or low vocal tone). Introduce the musical term *ostinato* (a repetition of similar rhythmic patterns and tones).

3. Introduce students to the musical terms *rhythm* (repeating beat), *dynamics* (softness or loudness of the voice), and *pitch* (high or low sound of the vocal tone). Use the *Sample Chants* to provide students with practice using these three components of chanting. Then explain that the chants can be layered on top of each other by overlapping lines. Different versions of the same lines can be spoken or sung simultaneously.

4. Tell students that they will be chanting the *Sample Chants* as a class. To facilitate the first chant, place students into groups to practice layering the phrases of the chant. One group chants the repeated first line in a slow, low-pitched rhythm: "The wolves are back; the wolves are back." Then, as the first group continues repeating their lines, the next group of students layer "The valley is sharing food again!" with a medium pitch and rhythm. Then the next group adds another layer to the chant with "The grasses are growing tall again!," similarly chanted with a medium pitch and rhythm. Continue adding layers until all lines are chanted. Discuss with students how the chant expresses the main idea of the text and how the chant shows the evolution of what happens over time—that when the wolves come back, the environmental balance is restored.

5. To facilitate the second chant, place students into groups of six to chant the opening stanza. Have one group begin chanting, "The wolves are gone," and have additional groups add to the chant when their lines are to be read. Eventually all lines will be read simultaneously, enabling students to stop chanting line by line until "The wolves are gone" is the last line chanted. Repeat the process with the second stanza. Ask students to discuss the characteristics of the chant. Work as a group to identify the main idea and supporting details of the chant, discussing how the chant shows the relationship between a series of ideas linked to a dramatic moment and how each line adds new perspective to the idea through the integration of words, movement, rhythm, pitch, and dynamics.

Chants *(cont.)*

6. Tell students that they will work in small groups to create their own chants, summarizing the meaning of the narrative informational text. Remind students to use words or phrases that show the main idea of the text, and then add details to support the main idea. Refer students back to the list recorded earlier in the lesson. Tell them that they will need to decide when to use specific words and phrases from the book and when to paraphrase. Have students complete *Planning for Chant* in small groups and then create their chant. Use the Planning Questions to guide students' thinking.

7. Invite students to add instrumental sounds (these can be found items that make sounds or musical instruments if available) and movements to go with each line. Then have students do the chant with words only, words and instruments, instruments only, or words and movements.

8. Have each group perform their chant for the class. Debrief using the Discussion Questions.

Planning Questions

‣ What pitch will you use?

‣ What dynamics will you use?

‣ What rhythms are suggested by the words in your line?

‣ What other sounds can you add to give your phrase more interest (the use of instruments, clapping, stomping, slapping the desk)?

‣ Are there movements you could add to emphasize your tempo or heighten the impact of a particular verse (slow, curved motions or quick, jagged movements)?

Discussion Questions

‣ Which words or phrases show the main idea of the text?

‣ Which words or phrases show details that support the main idea?

‣ How did you decide when to paraphrase and when to quote from the text?

‣ How and why did you include figurative language?

‣ How did the rhythm of the lines work when the lines were overlapped?

‣ How did the different pitch, dynamic, and rhythm affect the way lines sound together?

‣ What other ideas could you experiment with to make your chant more interesting?

Chants *(cont.)*

Specific Grade-Level Ideas

Grades K–2

Have students create the chant as a class and then add an additional part on their own. Consider using the book *Rah, Rah, Radishes! A Vegetable Chant* by April Pulley Sayre as a mentor text. Students also can use chanting to internalize letter-sound relationships, word patterns, and the spelling of high-frequency words. Invite them to brainstorm ideas for a kinesthetic component to the chant that enhances the meaning of the lyrics. Have students work on creating chants with interesting sounds and rhythms. Discuss the creative aspects of the chants as well as the sound relationships. Spend a few minutes chanting the spelling of commonly used words. Encourage students to create their own chants to remember spellings and patterns of words or steps of a process, such as writing a sentence remembering a capital letter at the beginning and a period at the end.

Grades 3–5

In addition to the ideas for grades K–2, extend this lesson by dividing students into small groups to create a chant for another nonfiction text, such as *The Buffalo Are Back* by Jean Craighead George.

Students also can create chants to remember conventions of spelling, commonly misspelled words, vowel combinations, and contractions.

Visit **www.brainworks.mcla.edu** to see chants in action and share examples with your students.

Grades 6–8

Ask students to select phrases that make the chants more complex with three overlapping lines. They will need to experiment with rhythm, dynamics, pitch, and word choice. The first line becomes the baseline of the chant, and the other lines layer on top creating overlapping sound and rhythm.

Students also can create chants to recall rules for irregular structural changes in spelling and for conventions of capitalization and punctuation.

Grades 9–12

Students can conduct research projects on the origins of different types of chants over time, including who created them, how they were created and performed, and in what contexts. Then students can write their own chants using what they learned.

> "Chants use repetition to engage the right side of the brain's 'musical' intelligence."
> —Kenneth Beare (2020)

Sample Chants

Sample Chant for *The Wolves Are Back*

The wolves are back; the wolves are back
The valley is sharing food again!

The wolves are back; the wolves are back
The grasses are growing tall again!

The wolves are back; the wolves are back
Hikers marvel at the sound.

The wolves are back; the wolves are back
Trees grow, erosion stops.

The wolves are back; the wolves are back
Balance is restored!

Sample Chant for *The Wolves Are Back*

The wolves are gone
Where did they go?
Gone . . . Every one
No voices howling
Chorus of the wilderness
Silenced

The wolves are back
Jogging through the grass
The valley is sharing food again
Hunting bison
Carcass of elk
H—O—W—L

Note: The inspiration for these chants was *The Wolves Are Back*, by Jean Craighead George.

Name: _____ Date: _____

Planning for Chant

Directions: Answer the questions to help plan for your chant.

What specific words in the text show the main idea?

_____

_____

_____

How can you work with different syllables to create interesting rhythms?

_____

_____

_____

Using just one sentence or phrase, summarize the main idea in your own words.

_____

_____

_____

Is there figurative language that you can use? List some examples.

_____

_____

_____

What supporting details will you include in your chant?

_____

_____

_____

What information will you paraphrase, or put in your own words?

_____

_____

_____

What line or lines will you repeat?

_____

_____

_____

What choices of pitch, dynamics, and rhythm will you make to distinguish between layers?

_____

_____

_____

Songwriting

Model Lesson: Show What You Know through Song

Overview

Creating original lyrics to familiar melodies encourages students to explore new learning or demonstrate what they have learned. In this lesson, students demonstrate their knowledge at the end of a unit of study by writing new lyrics to an original song. Melodies used for the song lyrics can be familiar tunes. Depending on the grade level, groups of students can each write a song or the whole class can create a song together.

Materials

▸ *Sample Songs* (page 159)

▸ *Lyrics Brainstorming Guide* (page 160)

▸ *Songwriting Planner* (page 161)

▸ list of familiar melodies to be used for songwriting activity

▸ *Elements of Music* (page 137)

Standards

Grades K–2

▸ Uses key details from research to support lyrics

▸ Demonstrates understanding of word relationships and rhyme in writing

▸ Demonstrates how a specific music concept (melody) is used for a specific purpose

▸ Demonstrates and explains reasons for personal choices of musical ideas

Grades 3–5

▸ Explains a character by referring accurately to details and examples in the text

▸ Uses knowledge of language and rhyme in writing

▸ Demonstrates how responses to music are informed by structure and elements such as melody

▸ Describes a connection of personally created music to expressive intent

Grades 6–8

▸ Cites text evidence to support facts stated in lyrics

▸ Demonstrates understanding of language, word relationships, and rhyme in writing

▸ Demonstrates how responses to music are informed by the structure and elements such as melody

Grades 9–12

▸ Cites evidence to support analysis of what a text says explicitly and inferentially

▸ Produces clear writing in which the development, organization, and style are appropriate to task, purpose, and audience

▸ Demonstrates how responses to music are informed by the structure and elements such as melody

Songwriting (cont.)

Preparation

This lesson is modeled using the topic of research skills, but any topic of study may be chosen. Gather sample songs about content areas. A sample song about the periodic table and a second sample about bees are found on page 159. You can use these as models with students, or you can create your own song to share with students. Additional ideas are provided in the Specific Grade-Level Ideas.

> Websites that outline how to write a song may be helpful for you to review prior to teaching this strategy. For example, you can check out the information at this blog: **www.musicalfutures. org/musical-futures-blog/why- its-more-important-than-ever-to- include-singing-in-the-classroom**.

Procedure

1. Ask students, "What are some of the things you are learning in our current unit of study?" Tell them that songs can help us distill our learning, and that today, they get to write an original song about what they've learned.

2. Introduce or review the terms *melody, lyric, chorus,* and *verse*. Discuss how the chorus in the song reveals the main idea and the verses provide details. Explain to students that songwriting always includes a topic, a melody, a chorus/verses, and a purpose.

3. Share the sample songs from page 159 or a song you created.

4. Display a list of songs that everyone is likely to know or could learn, such as "Old Macdonald Had a Farm," "Mary Had a Little Lamb," and "The Ants Go Marching." Consider different cultural traditions, and encourage students to use songs that are familiar to them.

5. Tell students that they will be writing their own songs. Distribute *Lyrics Brainstorming Guide*. Have students complete the *Lyrics Brainstorming Guide* to develop a rhyming structure for their lyrics, brainstorming words that rhyme with the word that ends each line.

6. Distribute *Songwriting Planner*. Have students use it to plan the lyrics and chorus of an original song with a known melody.

7. Provide students time to share their songs with the class.

8. Use the Discussion Questions to talk with students about using the process of songwriting as a strategy for better understanding how to find reliable web sources.

Discussion Questions

▸ How did you decide what information to include in your lyrics?

▸ What challenges of songwriting did you encounter?

▸ How did songwriting help you deepen your understanding of the subject?

▸ What choices did you have to make when creating lyrics and a chorus to make the song work with the melody?

Songwriting *(cont.)*

Specific Grade-Level Ideas

Grades K–2

Gather and explore a set of picture books that depict the power of music, such as *Your Name Is a Song* by Jamilah Thompkins-Bigelow, *Drum Dream Girl: How One Girl's Courage Changed Music* by Margarita Engle, and *Grandma's Records* by Eric Velásquez.

As a class, create songs about relevant content-area topics, such as the five senses, observations during a nature or playground walk, reading strategies, community helpers, animal habitats, or life cycles.

Grades 3–5

In addition to the ideas for grades K–2, students might work in small groups, pairs, or individually to create songs about landforms, the solar system, historical figures, poets, illustrators, or characters in a text.

Challenge students to write additional verses to their songs that explain additional details or important information.

Grades 6–8

To use this strategy as a culminating activity for a lesson/unit on evaluating websites for credibility, have students include information on authority, accuracy, scope, and referenced sources in their song. See below for insights from the middle school teacher who developed this idea.

Invite students to translate another art form (a poem, painting, collagraph, or photograph) into a song. Additional ideas for songwriting include the scientific process, ecosystems, or health concepts. Challenge students to write additional verses to another group's song to add more details or important information.

"Having taught this research lesson on locating valid sources, I was impressed with the students' deep understanding of the topic. This was demonstrated in the content-specific language they used to creatively weave their songs together. As a result of this activity, students would break out in their favorite songs throughout the year. It was fun to see! I'm sure that the catchy tunes helped them to remember the terminology and concepts that may have otherwise been forgotten."

—Shanda Palsulich (personal communication, February 2, 2021)

Grades 9–12

Invite students to interview local singers and songwriters to learn more about the art of songwriting. Have them create a list of interview questions and practice interview skills in small groups before conducting the interviews. Invite students to use one piece of craft they learned as they write their own song.

Sample Songs

This song is set to the melody of "The Wheels on the Bus." Facts and ideas were drawn from the visual periodic table found at **mymodernmet. com/illustrated-periodic-table**.

Periodic Table: Examples Make It Real!

Exploring chemical elements
Elements
Elements
Exploring chemical elements
In the periodic table

Beryllium goes with emeralds
Emeralds
Emeralds
Beryllium goes with emeralds
In the periodic table

Sun and stars with hydrogen
Hydrogen
Hydrogen
Sun and stars with hydrogen
Pictures help to label

Barium and X-rays
X-rays
X-rays
Barium and X-rays
The periodic table

It's hard to get your head around
Head Around
Head Around
It's hard to get your head around
But pictures help to label

This song is set to the melody of "My Bonnie Lies Over the Ocean." Facts are drawn from an article titled "Honeybee," from the National Geographic Kids website. You can find the article at **kids.nationalgeographic.com/animals/ invertebrates/facts/honeybee**.

Honey bees they collaborate closely
They all have their very own roles
Three types of bees work together
To achieve shared health and hive goals.

Chorus:
Honey Bee, Honey Bee
Pollinates our fruits, nuts and veggies
Honey Bee, Honey Bee
Bring the sweet taste of honey to me!

Male drones will mate with the queen
The queen lays the eggs for new bees
Female bees build, tend and clean the hive
Protecting the colony from disease.

Chorus

Female bees forage for food
Manage the live of the hive
They circulate air by beating their wings
And help keep the colony alive.

Chorus

Honey bees sustain food systems
They're in danger and no one knows why
Scientists are searching for solutions
to ensure that our honeybees survive.

Chorus

Name: _____ Date: _____

Lyrics Brainstorming Guide

Directions: Use the chart to help you plan your song lyrics.

Topic of Study	
Main Ideas for the Chorus	**Melody Ideas**
	■ "Twinkle, Twinkle Little Star" ■ "Skip to My Lou" ■ "BINGO" ■ "This Land Is Your Land" ■ "You Are My Sunshine" ■ "If You're Happy and You Know It" ■ "Row, Row, Row Your Boat" ■ "Yellow Submarine" List your own ideas:
Details for Lyrics	

Name: _____ Date: _____

Songwriting Planner

Directions: Use the chart to help you plan your song structure.

Title of Song
Chorus (important ideas about the subject)
Verse (details about the subject)

Music and Memories

Model Lesson: Meaningful Musical Memories

Overview

In this musical strategy, students use music to represent stories and culture that are passed down from earlier generations. Students interview an elder (someone from an older generation) about their musical story or the role music has played in their life. The interviewee could be a family member or a special person in the student's community, school, or neighborhood. Students will inquire about the interviewee's memories attached to music—songs, places, people, or experiences. Students also reflect on their own musical culture, asking themselves similar questions. The final presentation can be a playlist of music, an original song, a poem, or a picture summarizing the findings.

Materials

▸ story about how families bond through music

▸ *Interview Planner* (pages 166–167)

▸ *Elements of Music* (page 137)

Standards

Grades K–2

▸ Participates in shared research and writing project

▸ Makes connections between personal experiences and ideas in other texts

▸ Describes how specific music concepts are used to support a specific purpose

▸ Demonstrates and explains reasons for personal choices of musical ideas

Grades 3–5

▸ Conducts a short research project to build knowledge

▸ Organizes and develops clear and coherent writing

▸ Demonstrates and explains how responses to music are informed by the structure and elements of music

▸ Describes the connection of personally created music to expressive intent

Grades 6–8

▸ Conducts a short research project to answer a question

▸ Organizes and develops clear and coherent writing

▸ Explains how knowledge relates to personal choices and intent when creating and performing music

▸ Demonstrates the relationship between music and another discipline

Grades 9–12

▸ Conducts a short research project to answer a question

▸ Organizes and develops clear and coherent writing

▸ Shares music and demonstrates how the elements of music have been employed to realize expressive intent

Music and Memories (cont.)

Preparation

Select a text with a theme of family connections and music, such as the memoir *Grandma's Records* by Eric Velásquez. Additional ideas are provided in the Specific Grade-Level Ideas.

Procedure

1. Begin with a discussion about the personal connections all of us have to certain music. Ask such questions as, "Do you have a favorite song?" "Why is it special to you?" "How can a song remind us of a special person, place, or experience?" "What impact does music have on your life?" "What songs are special to your family members?" "How can you find out?"

2. Share the text you selected about family connections and music.

3. Tell students that they will be exploring the idea of deepening connections through music by interviewing a family member or another special person about music. Next they will ask themselves similar questions and reflect on their own musical culture. Then they will prepare a presentation of their findings. They may prepare a playlist of music, a short video of music and photos, an original song, or a poem or picture that summarizes what they discovered.

4. Introduce the idea of interviewing and what makes a successful interview. Above all else, a successful interview requires the interviewer to be curious. As a class, create a list of interview questions students can ask their interviewees, but remind students to be ready to follow the lead of the interviewee. Explain that it is important to avoid yes-or-no questions. Here are some sample questions:

   ‣ What role has music played in your life?

   ‣ What was a favorite song from your childhood? What have been some of your other favorite songs over your life?

   ‣ Did you play an instrument? If so, which one? If not, why not?

   ‣ Is there a song or kind of music that takes you back to a particular place in your life? What is that song?

   ‣ How have your musical "tastes" changed over time?

5. Distribute *Interview Planner*.

6. Have students complete their interviews. Two separate interviews are ideal. It takes time for someone to remember the impact music has had on their life!

7. Discuss the Planning Questions with students and give them time to prepare their presentations. There are many options for sharing the information gleaned from the interviews. Students can create a playlist of their interviewee's favorite music, which could range over several decades. Or they could make a video or create a visual image that captures the "essence" of their interviewee's musical story. Presenting the information in a monologue as the voice of the interviewee is a possibility, as is writing a poem or song that encapsulates the interviewee's musical story.

8. Invite students to share their final presentations with others if they are comfortable doing so. Use the Discussion Questions to help students understand the process.

9. Encourage students to share their final presentations with the family member or special person they interviewed. If they do, have them report back to the class about the experience.

Music and Memories *(cont.)*

Planning Questions

▸ Which findings from the interview do you want to include?

▸ Which findings from your own musical story do you want to include?

▸ How are these findings important to you and your interviewee?

▸ How well do these findings come together to create an artful presentation and not simply a retelling of the interviews?

▸ How will you put the information together effectively in a short three- to five-minute presentation?

> "Community is a fundamental aspect of our experience of music—it tends to unite people, forming bonds that might not exist otherwise. It connects different cultures, promoting diversity and growth. Music encourages creative thinking, discipline, leadership, and problem solving."
>
> —Chesley Talisse (2018)

Discussion Questions

▸ What did you learn about music and memories from your interview process?

▸ What types of things did people remember through their experience with music?

▸ What challenges were involved in creating the final presentation?

▸ How was this interview experience meaningful to you?

▸ What do the interviews tell us about the power of music in grounding us in culture and tradition?

> "Music holds value in culture. It must be held dear and treasured. It is not frivolous; it's serious business."
>
> —Louise Pascale (2014)

Music and Memories *(cont.)*

Specific Grade-Level Ideas

Grades K–2

Ask students to name their favorite song. Ask them where and when they sing it and who they learned it from. Share with students your own favorite song from your childhood. Have students go home and ask an older family member, neighbor, or school or community member about their musical memories. When they've gathered the information, have the class discuss about what they learned about the importance of music in our lives.

Grades 3–5

Have students keep notes from their interviews in their writing journals. This notebook entry can serve as an idea for future writing pieces. Use this process to begin a study of personal narrative writing, interviewing, and voice in writing.

Grades 6–8

Use this process to spark a discussion about memoir writing. Have memoirs available for students to read and examine. As a class, brainstorm the characteristics of memoir writing. Have students write a memoir that shows the special relationship between themselves and another person in their lives.

Invite students to reflect on the impact music has in their lives. Ask students, "What would life be like without music? How does music reflect our cultures, traditions, and communities?" Have students share their ideas in small groups.

Grades 9–12

After students complete their interviews, have them compare and contrast the findings with their own feelings about the importance of music in their lives. Ask students: "What would life be without music? What impact does music have in culture? How does it define our identity?"

Have students research the role music plays in various world cultures. Ask them what they learned about the power music holds in people's lives. Then have students express their findings through a poem, narrative, or song. Alternatively, students could consider what their lives would be like without music. They could explore this further with the 18-minute TEDx talk, "Returning Music to the Children of Afghanistan" (Pascale 2014), which tells about the effects of a decade of music censorship on the Afghan people.

Name: _____ Date: _____

Interview Planner

Directions: Interview a family member or special person in your life, using the following questions. Then, write and ask two of your own questions.

Person's name: _____

Relationship to me: _____

What are some musical memories you have? _____ _____ _____ _____	Does music take you back to a particular time and place? If so, what is most memorable? _____ _____ _____ _____
Is there a particular song you remember from childhood? Where did you sing it? Why? _____ _____ _____	What songs are connected to family traditions? _____ _____ _____

If you can remember a childhood song, what is most meaningful—the lyrics or melody?

_____

_____

_____

_____

Name: _____ Date: _____

Interview Planner *(cont.)*

Tell me about the special people, places, or experiences that you think about when you hear a particular song or type of music.

_____

_____

_____

_____

_____

_____

Write and ask two of your own questions:

1. _____

_____

_____

_____

_____

_____

2. _____

_____

_____

_____

_____

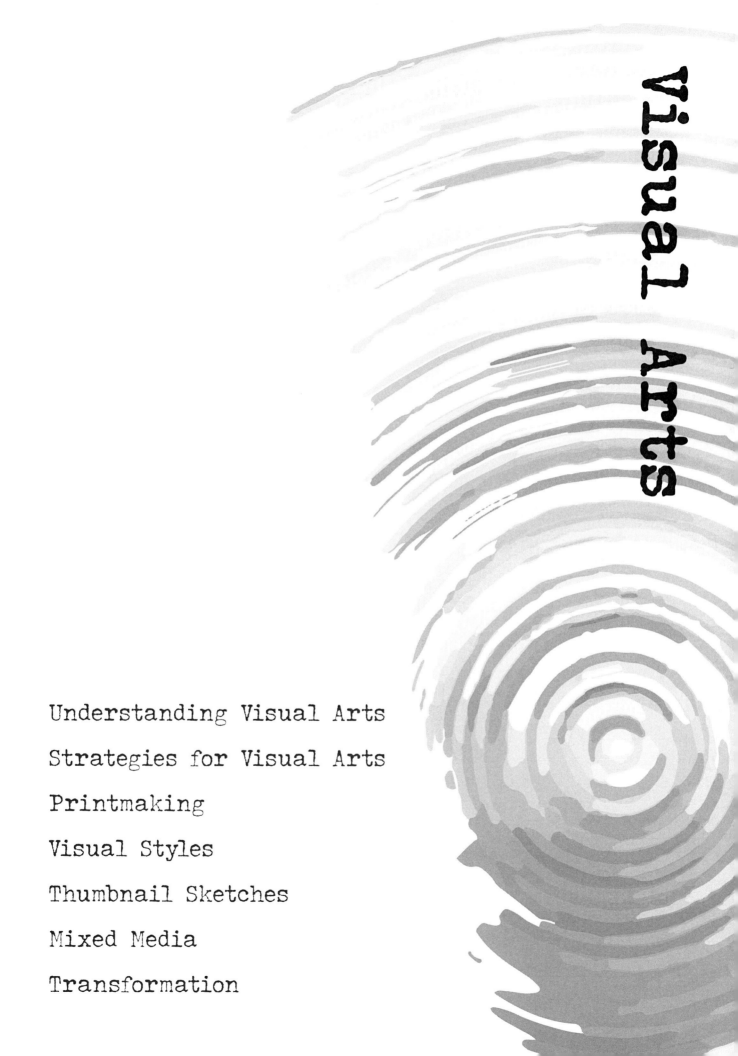

Visual Arts

Visual Arts

Understanding Visual Arts

We are bombarded with images on a daily basis, and though we have become more skilled at reading the nontextual representation of ideas, our visual-literacy abilities need to develop further. Why then, is education so often text-based? Working with images can provide opportunities for students to observe, notice details, and make meaning. Visual work can communicate nuances that words cannot. In this section, we explore how students can use visual art as a language.

Particular to visual arts is hands-on work with various materials. Visual artists use their art in many ways—to create narratives, observe, explore patterns, translate, represent, and juxtapose ideas using visual communication. Using the elements of art—line, form, shape, color, texture, and pattern—students can investigate and create visual representations of ideas. They also can create images as a way to tell what they know.

When students process visual information as well as verbal, they are using different parts of the brain. Allan Paivio suggests that learning can be expanded by the inclusion of visual imagery, allowing students what he termed "dual coding" (as cited in Reed 2010). All curricular areas have visual aspects, so providing students with the opportunity to work with multiple representations of content is easy to incorporate and will give students new ways to engage in and access ideas related to language arts.

> Through artmaking, students explore line, shape, color, texture, value, space, and form, tapping into their intuition and sparking curiosity.
> —Dana Schildkraut, Arts Educator (personal communication, October 22, 2020)

Elements of Visual Art

The elements of visual art were informed by a review of the field, including the J. Paul Getty Museum (Getty, n.d.-a), the Institute for Arts Integration and STEAM (Riley 2017), and the Kennedy Center (Glatstein 2019).

- **Line:** A mark made by the path of a point moving in space; lines can be horizontal, vertical, or diagonal; they can vary in width, direction, and length

- **Shape:** A closed line; shapes can be geometric, often made up of straight edges, or they can be organic and made up of irregular, free-form edges; shapes are flat and can be a defined by length and width

- **Color:** The response of the eyes to different wavelengths of light reflecting off objects; color can be defined by any of its three properties: hue (or name, such as red, blue, or green), intensity, and value

- **Form:** A three-dimensional shape that can be expressed by length, width, and depth

- **Texture:** The quality of a surface that can be seen and felt (rough, smooth, bumpy, and so on); texture can be real or implied, meaning that a surface can have a physical texture or visually appear to have a texture even though the surface is flat

- **Value:** The lightness or darkness of a color

- **Space:** The area between, around, above, below, or within objects; space can be defined as negative (such as the emptiness of holes) or positive; space also describes depth, or the illusion (idea) of depth

Visual Arts *(cont.)*

Principles of Design

These are informed by the J. Paul Getty Museum (Getty, n.d.-b), the Institute for Arts Integration and STEAM (Riley 2017), the Kennedy Center (Glatstein 2019), and PBS Learning Media (KET, 2014).

- **Balance**: Arrangement of art elements with attention to visual weight. Symmetrically balanced artworks feel stable; asymmetrically balanced artworks can create a feeling of instability or movement

- **Movement**: An artwork can be composed suggesting a sense of action. The elements of art can be intentionally placed in ways that guide the viewer's eyes around the work

- **Repetition**: Applying art elements so that the same element(s) are used again and again; repeating elements in a predictable way creates pattern

- **Proportion**: Size relationship between objects or elements in an artwork

- **Emphasis**: The part of the artwork that stands out in an eye-catching way; the center of interest

- **Contrast**: The juxtaposition of elements in an artwork showing differences that make them stand out from each other; many things can be in contrast to each other, including colors, shapes, or textures

- **Unity**: The use of elements of art to create harmony in a composition

- **Variety**: Combining art elements in ways to create visual interest

Strategies for Visual Arts

Printmaking

In this strategy, students make a collagraph print incorporating textured materials, including those found in nature. The resulting print is later traded with another classmate and serves as a story starter to prompt creative writing, either a story or a poem. Students explore how looking closely at an image enables them to extract elements, feelings, and words that they can translate into a compelling piece of writing. Often students feel intimidated when asked to create a piece of creative writing, and some may struggle with where to begin. Starting with a piece of visual art is an easier way for students to generate ideas for writing. Furthermore, there is an element of excitement when students know that their artwork will be the inspiration for a classmate's writing, and that they, in turn, will be using a classmate's artwork to prompt their own writing. Learning about the visual art form of printmaking is powerful, because the original plate can be inked and printed repeatedly, giving students the opportunity to create many variations of the same image. This opens up doors for students to explore variety, repetition, and the concept of making a series of artworks.

Visual Styles

In this strategy, students learn that artists often have a distinct visual style with signature characteristics that make their artwork recognizable. Artists can develop their works' signature characteristics by the way they intentionally use the elements of art: line, shape, color, form, texture, value, and space. Through the visual arts, students can demonstrate a variety of curricular concepts by creating and manipulating the elements of art. Illustrators use their understanding of these elements to deepen meaning and enhance the relationships between text and image. Often, images in books tell a compelling story of their own that can deepen the themes of a text.

Visual Arts *(cont.)*

Thumbnail Sketches

Thumbnail sketches are small drawings that challenge one to explore a concept, generating multiple ideas quickly. They can be used as a brainstorming tool that encourages one to think beyond basic solutions and move into more creative responses. "It's basically a way to visually brainstorm where you don't obsess and tweak but instead rough out a large number of possibilities" (Johnson 2011, para. 7). Working with thumbnail sketches reduces worry about one's level of artistic skill, as each sketch is done quickly and simply with basic shapes and line drawings to get rough representations of the idea down. Creating thumbnail sketches also can serve as an invitation to distill ideas down to a simple form.

Mixed Media

This strategy challenges students to experiment with putting a range of materials together in new ways. Students manipulate materials, experiment with the juxtaposition of materials, and create two- or three-dimensional pieces such as mobiles, collages, assemblages, dioramas, and digital installations. This process gives students the opportunity to use metaphors, prompting them to make meaning of experiences in new ways and boil concepts down to their essence to consider qualities rather than literal representations. Students test and explore ideas in experiential, hands-on ways; make choices about how they will use materials to communicate; and explore cause-and-effect relationships in the process of working with different media. The use of multiple representations is essential to the development of flexible thinking in language arts. This interpretive exploration will draw other themes. The construction of three-dimensional pieces requires students to interpret and explore ideas visually.

"The importance of images and visual media in contemporary culture is changing what it means to be literate in the 21st century. Today's society is highly visual, and visual imagery is no longer supplemental to other forms of information. New digital technologies have made it possible for almost anyone to create and share visual media. Yet the pervasiveness of images and visual media does not necessarily mean that individuals are able to critically view, use, and produce visual content. Individuals must develop these essential skills in order to engage capably in a visually-oriented society. Visual literacy empowers individuals to participate fully in a visual culture."

—Association of College and Research Libraries (2011, para. 1)

Transformation

In this strategy, students transform found materials such as books, images, posters, record album covers, and other found items into new forms. Students work with a variety of media and found materials to give new life and new meaning through the translation of their ideas in the creative process. In the process, the appearance of the materials and the meaning are altered. Repurposing, recycling, and reinterpreting materials provide students with rich ways to access curricular ideas and bring their ideas to life. Through artwork, students transform the meaning of the words on a page, in an article, or throughout a discarded book. They discover how words and visuals work together to communicate new meaning and reflect on the process of altering the meaning and the message of words.

"Teaching through the arts can present difficult concepts visually, making them more easy to understand. Art instruction helps children with the development of motor skills, language skills, social skills, decision-making, risk-taking, and inventiveness."

—Seneca Academy (2021)

Printmaking

Model Lesson: Collagraph as a Story Starter

Overview

In this strategy, students make multiple collagraph prints incorporating textured materials, including those found in nature. The resulting prints are later traded with classmates and serve as story starters to prompt creative writing. Students explore how looking closely at an image allows them to extract elements, feelings, and words that they can translate into a compelling piece of writing.

Materials

- example of collagraph plate and print (see digital resources)
- collagraph print supplies (cardboard, leaves, string, scissors, glue, bubble wrap, etc.)
- sturdy cardboard squares (one per student)
- *Sample Collagraph* (page 178) *(optional)*
- paint or ink, paintbrushes or paint brayers
- white paper
- rolling pin or clean paint brayer or printing press *(optional)*
- *Elements of Visual Art* (page 171)

Standards

Grades K–2

- Writes in a variety of forms or genres
- Uses descriptive words to convey basic ideas
- Explores uses of materials and tools to create works of art or design
- Describes what an image represents

Grades 3–5

- Writes narrative accounts, such as poems and stories
- Uses descriptive and precise language that clarifies and enhances ideas
- Creates personally satisfying artwork using a variety of artistic processes and materials
- Determines messages communicated by image

Grades 6–8

- Uses a variety of prewriting strategies
- Uses descriptive language that clarifies and enhances ideas
- Demonstrates openness in trying new ideas, materials, methods, and approaches in making works of art
- Analyzes multiple ways that images influence specific audiences

Grades 9–12

- Uses a variety of prewriting strategies to draft and revise written work
- Uses descriptive language that enhances ideas and supports different purposes
- Demonstrates openness in trying new ideas, materials, methods, and approaches in making works of art
- Analyzes multiple ways that images influence specific audiences

Printmaking *(cont.)*

Preparation

Gather textured materials, such as corrugated cardboard, fabric, and pipe cleaners. Include a variety of textured items from nature too, such as twigs, leaves, and flat pebbles. Conduct an online search for examples of collagraph plates and prints or use the *Sample Collagraph.* Additional ideas are provided in the Specific Grade-Level Ideas.

Procedure

1. Explain that printmaking is an artistic process that involves transferring an image from one surface onto another surface, usually paper or fabric. There are many printmaking techniques, including making a collagraph. A collagraph is made by gluing natural or found materials onto a base of cardboard, wood, or metal to produce textures. The base is known as a block or plate. When ink or paint is applied to the plate and a sheet of paper is pressed onto it, the ink or paint transfers onto the paper, along with the image of the textured details.

2. Share the example of a collagraph that you chose and discuss how the artist decided to use a variety of textures to achieve a desired effect. Define *texture* as "the quality of a surface that can be seen and felt: rough, smooth, bumpy, and so on." Texture can be real or implied, meaning that a surface can either have a physical texture that can be felt—such as the plate—or appear to have a texture, even though the surface is flat—such as the print. Show students both the initial plate and the resulting print to compare and contrast them.

3. Tell students that they will create a collagraph plate and produce at least two prints to prompt the writing of a short, creative story or poem. The image they create should not illustrate an entire story; rather it should simply be an interesting image that will inspire classmates to invent a story or poem based on what they see in the picture. Explain to students that this is called a *story starter.*

4. Gather the class to demonstrate how to make a collagraph plate. A sturdy piece of rectangular cardboard serves as the backing. Additional materials, such as other pieces of cardboard, fabric, tissue paper, leaves, and twigs, are cut into shapes and glued onto the cardboard backing to make an image. Introduce the word *composition,* which is "the arrangement of the visual art elements on the cardboard backing." Use a simple artistic composition for this demonstration, such as making the image of a house. Several straight twigs can be glued down to represent the house's walls. A large leaf cut into a triangle can be glued down to represent the house's roof. Small, flat pebbles can be glued inside the house to represent the windows. Crumpled tissue paper can be glued below the house to show a grassy yard. Images also can, of course, be more abstract.

5. Demonstrate how to apply the paint or ink to the plate with either a printmaking brayer or a paintbrush. Show the class how the image is transferred from the plate by placing a blank sheet of paper on top of the inked plate. Press down with your hands to apply an even amount of pressure. Other tools can be used in this step, such as a rolling pin, a clean printmaking brayer, or even a printing press. Remove the paper, which is now called the *print,* and reveal the transferred image.

Printmaking *(cont.)*

6. Discuss as a class what students notice, including how the print depicts a mirror image of what is on the plate. Remind students that one of the key principles of printmaking is that the plate can be inked repeatedly and many prints produced.

7. Spread out the available textured materials where students can easily see what is available to them, including materials from nature. Distribute a sheet of paper to each student in case students would like to sketch their plans. Use the Planning Questions to guide their thinking.

8. Distribute the cardboard backings, textured materials, scissors, and glue. Have students assemble their images on their collagraph plates by cutting apart and gluing down the textured materials.

9. Allow students time to apply paint or ink to their collagraph plates and produce at least two prints. Encourage them to experiment with different paint or ink colors and different-colored papers. If extra paint is left on the collagraph, students can wipe it clean with a tissue, or have students make a ghost print, which is a print after the main print for the purpose of removing extra paint/ink.

10. Have students keep one of their prints for their own portfolios and trade the other print(s) with a student in class. As students circulate to trade and collect prints, encourage them to ask each other questions about the artistic choices they made.

11. Have students return to their seats and place the print they collected from their classmate in front of them, where they can closely examine the collagraph. Explain that now they will use the new print as inspiration for a piece of creative writing, such as a story or poem.

12. Work with students to brainstorm for the piece of creative writing. For example, a successful short fiction story will likely include characters, a setting, a plot, a conflict, and a resolution. A successful poem will likely include imagery, rhythm, attention to line, and, if you decide, a specific form. A nonfiction text will include facts and text features such as a chart or glossary. Students may choose to write a persuasive piece. Or, they might create a list of words that come to mind.

13. Give students time to develop their piece of creative writing.

14. Have students practice reading their writing aloud and encourage them to make revisions for clarity. Then have students paste or display their writing next to the collagraph from which it was inspired.

15. Invite students to share their writing with the class, or perhaps with just the person who created the collagraph. Use the Discussion Questions to debrief at the end of the lesson.

Planning Questions

▸ What do you want to show/illustrate in your collagraph and why?

▸ How will you use textures in your collagraph to support and enhance your composition?

▸ How can you arrange the materials in your composition to communicate a compelling idea?

"Collagraphs are a wonderful way to explore printmaking, texture, color, and collage all at once. It also is a great strategy to use up some of those random art materials floating around your classroom like bubble wrap, felt, yarn, and cardboard."

—Megan Dehner (n.d.)

Printmaking *(cont.)*

Discussion Questions

▸ How did you choose your composition for your collagraph?

▸ What would you write about your own collagraph?

▸ What did you learn about your own collagraph after hearing how your classmate interpreted it as a story starter for their creative writing?

▸ After listening to the creative writing based on your collagraph, what feedback would you give to the author?

▸ Were you surprised to hear how your classmate interpreted your collagraph in their creative writing? Why or why not?

▸ As you listened to classmates reading their creative writing, how did looking at the accompanying collagraph affect you?

Specific Grade-Level Ideas

Grades K–2

Create one collaborative class collagraph in a large format. Print the plate enough times so that each student receives one. Students also can write a class story together.

If students create individual collagraphs, you may want to cut apart a variety of shapes ahead of time, because cardboard, fabric, and string can be challenging to clip with scissors. Help students envision creative ways to assemble the precut shapes into new imagery. Consider binding all students' prints and accompanying writing together in a class book of short stories or poems.

Grades 3–5

Have students explore color choices and how they connect to mood. How does the overall mood of the image change if they produce the print with black ink on red paper versus pale blue ink on white paper? How might the students' writing change based on the mood evoked from the colors?

Grades 6–8

Ask students to make several prints and give them to different students in the class, instead of trading with just one other person. Later, students will have developed several pieces of creative writing from the same image. Compare and contrast the writing to reflect on how and why different interpretations evolve from the same image.

Grades 9–12

In addition to the ideas for grades 6–8, students can investigate how they might develop a collagraph using abstract imagery instead of representational imagery. Ask them to consider how the elements of art and principles of design play an essential role in communicating abstracted ideas.

Sample Collagraph

Step 1

Step 2

Step 3

Artwork by Dana Schildkraut. Used by permission.

Visual Styles

Model Lesson: Signature Characteristics

Overview

Students choose an illustrator and analyze the artist's use of art elements, including line, shape, form, texture, and color throughout their work. After identifying how illustrators have specific elements that are characteristic in their work, students illustrate their own writing, paying attention to the elements of line, shape, form, texture, space, value, and color.

Materials

▸ books or artwork with illustrations that feature design elements characteristic of different illustrators' style of work

▸ *Finding Signature Characteristics* (pages 182–183)

▸ *Elements of Visual Art* (page 171)

Standards

Grades K–2

▸ Uses information from illustrations to gain understanding

▸ Uses observation and investigation in preparation for making a work of art

▸ Interprets art by identifying subject matter and describing relevant details

Grades 3–5

▸ Explains how specific aspects of a text's illustrations contribute to what is conveyed by the words in a story

▸ Identifies and demonstrates diverse methods of artistic investigation

▸ Interprets art by analyzing characteristics of form and structure, and visual elements

Grades 6–8

▸ Analyzes how specific aspects of a text's illustrations contribute to what is conveyed by the words in a story

▸ Develops criteria to guide making a work of art that meets an identified goal

▸ Interprets art by analyzing subject matter and characteristics of form and structure

Grades 9–12

▸ Interprets information presented in diverse media and formats, and explains how it contributes to a topic, text, or issue under study

▸ Evaluates the effectiveness of an image or images to influence ideas, feelings, and behaviors of specific audiences

▸ Identifies types of contextual information useful in the process of constructing interpretations of an artwork or collection of works

Visual Styles *(cont.)*

Preparation

Gather a collection of books that feature the same illustrator. If you'd like to showcase the style of more than one illustrator, gather multiple collections of books. To find a curated list of websites featuring diverse, award-winning illustrators—for example the Coretta Scott King Award, Pura Belpré Illustrator Award, and more—visit *Teaching with Trade Books* (**www.teachingwithtradebooks.com/resources-in-childrens-ya-literature**) or the American Library Association. Additional ideas are provided in the Specific Grade-Level Ideas.

Procedure

1. Define an *illustrator* as "an artist who creates pictures for books, magazines, posters, and more."

2. Ask students to think about illustrations they have created in the past. Ask them, "Where did you get your inspiration as illustrators? Where do you think artists get their inspiration as illustrators?"

3. Discuss illustrators with whom students are familiar and who have a unique style that is easily recognizable (Eric Carle, Mo Willems, Dav Pilkey). Have students share a time when they were able to identify a particular illustrator's work because of their signature characteristics. Define a *signature characteristic* as "a trait that someone possesses that helps define who that person is." Explain that artists often have signature characteristics that repeatedly show up in their artwork.

4. Display *Finding Signature Characteristics.* Share one of the books you selected and focus on the illustrations as you page through it as a class. Then record the seven elements of art that you want students to focus on: color, line, shape, form, texture, space, and value. Define them as needed. Students can reference these terms throughout the lesson. As a class discuss the questions from *Finding Signature Characteristics* to examine how students can find and analyze these elements in illustrations.

5. Place students into small groups. Have each group choose an illustration from the books you have provided. Give each student a copy of *Finding Signature Characteristics.* Have students work within their small groups to discuss the art elements within the illustration they have chosen and complete *Finding Signature Characteristics.* Offer assistance as needed.

6. Have each group display their chosen illustration for the other groups to observe and share their findings.

7. Have students illustrate their own writing pieces, using their interpretation of the art elements of line, shape, form, texture, color, space, and value. Encourage students to either explore their own personal illustration style and signature characteristics or attempt to replicate the style of one of the illustrators they've been exploring.

8. Debrief, using the Discussion Questions and *Elements of Visual Art.*

Discussion Questions

▸ What are some "signature" characteristics of each artist's approach?

▸ How do the pictures and words interact to convey meaning?

▸ How do pictures convey messages? Discuss an example.

▸ What elements of line, shape, form, texture, color, space, and value did you use in your own illustrations? Why?

Visual Styles *(cont.)*

Specific Grade-Level Ideas

Grades K–2

Offer students an opportunity to view artists at work in their studio by visiting the Eric Carle Museum of Picture Book Art at **www.carlemuseum.org**.

Conduct an illustrator study as a class. Have students try out the illustrator's style in their own illustrations. They can do this by creating an additional page for the book and adding text and images.

You also might focus on the color of illustrations. For students to better understand how colors reveal mood or create feeling, read aloud *The Color Monster: A Story About Emotions* by Anna Llenas. Have students discuss their artistic choices.

Grades 3–5

In addition to the ideas for grades K–2, invite students to create their own books by adding their own artistic flair while borrowing from the illustrator's style and focusing on the message the illustrations convey. Students can write an artist's statement that discusses their approach to their illustrations.

Invite students to write text to accompany a wordless picture book such as *Draw!* by Raúl Colón. Gather sets of wordless books from a variety of cultures for kids to explore.

Grades 6–8

Invite students to examine the social themes that motivate and inspire the artists of various cultures. Students also can choose another book that they feel demonstrates criteria for an illustrator award and write persuasive essays to compete for the award themselves based on criteria from a real or imagined review board.

Grades 9–12

In addition to the ideas for grades 6–8, invite students to research the evolution of an artist's work. Artists' signature characteristics develop over time, so earlier works look very different from the signature elements for which they later become known. Encourage students to analyze why and how their chosen artist's work changed over the years.

Invite students to review the work of painter and printmaker Jonathan Green, who was raised in the Gullah community on the Sea Islands in South Carolina. Students can identify both the "modern and cosmopolitan" appeal of his work, while examining how "Green looks to the familiar images of his ancestral home for the subjects of his paintings" (The Red Piano Art Gallery, n.d., para. 2).

Name: _____ Date: _____

Finding Signature Characteristics

Directions: Choose an illustration from a book. Then answer the questions.

Title of book and name of illustrator:

_____

Color Describe the colors of the illustration. What color choices did the artist make? How does the artist communicate mood?	
Line How would you describe the artist's use of line in the illustration (for example, thickness; type of medium used, such as ink, charcoal, brushstroke; or quality of line, such as hard or soft)?	
Shape What shapes are found in the illustration?	
Form How is the illustration bordered or framed? How are the elements in the illustration arranged into a composition that hangs together?	
Texture What materials do you think the illustrator used for texture in the illustration?	

Name: _____ Date: _____

Finding Signature Characteristics *(cont.)*

Value How light is the color? How dark is the color?	
Space What is the perception of distance between or around objects? What areas of positive space do you see (space with an object in it)? What areas of negative space to you see (space without an object in it)? What is the relationship of the object to the foreground and/or background of the image?	

Directions: Answer these questions based on the book.

1. How do the illustrations tell the story?

   _____

   _____

   _____

2. What is the theme or overall message of the book?

   _____

   _____

   _____

Thumbnail Sketches

Model Lesson: Symbolism

Overview

Students will explore how illustrators use imagery to symbolize meaning and to inform, persuade, explain, or exemplify meaning. After identifying and discussing symbolic images in *Dreamers* by Yuyi Morales, students will explore ideas in the text through the creation of symbolic thumbnail sketches.

Materials

- *Dreamers* by Yuyi Morales
- *Sample Thumbnail Sketches* (page 187)
- *Elements of Visual Art* (page 171)

> "Imagine your subject or picture stripped of all details, through squinted eyes, or in poor light. All you see are big rough shapes and some lines. That's all you need for a thumbnail."
>
> —Victoria Torf (n.d.)

Standards

Grades K–2

- Uses information gained from illustrations to gain understanding
- Interacts with sources in meaningful ways
- Describes what an image represents
- Uses observation and investigation in preparation for making a work of art

Grades 3–5

- Explain how specific aspects of a text's illustrations contribute to what is conveyed by the words in a story
- Interacts with sources in meaningful ways such as annotating or freewriting
- Determines messages communicated by an image

Grades 6–8

- Analyzes how specific aspects of a text's illustrations contribute to what is conveyed by the words in a story
- Interacts with sources in meaningful ways such as annotating or freewriting
- Analyzes multiple ways that images influence specific audiences

Grades 9–12

- Interprets information in diverse media and formats, and explains how it contributes to a topic, text, or issue under study
- Interacts with sources in meaningful ways such as annotating or freewriting
- Engages in making a work of art or design without having a preconceived plan

Thumbnail Sketches (cont.)

Preparation

Preview the text, *Dreamers*, by Yuyi Morales. Select at least one compelling image from the book that communicates lots of symbolic imagery. Find samples of thumbnail sketches to show to students. You can use the samples shown on page 187 or do an internet search to find some.

Procedure

1. Introduce the idea that authors and illustrators of picture books carefully plan the relationship between image and text to reinforce, amplify, and add nuance to a story.

2. Introduce the book *Dreamers* by Yuyi Morales. Note that Morales is both author and illustrator. Read the book once through for enjoyment.

3. Share a video of Morales talking about the symbolism in her illustrations, such as the one found at this site: **www.youtube.com/watch?v=CAiTFJaNiD8**.

4. Show students an image from the book. Ask them to identify techniques Morales used in her illustrations to communicate ideas such as memory, hopes, dreams, and cultural connections using symbolic imagery. For example, Morales notes the volcano represents the sleeping woman and also the idea of a warrior. The monarch butterfly captures the idea of long travel crossing boundaries. The backpack full of memorable items shows the gifts that immigrants bring.

5. Ask students to consider how the illustrations add to the meaning of the text. As a class, discuss the use of symbols as images that represent abstract ideas.

6. Ask students to identify symbols in their own lives. For example, things that symbolize love or happy thoughts of a specific family member might include a coin, a flag, wedding rings, the peace sign, or an article of clothing. Encourage students to think about personal, cultural, and universal symbols.

7. Have students discuss the symbols Morales uses in her illustrations. Ask students to identify an idea in the text that they would like to symbolize through an image.

8. Introduce the art form of thumbnail sketches to translate their ideas into visual form. Explain to students that thumbnail sketches will help them explore ideas in a simple format. Display the sample images of thumbnail sketches you selected.

9. Have students draw a small series of boxes on a sheet of paper. In each box have them explore an idea with simple shapes and lines, creating a thumbnail sketch documenting the idea(s) from the text that they wanted to symbolize.

10. Debrief using the Discussion Questions.

Discussion Questions

▸ What role do symbols play in our lives?

▸ Why do illustrators use symbolism in their images?

▸ Do you think visual symbols communicate meaning in different ways than text?

▸ How did you use the elements of art to show the ideas you wanted to symbolize?

▸ What ideas does your visual communicate and how?

Thumbnail Sketches (cont.)

Specific Grade-Level Ideas

Grades K–2

Invite students to create a thumbnail sketch using a visual idea from a children's book that they find personally meaningful.

For example, share with students the text *Most Days* by Michael Leannah. Discuss the theme of the book (appreciating the everyday, small moments of life) and explore the symbolism of how a blue jay reappears in the illustrations throughout the text. Create thumbnail sketches of the blue jay and work as a class to infer what the blue jay might symbolize and why the illustrator chose to repeat the image of a blue jay.

Grades 3–5

Ask students to create thumbnail sketches of symbols based on themes from a book they have read.

Invite students to conduct a search for "symbolism" on *The Classroom Bookshelf* blog and read entries about the latest picture books that model symbolism. Students will discover blog entries about the use of symbolism in *The Rabbit Listened* by Cori Doerrfeld, Square by Marc Barnett, *Here I Am* by Patti Kim, and more. Have students choose a text based on their interests. Group students by their book choice and have them discuss the symbolic meanings in the book, and create individual thumbnail sketches to express the ideas.

> "Thumbnail sketches are quick, abbreviated drawings, usually done very rapidly and with no corrections. You can use any medium, though pen or pencil is the most common. Thumbnail sketches usually are very small, often only an inch or two high."
>
> —Helen South (2018)

Grades 6–8

Have students use thumbnail sketches to brainstorm visual ideas for the development of a personal symbol for themselves based on one or more character traits they are proud of.

Grades 9–12

Invite students to explore the use of symbolism in protest or propaganda posters. Invite them to create thumbnail sketches to plan for the development of a symbol as a call to action.

> "Thumbnailing is one of the most important steps in the creative process. Thumbnailing and eventually picking an idea defines what you'll be doing in every other stage of a project."
>
> —Concept Art Empire (2021)

Sample Thumbnail Sketches

Note: These thumbnail sketches of a volcano and Monarch butterfly were developed during an exploration of *Dreamers* by Yuyi Morales.

Mixed Media

Model Lesson: Life Stories Told and Retold

Overview

Students listen to a story that explores memory and how people retell the events of their own lives. Students interview an elder in the community or a family member and represent the essence of their life through the careful composition of found objects. Then they create a sculpture out of the assembled items called an *assemblage*.

Materials

▸ text that retells life events (see the *Recommended Resources* on pages 15–16 for suggestions on finding diverse texts)

▸ *Creating Interview Questions* (page 192)

▸ images of assemblages from the internet

▸ various found objects that may represent life stories

▸ *Mixed Media Catalog* (page 193)

▸ *Elements of Visual Art* (page 171)

Standards

Grades K–2

▸ Participates in a shared research project

▸ Describes key ideas or details from a text

▸ Creates art that tells a story about a life experience

▸ Makes art with various materials and tools to explore personal interests, questions, and curiosity

Grades 3–5

▸ Conducts a short research project that builds knowledge

▸ Determines the main ideas and supporting details of a text

▸ Applies knowledge of available resources, tools, and technologies to investigate personal ideas through the art-making process

▸ Identifies and analyzes cultural associations suggested by visual imagery

Grades 6–8

▸ Conducts a short research project to answer a question

▸ Interprets information and explains how it contributes to a topic under study

▸ Formulates an artistic investigation of personally relevant content for creating art

▸ Analyzes ways that visual components and cultural associations suggested by images influence ideas and emotions

Grades 9–12

▸ Conducts a short research project to answer a question

▸ Includes multimedia components and visual displays in presentations to clarify information

▸ Analyzes how one's understanding of the world is affected by visual imagery

▸ Shapes an artistic investigation of an aspect of present-day life using a contemporary practice of art or design

Mixed Media *(cont.)*

Preparation

Select a text that features a retelling of life events, such as *The Matchbox Diary* by Paul Fleischman, which features a child's great-grandfather retelling his immigration story through collected objects and memory. Familiarize yourself with *Creating Interview Questions*, and make one copy for each student. Decide if you will supply students with materials for making assemblages or if you would like them to use found objects. Conduct an internet search to find images of assemblages created by a range of artists such as Louise Nevelson, Joseph Cornell, Wolf Vostell, and Pablo Picasso to share with students. Additional ideas are provided in the Specific Grade-Level Ideas.

> For more teaching ideas using *The Matchbox Diary*, see *The Classroom Bookshelf* website at **www.theclassroombookshelf. com/2013/09/the-matchbox-diary/**.

Procedure

1. Have students remember a special time in their own lives. Ask, "What is a memory of the event, and how has the memory changed over time? How did the event make you feel? Why do you think you still remember this event? What makes some life events more memorable than others?"

2. Share a story that features a retelling of a character's life events. Discuss with students the events in the story that were important in the character's life.

3. Tell students that they will have the opportunity to represent the important parts of a loved one's life (or the life of a community member) through a type of visual art called an *assemblage*. Share examples that you have gathered. Explain to students that an assemblage is "a form of visual art in which the artwork is created by putting together found objects to communicate about a story or memory."

4. Ask students how they might find out about the important events in someone's life. Suggest that interviews are a great way to gather firsthand knowledge about a person's life experiences. Discuss how interviews work. Distribute copies of *Creating Interview Questions*. As a class, review the interview tips and then help students draft interview questions. Tell them they will conduct interviews at home or in the school community.

5. Once interviews are complete, discuss how students could represent the ideas in the interviews through artifacts or objects that symbolize significant life moments in the person's life. Ask students to identify and collect a variety of artifacts and found objects that represent themes that emerged from their interviews. If you collected any, share the found objects you gathered and allow students to use those as well.

6. Once they've collected a range of objects, distribute the *Mixed Media Catalog*. Have students record the objects they are using and write about the big ideas behind these objects.

> "Art has been created from cast-off materials since art has been in existence. Certain artists are drawn to making something out of what would generally be considered nothing — taking what most people would view as useless and arranging it in an artistic manner, or placing it with traditional materials or in a particular setting that elevates it from junk to art."
>
> —Berea Public Art (2009)

Mixed Media *(cont.)*

7. Now students are ready to use the found objects to experiment with creating a two- or three-dimensional composition. This can be a collage, a sculpture, or a composed collection of objects presented in a way that feels representative of ideas they want to convey.

"When you put together things that others have thrown out, you are really bringing them to life...a life that surpassed the life for which they were originally created."

—Louise Nevelson (as cited in Beckett 2015)

8. Have students write short artist statements about their assemblages. What meaning does the piece hold for them? What is important to communicate? Allow time for students to present their work to the class.

9. Debrief, using the Discussion Questions.

Discussion Questions

- ▸ What objects are included in each piece?

- ▸ How did you select the objects for your assemblage?

- ▸ How do the objects and composition of your piece reflect themes from your interview?

- ▸ What moments were represented— big life-changing events or small but significant moments?

- ▸ What similarities and differences do you see in the ideas selected?

- ▸ What artistic choices were made in each assemblage, including the objects selected, the composition of the piece, and how the assemblage was created to communicate ideas from the interviews?

Mixed Media *(cont.)*

Specific Grade-Level Ideas

Grades K–2

Invite a special guest speaker, such as a community or family member, to visit the classroom. This can be done in person or virtually. Conduct an interview as a class. Be sure to have students prepare questions ahead of time.

As a class, conduct a genre study and gather additional books and resources with the theme of bonding with grandparents, such as *The Hello, Goodbye Window* by Norton Juster. Students can bring in a single artifact and story. The class can then create an assemblage together under the theme "family stories."

Grades 3–5

Explore the genre of biography and have students write a biography to accompany the assemblage they have created for the person they interviewed. Discuss how life stories can be shared through words or visually through art. Ask them what artistic choices they can include to show the idea of a life over time.

Invite students to use found objects to capture a scene from a favorite book, song, poem, or play or their own writing. Invite them to capture a scene from their own writing by representing it in an assemblage of found objects.

Grades 6–8

Have students further investigate the practice of conducting an interview. Discuss the ethics involved, and have students write consent forms before interviewing their participants. If the participant gives consent to be recorded, students can explore the use of technology to record their interview and transcribe the data.

Students also can investigate memoir, write a memoir, and then create an assemblage, such as a triptych, that captures aspects of their own lives. A triptych is a set of three associated artistic, literary, or musical works intended to be appreciated together. Images can be in hardcopy form or captured and displayed digitally.

Grades 9–12

Harness the power of mixed media to drive environmental advocacy projects. First, have students read about an environmental issue of their choice across a set of texts, such as trash in the environment, by visiting the website **teachingwithtradebooks.com** and locating the text set called "Trash Text Set," which is full of texts of different genres and modalities. Invite students to partake in a call to action by designing a piece of visual artwork using their choice of mixed media, such as a collage of trash found on a local beach, park, or street.

Name: _____ Date: _____

Creating Interview Questions

Directions: Read the Interview Tips before you begin the interview. Write four or more interview questions that you want to ask.

> ### Interview Tips
>
> - Ask open-ended questions beginning with words such as *how, when, why*, and *what*. Try not to ask questions with *yes* or *no* answers.
>
> - Ask questions about the different stages of your subject's life, such as childhood and adulthood.
>
> - Ask about feelings such as times when your subject was surprised, thrilled, sad, and so on.
>
> - Ask about the different roles a person has played in your subject's life (artist, mother, friend, and so on).
>
> - Ask about important moments such as turning points, signature moments, and cherished memories.

1. _____

   _____

2. _____

   _____

3. _____

   _____

4. _____

   _____

5. _____

   _____

Name: _____ Date: _____

Mixed Media Catalog

Directions: Look at the found objects for your project. Complete the chart.

	Describe or sketch the object.	What is the meaning of the object? Why did you choose it?	What theme or big idea does the object symbolize?
Object 1			
Object 2			
Object 3			
Object 4			

Transformation

Model Lesson: Altered Text

Overview

In this lesson, students experiment with putting together material in new ways by working with discarded books and transforming the meaning of the words on the page. They choose specific letters, words, or sentences and color or paint over the rest of the page, allowing the chosen words to stand out and with a new meaning. Students then alter the books, giving new form and meaning by transforming them artistically. They explore how visual art elements such as color, texture, and composition communicate meaning and mood and work with text to communicate an overall message.

Materials

▸ Materials for students to alter such as discarded books, articles, copies of primary sources from websites such as the Library of Congress, and so on

▸ art materials (paint, paper, stamps, scissors, glue, ribbon, buttons, and so on)

▸ *Altered Text Sample* (page 198)

▸ *Reflection for Altered Text* (page 200)

▸ *Elements of Visual Art* (page 171)

Standards

Grades K–2

▸ Describes how words or phrases suggest feelings or supply meaning

▸ Demonstrates understanding of word relationships

▸ Discusses and reflects with peers about choices made in creating artwork

▸ Explores uses of materials and tools to create works of art or design

Grades 3–5

▸ Determines the meaning and nuances of words and phrases

▸ Produces clear and coherent writing

▸ Creates an artist statement using art vocabulary to describe personal choices

▸ Creates personally satisfying artwork using a variety of artistic processes and materials

Grades 6–8

▸ Determines the meaning and nuances of words and phrases

▸ Produces clear and coherent writing

▸ Reflects on whether personal artwork conveys the intended meaning and revises accordingly

▸ Demonstrates openness in trying new ideas, materials, methods, and approaches in making works of art

Grades 9–12

▸ Demonstrates understanding of figurative language, word relationships, and nuances in word meanings

▸ Produces clear writing in which the development, organization, and style are appropriate to task, purpose, and audience

▸ Engages in constructive critique, then reflects on, revises, and refines works of art

▸ Engages in making a work of art or design without having a preconceived plan

Transformation (cont.)

Preparation

Familiarize yourself with the many techniques used to alter books by searching for images online that showcase altered books. Bookmark images that can be easily shared with students. Gather discarded books for students to alter. Plan ahead and ask your school and/or local librarians for books that they plan to discard. Be sure to check discarded books for appropriate content. Decide whether you will take pages out of one book and have students alter one page only, or if you would like each student to begin a long-term project of altering an entire book of their own over time. Additional ideas are provided in the Specific Grade-Level Ideas.

Procedure

1. Explain to students that they will have the opportunity to transform, or change, the meaning of a page in a book. Share *Altered Text Sample*, and images of altered text from the internet, and show students how altered texts are showcased in museums.

2. Read aloud any page from a discarded book. Discuss the meaning of the page with students.

3. Model how to give the page new meaning as you choose letters, words, or sentences on the page that combine to make a new thought or create new meaning. Underline or circle the words. They do not need to be in order on the page to create meaning.

4. Discuss the meaning of the words you have chosen. Use art materials such as paint, markers, or colored pencils to cover everything else on the page except the words. Discuss *Elements of Visual Art*.

> "Assemblage is art that is made by assembling disparate elements – often everyday objects – scavenged by the artist…"
>
> — Tate (n.d.)

5. Tell students that the page is now a fresh canvas. Using students' suggestions, continue to alter the page with illustration pens, paint, collaged papers, or other media to create an illustration. Explain to students that an *illustration* is "a visual explanation of a text and how the words and artwork work together to communicate a message to the reader." Make choices collaboratively to complete the artwork example.

6. Reread the complete example back to students. State that this new creation could be considered a freeform poem with an accompanying illustration. Define a *freeform poem* as "a poem that doesn't involve specific rules of format or structure."

7. Provide students with art supplies and a page (or a book) to alter. Discuss how students will repurpose the books that would have been thrown away. Have students sketch plans on a separate sheet of paper to explore a range of possible ideas, noting that artists and writers often experiment with ideas. Use the Planning Questions to help students think about potential directions for their altered texts.

8. Have students begin the process of transforming their pages. Monitor students as they work and ask how they are choosing colors, textures, and other elements of art to enhance meaning.

9. Distribute *Reflection for Altered Text* and have students consider how they are transforming the meaning of the page or book. Talk about this as a class before asking students to complete the page on their own.

10. Debrief the process with students by using the Discussion Questions.

Transformation (cont.)

Planning Questions

▸ What theme will you explore in your page or book? Why?

▸ Which words or phrases on the page(s) stand out to you?

▸ How will you alter the meaning of a page or pages?

▸ What choices will you experiment with in terms of the elements of art (color, shape, space, line, form, texture, and value), and which art materials will you use to achieve your desired effect?

> "Altered books go further than just drawings as they can be composed of a variety of art media, such as photos, collage, symbols, and repeating patterns, allowing their creators to stretch their imagination and creativity."
>
> —Natasha Anne Toth (2015, 21)

Discussion Questions

▸ Discuss the dual roles of author and artist you played in the creation of your altered book.

▸ What choices did you make in both roles?

▸ How were they similar and different?

▸ What new meaning did you give to the page or book?

▸ Which artistic techniques produced the most interesting results? Why?

▸ What is communicated by the composition of the pages?

▸ What did you learn during the process of creating your altered page or book?

Transformation (cont.)

Specific Grade-Level Ideas

Grades K–2

Locate discarded books with large print. Have students look for sight words. For example, they can create an altered page all about the word *and*. Students can also create alphabet books, exploring words that begin with specific letters by locating words and images throughout the book that begin with that letter and transform the page accordingly.

Explore a particular theme that students can research through image, text, and found materials.

Have them select ideas they want to explore further by composing pages in a book. Students could work on single pages that get re-bound in an altered class book.

Grades 3–5

Have students share their work in a "silent celebration." Have each student place one of their altered book pages on a desk next to a blank sheet of paper for student comments. The blank sheet of paper should have two columns: Viewer's Name and Viewer's Comments. Ask students to move from desk to desk, viewing the altered pages and writing comments. Before the celebration, brainstorm ideas for comments as a class, such as commenting about how a particular color may make them feel or the artist's choice of words. Remind students that this is a celebration and a time to give positive feedback only, not a time for constructive feedback or criticism. After the celebration, allow time for students to talk with their peers about the work they viewed.

Grades 6–8

Students can identify a theme for their altered books and design pages based on this topic. Students also can choose one or more writing pieces from their writing folders and incorporate excerpts into the altered book. As students think about composing a page, they should consider where to place text, what size the text should be, and how images can connect to, expand on, or contrast with the text. Ask students to consider their multiple roles as author, artist, and graphic designer as they construct their books. Explore unifying themes for the book such as mythology.

Grades 9–12

In addition to the ideas for grades 6–8, students can go through the first few steps of choosing words and blocking out the other surrounding text. Then students can make a photocopy of the page and give it to a partner. Both partners can create artwork around the same selected text as they see fit, each working on their own page. Afterward, the partners compare and contrast the artworks to see how the words were interpreted in similar or contrasting manners, and discuss their choices. Students also can choose to intentionally illustrate the text using abstract imagery, which will encourage stronger reliance on how elements of art and principles of design combine to intentionally communicate meaning.

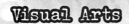

Altered Text Sample

Artwork with Helen Keller's 1893 Letter by Christine Flood. Used by permission.

Altered Text Sample (cont.)

Artist's Statement and Poem by Christine Flood

I was really moved by the way Helen explained her experience in this letter. I started by reading through the letter and with a pencil circling my favorite words that spoke to what she was trying to say, like "eyes in her fingers" and "the noise which you feel." Once I had some words picked that spoke to my emotions, I then went back through and started composing a poem by choosing other words. My next step was to make my choices more permanent by using a bold marker to surround the words and make them stand out. Here is the poem I chose:

My Dear

I wrote so please accept it
feel my mind recurring delight
and realize the eye of the mind and soul,
eyes in fingers
spy
hold
pick
the noise which you feel
running high.
it dies away into a gentle murmur
to feel the roadside gleam.
believe me,
your affectionate
little friend,
Helen Keller.
August twentieth, eighteen hundred and ninety-three.

The feelings that overcame me in reading the letter was of happiness, joy, and hope so I wanted to express that in my art choices. I started blocking out text with colorful washi tape. Then I found images of sky, sun, birds and most importantly hands. I wanted to focus on natural elements that one could hear and feel, not just see. I collaged them over and around text. I wanted to help Helen convey the message that her fingers were not just used to feel physical objects, but were used to feel emotions, feel time, feel life. Her hands let her see the world and she wanted to share this beautiful discovery. I finished blocking out text with paint and oil pastels, experimenting with different brushstrokes and layering of colors and textures.

View the primary source letter at: **www.loc.gov/resource/magbell.12400303/?sp=1**

Name: _____ Date: _____

Reflection for Altered Text

Directions: Consider the meaning of the pages before and after you transform a book. Record your ideas on the chart.

Before What was the meaning on the page before you transformed it?
Transformation Process What artistic choices did you make to transform the meaning?
After What is the meaning of the page now?

    © Shell Education

Creative Movement

Creative Movement

Understanding Creative Movement

Integrating creative movement across the curriculum is an engaging approach to learning that allows students to experience, translate, and communicate language arts ideas kinesthetically. In 1983, Howard Gardner identified bodily kinesthetic intelligence within his theory of multiple intelligences (2011) as one way that students learn. Neuroscientists are finding that memory and recall are improved when the body is engaged in the learning process (Zull 2002) and that the mind uses the body to make sense of ideas (Carpenter 2011).

While important for all learners, opportunities to express themselves nonverbally can be particularly powerful for some students, especially those for whom the current educational systems do not respond to their learning styles. Such opportunities can provide students with access to language arts content that would not be possible otherwise. Stacey Skoning (2008) states that creative movement, or dance, "is important to incorporate into our inclusive classrooms if we want to meet the needs of more diverse groups of students" (9).

Creative movement allows students to be physically active, which often increases students' attention span, but it is much more than just the incorporation of movement into classroom activities. When students are involved in creative movement, they become more mindful of their bodies' ability to communicate, explore what happens when they move with intention, engage in problem solving through movement, and develop awareness of their creative choices. It is important to keep the possibilities for this work in mind as students explore these lessons.

As students deconstruct and reconstruct concepts, they take ownership of the ideas through kinesthetic means and creative choices. Writer and choreographer Susan Griss (1994) makes the point that because creative movement is "expressive, informative, and analytical," it can heighten learning in the language arts classroom by increasing comprehension, supporting the development of whole language skills, providing multicultural insights, bolstering social skills, and focusing energy into creative outlets.

Elements of Creative Movement

These elements are drawn from several sources, including the Kennedy Center (Bodensteiner 2019), PBS Learning Media (KQED 2015), the Institute for Arts Integration and STEAM (Riley 2017), the National Core Arts Standards, and the Perpich Center for Arts Education (2009).

- **Body**: Creative movement works with the parts of the body to move, isolate, manipulate to create shape and movement through space

- **Space**: Creative movement interacts with and occupies space on different levels, in different pathways, in different size and scope of movement.

- **Action**: Non-locomotor, which is axial-movement around the body's axis and Locomotor, movement that travels through space

- **Time**: Movement happens over time and can communicate through tempo and rhythm.

- **Energy**: The qualities (sustained, percussive, suspended, etc.), weight (heavy, light, etc.), and flow (continuous, controlled, etc.) of how movement occurs

Creative movement embraces an *every body* spirit. All the activities can be done seated or standing, stationary or ambulatory.

—Celeste Miller, Choreographer and Educator (personal communication, May 4, 2021)

Creative Movement (cont.)

Strategies for Creative Movement

Each creative movement strategy results in a short piece of choreography: repeatable dances made up of original movements created by students. The final strategy, Choreographic Structure is an advanced step in this process that introduces students to several tools of choreography and the suite form.

Answer Me in Movement

Students respond to a question from the teacher, and, instead of answering with words, they "answer" by creating their own movements to express their responses. This could be as simple as an arm gesture such as circling the arms over the head to represent the sun. Answer Me in Movement invites students to develop the skill of translating ideas into new forms, exploring the meaning of concepts in new ways.

Movement Strings

Students invent a series of movements that can be strung together, similar to beads on a string. This strategy works well with lists of ideas that can be organized sequentially.

Progressions

Students focus on the transitions between their movements. It is a further development of Movement Strings. This strategy provides an opportunity to connect concepts, processes, and events into a movement phrase that links ideas together in meaningful ways.

Sensory Movement

Students use the five senses, combined with motion, as the inspiration to create movement. This strategy explores the sensory details of ideas. Perfect for figurative and connotative language, Sensory Movement invites students to experience the qualities of concepts such as colors, emotions, and more.

Choreographic Structure

In each creative movement strategy, students are creating dances. This is choreography. Choreography begins with improvisation to create original movements and experiment with different ways to do them: fast or slow, big or little, and so on. From this experimentation the choreographer (or collaborative choreographers) selects the movements they want to use and orders them into sequences and patterns. This is called a *dance suite*. These now predetermined movements are repeatable. Students then rehearse the movements to prepare for their presentation. In this strategy, students are introduced to five choreographic structures to create a dance suite. A dance suite can be thought of as a set of "mini-dances" about the same topic or theme.

> "Creative movement is movement that reflects the inner state of a child. In creative movement, children are free to express their own personalities, style, thoughts, and feelings. Creative movement encourages children to act on what they are learning and express their individuality."
>
> —Ann McKitrick (2016)

Creative Movement (cont.)

Choreography in the Classroom

Each of the creative movement strategies has been used successfully in classrooms by choreographer and educator Celeste Miller. The strategies are organized to build on each other, increasing in depth and complexity. Thus, it is highly recommended that you introduce the strategies to students in the order presented in this section:

1. Answer Me in Movement

2. Movement Strings

3. Progressions

4. Sensory Movement

5. Choreographic Structure

Students can move through the strategies sequentially, culminating in a short choreographed piece, or the strategies can be completed individually as one-time lessons.

All activities can be done in the classroom by moving tables/desks and seats to the outskirts of the room in an organized fashion. You also may take this process outside, use an open meeting area, or plan to use another open space such as the gym or cafeteria. A large space is not necessary for this process, but rather just another possibility. Students should stand in a circle formation with the teacher when given instructions and when sharing their creative products. Student breakout groups can be scattered throughout the room.

In the creative movement lesson plans, the word *dance* is used as a noun—"that which is created"—and also as a verb—"to dance." We often think of dance as steps done to music, with a beat. In creative movement, dance encompasses unique motions created by the individual to express ideas. Creative movement dances can be done to silence or to words, in addition to music. It is unique and does not have to mimic the steps

or a particular dance genre (though it can). In the lesson plans, students are often referred to as "dancers." This is to empower students to own their agency as creative makers using dance. Teachers should make the decision to use the word based on the climate of their classroom; sometimes the word *dance* carries cultural or gendered overtones that inhibit student participation. Good substitute words for *dance* are *movement* (verb) or *movers* (noun). Teachers can refer to what their students are making as "creative movement explorations," instead of "dances." This is at your discretion.

Teaching the Strategies

Because these strategies build on each other, the first set of how-to lessons (pages 207–218) models how to introduce each strategy to students. The second set of lessons (pages 219–252) models one way to use the strategies with a single piece of text—Richard Blanco's inaugural poem "One Today." Each strategy allows the students to use movement to further investigate the poem, its meaning, and its importance, culminating in a combination of all the movements (strategies) into one choreographed piece. Should you choose to use a different text with students, the lessons can serve as a guide to your thinking. Look for these characteristics in identifying texts that work well with movement such as:

▸ richly detailed visual and sensory images

▸ a sense of progression (the story moves along)

▸ language that evokes movement

▸ multigenre and multimodal texts—can be an excerpt of a larger work (a letter, poem, monologue, visualization, primary source photograph, painting, quotation, or oral history)

Creative Movement (cont.)

Helpful Terms

- **Dance**: Movement aware of itself done with purpose. These movements may be unique to each person who creates them.

- **Movement**: Individual movements, often gestures. These are discrete units that can be organized in any order. Movements or gestures are the equivalent of a "word" in a sentence.

- **Movement sequence**: The stringing together of several discrete movements. Movement sequences can be thought of as "sentences."

- **Choreography**: Purposeful movements arranged for effect to communicate ideas.

- **Choreography tools**: Forms that can be used to create movement patterns.

- **Shape**: A frozen pose that you hold. A shape is not limited to circle, square, triangle, and so on. Rather it is the design of the body, similar to a sculpture, that can be held in stillness. Shapes are done with the whole body. For example: Stand on one foot, with the free leg bent and the toe touching the standing leg knee. Arms are straight out to the side.

- **Level**: Levels are where the body is on a vertical plane: low, middle, or high. You could be close to the ground (low), or as high as you can reach (high), or in between high and low (middle).

- **Neutral stance**: This is a resting stance, whether seated or standing. A student once defined a neutral stance as: "It's like when a car is in neutral. It's not moving yet, but it is ready to go."

- **Call and response**: The leader does a movement, then the group responds by repeating the same movement back to the leader.

- **Copying**: The leader's back is to the group, and the group copies the leader. Thus the leader's right arm is the copier's right arm. If the leader moves to their right, everyone moves to their right.

- **Mirroring**: The leader faces the group. The group sees the leader as a mirror image. Thus the leader's right arm is the group's left arm. If the leader moves to their right, the group moves to their left.

- **Unison**: Everyone is doing the same thing at the same time in sync with one another.

- **Counter unison**: Endless versions and configurations of how different people are doing different things.

- **Transition**: The ability to connect movement ideas (for example, a person can go from skipping to walking or from reaching upward to twisting around themselves).

- **Fan**: One person does a movement while everyone else is still, then the second person does a movement while everyone else is still, and so on. Every student gets a turn, then the movements are completed in reverse order.

- **Rondo**: Dancers perform their individual movements in unique sequences, so everyone in the group must learn everyone else's movement. Each dancer completes each movement but in a different order from the rest.

- **Recurrence**: The repetition of something that has been done in a dance before, but usually with a slight twist.

Music is a helpful tool to use with students in creative movement. Check out this creative movement Spotify playlist by choreographer and educator Celeste Miller: **open.spotify.com/playlist/7bvVFJ1Zj0 gJgC1wv1Bwsz**. You can use this playlist with any of the lessons in this section.

Introducing the Strategies

Answer Me in Movement Introduction

1. Explain to students that in the Answer Me in Movement strategy, we use our bodies instead of words to communicate an idea. We do this by creating a single-movement response based on a prompt. Tell students to think of the movement as a "gesture," similar to the common gestures of using a wave to say "hello" or making the shape of a phone with your hand to say "call me."

One way to help students understand Answer Me in Movement is to reference the "live" function on a smartphone camera, where there is a slight bit of movement before the photo still is captured.

—Celeste Miller, Choreographer and Educator (personal communication, May 4, 2021)

2. Share with students that you are going to give them a prompt and you want them to show their movements en masse, which means "all together." Explain to students that they stay frozen at the end of their movement, thus creating a "snapshot" moment that nonverbally expresses their response to the prompt. Then, on your instruction to release, students should return to a neutral position. Say: "When I clap, I want you to answer me in movement, what is . . . ? When I clap again, go back to a neutral position."

Example:

Teacher: Answer me in movement, what is the weather today? *(Clap)*

Students respond in movement with a unique original gesture that indicates today's weather, such as on a sunny day, one student may make a circle with her arms to indicate the sun, and another student may turn his face upward and smile to indicate sunshine falling welcomingly on his face.

After a short pause in which all students are frozen in their "answer," clap and have students relax into a neutral position.

3. Give each student a chance to show their movement and then share verbally what the movement represented and why it was their movement choice. **Note**: We never try and guess what a movement means, rather this final step in the process gives students an opportunity to verbally share their movement-choice reasoning.

Introducing the Strategies (cont.)

Movement Strings Introduction

1. Explain to students that the Movement Strings strategy builds on the Answer Me in Movement strategy. Remind them that in that strategy they created gestures in single, original, and unique movements.

2. Share with students that in Movement Strings, their movements will last longer and contain more action before they freeze in their final poses. **Optional**: Consult the *Helpful Terms* (page 206) for movement types, sequences, or ideas to support students' creation of actions. Make sure you introduce the vocabulary as well as model the movements.

3. Read a sequential text with students (or refer to a previously read text), then have them brainstorm a list of the sequence of information or events that happened in the text.

4. Help students create a movement for each item on the list. Then have them link those series of individual movements together so that they can perform the movements in sequence, similar to beads on a string, one after the other. Remind students, however, that each movement idea is discrete, so the order of the sequence could be rearranged. This will give students the opportunity to learn how altering how information is distributed can alter a narrative's message.

Example:

A student creates a movement for the idea "Connections are built." The student begins crouched down low to the ground with both hands on the ground, then slowly rises while keeping one hand to the floor, as she makes a staircase-like sequence of movements with her other hand getting higher and higher. Her movement concludes with a long stretch connecting the hand on the floor to the hand up in the air, and she looks first down to the hand on the floor and then up to the hand over head. She decides to do her movement sequence slowly, gradually increasing in speed, while turning in place.

5. Provide each student the opportunity to show their movement to the class, share what the movement represents, and tell why they made that movement choice. **Note:** This final step in the process gives students the opportunity to verbally share their movement-choice reasoning.

Introducing the Strategies *(cont.)*

Progressions Introduction

1. Select and share a text that involves a sequence such as a series of events, steps, or actions.

2. Instruct students to create a list of how the sequence of events (narrative) or information (nonfiction) is organized in the text (What do we know first? What do we know next?)

3. Ask students to think of how the text uses language, images, or visual support to move readers from one idea to the next. Explain that their focus should be on the transitions between ideas, not just the ideas. Use chart paper to record students' ideas.

4. Explain that in Progressions, we infer emotions.

5. Organize the sequence of events in a two-column chart, as shown in the sample progression chart of "Jack and Jill." Explain to students that the left side of the chart details the sequence of events/information from the text. The right side of the chart details the movements that students choose to represent each part of the text. In this strategy, students focus on developing the ideas in column two so that the movements flow from one to the next. We avoid static positions, keeping the action going throughout.

6. Have students generate movement ideas for column two, always linking their movements from what came before to what comes next. Students make their own interpretation about to how to end their progression.

Introducing the Strategies *(cont.)*

Sample Progression

The example of the nursery rhyme "Jack and Jill" is provided here.

"Jack and Jill" Sequence of Events	Movement Ideas: For Two Students
Jack and Jill went up the hill to fetch a pail of water	Three joyful skips Followed by three cumbersome steps Put hands on thighs and take three labored breaths
Jack fell down and broke his crown	One student stands on one leg and sways Student falls and rolls like a ball to a different place in the room Student ends in a seated position, head in hands
Jill came tumbling after	The next student loses their balance by repeating the same movement that the first student did Student does a rolling movement that takes them to a different place in the room Student ends in seated position, holding their head
End	Students join hands and help each other stand Skip around in a circle Stop and look over their shoulders and shake their heads "no" Hold this final pose to complete the movement progression

Introducing the Strategies *(cont.)*

Sensory Movement Introduction

1. Explain to students that the Sensory Movement strategy uses the five senses (taste, smell, touch, sight, hearing) to convey information.

2. Explain that in Sensory Movement they will translate the senses into an action. As an example, say: "How would the color red move? Is it big and bold or soft and quiet?" Allow students time to share their ideas about how the color red might move.

3. Also explain that in Sensory Movement they will use their bodies, not their voices, to express the ideas. Ask: "How can we move *like* a screech, instead of screeching?" Have students respond with their ideas.

4. Display the following sentences (or similar sentences appropriate for students):
   ▸ The smell of sweet roses filled the air.
   ▸ The server accidentally dropped the large tray filled with dishes.
   ▸ The car came to a sudden stop.

5. As a class, brainstorm a list of words (or images) from each sentence that fall into any of the five senses and record them on chart paper. Also have students consider motion as another category. **Optional:** Provide students with their own copies of the sentences and have students circle sensory words/ideas that support the brainstormed list.

6. Prompt students to use inferencing skills to add more information to the list. For example, using the sentence, "The car came to a sudden stop," they can infer things such as the sound of screeching brakes, the smell of burning rubber, the sight of flashing metal, and the motion of being thrown forward and then caught by the restraint of a seat belt.

7. Have students select a sequence of motions to go with each sentence. They can work individually or in pairs or small groups. Provide students time to share their motion sequences with the class.

Introducing the Strategies *(cont.)*

Choreographic Structure Introduction

1. Explain to students that a dance suite is a choreographic structure for making longer and more complicated dances than they have made previously. An example of a dance suite is Carol Burch Brown's *Salt Marsh Suite*, which has six sections: tides, water, mud, birds, crabs, and grasses. Each section is its own topic, but all topics fit in the overall concept of the salt marsh.

2. Explain to students that they are going to practice creating a dance suite. They will use five choreographic tools for each of five sections of their dances. Choreographic tools are specific ways that movements can be arranged with one another.

3. Provide students with a theme around which to anchor their movements, such as the ocean, playground games, or animal habitats. If desired, select music to play in the background that matches the theme you select. This also may help students think about different movements they can use.

4. Place students into groups of five. (Groups of four or six also work, depending on the number of students in your class.) Distribute a copy of the *Choreography Planning Guide* (pages 215–218) to each student. Introduce students to each of the five choreographic tools.

5. Explain that the first choreographic tool is called Call and Response. This is when one person (the soloist) performs a movement or movement sequence and then the rest of the group performs that movement or sequence as a response back to the soloist.

6. To practice Call and Response, have one student in each group make some kind of motion and the rest of the group "answer back" with that same motion. If desired, play music while groups practice this choreographic tool. Have students record their movement in the Call and Response section of their planning guide.

7. Explain that the next choreographic tool is called Unison. This is where everyone does the same thing at the same time. Provide groups time to create an action or short movement sequence that they want to do in unison and briefly practice it. Have students record their movement in the Unison section of their planning guide.

8. Have groups put the movements they selected for the first two tools together. First they do their Call and Response movement(s) and then they do the Unison movement(s). Play music during this portion, as desired.

9. Explain that the third choreographic tool that they will learn is called the Fan. This is a sequence of movements where one student does a movement while everyone else is still, then the second person does a movement while everyone else is still, and so on. Have students think of this like a waterfall. In sports arenas, this is similar to the crowd doing the wave. However, in Fan, everyone does their own unique movement.

10. Provide groups time for each student to decide on their Fan movement as well as the order in which they want to do their movements. Have students record their movements in the Fan section of their planning guide.

Introducing the Strategies *(cont.)*

Choreographic Structure Introduction *(cont.)*

11. Select one group to help model this strategy. To do this, Student A does movement 1, Student B does movement 2, Student C does movement 3, Student D does movement 4, Student E does movement 5. Then Student E does movement 5 again, then Student D does movement 4, Student C does movement 3, Student B does movement 2, and Student A does movement 1. They arrive back where they started to complete the Fan.

12. Have students practice completing the Fan movement sequence.

13. Have groups put the movements they selected for all three tools together in sequence: Call and Response, Unison, Fan. Play music during this portion, as desired.

14. Explain that the next choreographic tool they will learn is called Rondo. This is when students perform their individual movements in unique sequences, so everyone in the group must learn everyone else's movement. For this practice, have students use the same movements they did in Fan, but have them teach them all to each other.

15. Display the Movement Sequence Guide shown on the next page to show how each student performs the movement sequence in a different order, but everyone is moving at the same time. Whereas in Unison everyone is doing the same thing at the same time, in Rondo it is similar to a round.

16. Have students record their movements in the Rondo section of their planning guide. Provide students time to practice.

17. Have groups put the movements they selected for all four tools together in sequence: Call and Response, Unison, Fan, Rondo. Play music during this portion, as desired.

18. Explain that the last choreographic tool students will learn is called Recurrence. This is the repetition of something that has been done before, but usually with a slight twist.

19. Have groups select a movement or movement sequence they have already done and then put a creative twist on it. For example, if students swayed their hands in the air earlier, this time they could sway their hands in the air while turning in a circle. Provide students time to practice their selected movements. Have them record their movements in the Recurrence section of their planning guide.

20. Have groups put all the movements for all five tools together in sequence: Call and Response, Unison, Fan, Rondo, Recurrence. Play music during this portion, as desired.

21. If desired, give each group time to share their dance suite with the rest of the class. This could be further developed into a school assembly.

> Consider breaking up the introduction to the strategies over three to four days so that students feel comfortable with each choreographic tool before moving on.

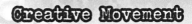

Introducing the Strategies *(cont.)*

Movement Sequence Guide

Student A Sequence	Student B Sequence	Student C Sequence	Student D Sequence	Student E Sequence
1	2	3	4	5
2	3	4	5	1
3	4	5	1	2
4	5	1	2	3
5	1	2	3	4

Name: _____ Date: _____

Choreography Planning Guide

Directions: Work with your group to select a movement or movement sequence for each choreographic tool. Draw or describe the movements, and think about and respond to the questions provided.

Call and Response: One student performs a movement or movement sequence, and then the group performs that movement or sequence as a response back to the student.

Draw a diagram that describes how you will use Call and Response.

Who will be the "caller"? Will the caller always be the same?

What is the formation (circles, lines, or random)? Will the formation always be the same?

Name: _____ Date: _____

Choreography Planning Guide *(cont.)*

Unison: Everyone is doing the same thing at the same time.

Draw or describe the movement that everyone will learn.

Fan: One person does a movement while everyone else is still, then the second person does a movement while everyone else is still, and so on. Each student gets a turn, then the movements are completed in reverse order.

Draw a diagram that shows the order of everyone in the Fan. Describe each person's movement(s).

Name: _____ Date: _____

Choreography Planning Guide (cont.)

Rondo: You will perform your individual movements in unique sequences, so everyone in the group must learn everyone else's movement(s).

Draw or describe each person's movements.

Name: _____ Date: _____

Choreography Planning Guide *(cont.)*

Use the chart to record the order in which each person will perform the movements.

Student A Sequence	Student B Sequence	Student C Sequence	Student D Sequence	Student E Sequence

Recurrence: This is the repetition of something that has been done before, but usually with a slight twist.

Select one of the choreographic tools and plan to repeat it, but with a twist! What will that twist be?

Answer Me in Movement

Model Lesson: "One Today" Answer Me in Movement

Overview

In this lesson, students read the poem "One Today" by Richard Blanco and use the Answer Me in Movement strategy to identify the main ideas the text illuminates. The sample teacher and student dialogue is not intended to be prescriptive, rather to guide your thinking and model how the strategy may play out.

Materials

▸ "One Today" by Richard Blanco (available as a picture book, on **Poets.org**, or as a video of the 2013 Inaugural Reading)

▸ chart paper

▸ copy of "One Today" for each student *(optional)*

Standards

Grades K–2

▸ Describes how words and phrases (regular beats, alliteration, rhymes, repeated lines) supply rhythm and meaning in a story, poem, or song

▸ Explores movement inspired by a variety of stimuli and identifies the source

Grades 3–5

▸ Determines the meaning of words and phrases as they are used in a text, including figurative language such as metaphors and similes

▸ Experiments with a variety of self-identified stimuli for movement

Grades 6–8

▸ Determines the meaning of words and phrases as they are used in a text, including figurative and connotative meanings; analyzes the impact of specific word choices on meaning and tone, including analogies or allusions to other texts

▸ Relates similar or contrasting ideas to develop choreography using a variety of stimuli

Grades 9–12

▸ Determines the meaning of words and phrases as they are used in a text, including figurative and connotative meanings; analyzes the impact of specific word choices on meaning and tone, including words with multiple meanings or language that is particularly fresh, engaging, or beautiful

▸ Explores a variety of stimuli for sourcing movement to develop an improvisational or choreographed dance study; analyzes the process and relationship between the stimuli and the movement

Answer Me in Movement (cont.)

Preparation

Have students practice using the Answer Me in Movement strategy (page 207) before beginning this lesson. Additional ideas are provided in the Specific Grade-Level Ideas.

Procedure

1. Share the poem "One Today" by Richard Blanco with students. Ask students to identify the main organizing idea of the poem (one), and find the four different "ones" listed in the poem (one sun, one light, one ground, one sky). Using chart paper, record each of the "one" words large enough for students to see easily.

2. As a movement warm-up, engage students in the following dialogue:

    Teacher: Where is the sun?
    Students: Up in the sky.
    Teacher: Let's reach overhead to start and make a movement for the sun, and we will call that movement number one.
    Teacher: The light from the sun reaches down to Earth. Let's move our arms from overhead, down to our sides, to spread the sun's light all around us here on Earth for movement number two. As we do the movement, imagine spreading light. Let's do movement number one, followed by movement number two.
    Teacher: Where is the ground? Can you show me a movement that shows where the ground is? Let's call this movement number three. Let's do movement number one, followed by movement number two, followed by movement number three. You each have slightly different and unique movements from one another. That's good!

    Teacher: Where is the sky? Let's do a last movement that means "sky" to you. We will call that movement number four. Now let's do all four movements in sequence, using an inhale to begin each movement, an exhale, and then a new inhale for the next movement and so on.

    ‣ one sun
    ‣ one light
    ‣ one ground
    ‣ one sky

    Option: Add music (without lyrics) and let students do the movement sequence to music.

3. Read the poem again and have students listen (or read) for how each of those four attributes inspires many images in the progress of the poem.

4. If age appropriate, distribute copies of the poem to students so they can highlight their ideas. Students should choose just one image, scene, phrase, or idea from the poem for each attribute. You can instruct them to choose one that has meaning for them or is something they never considered.

    Example:

    One sun—a student might choose the phrase "peeking over the Smokies";
    One light—a student might choose the phrase "millions of faces in morning's mirrors";
    One ground—a student might choose the phrase "hands digging trenches";
    One sky—a student might choose the phrase "facing the stars."

Answer Me in Movement *(cont.)*

5. Say: "When I clap, answer me in movement; show me your 'one sun' image or scene with a movement. Hold your position until I clap again, and then relax." Guide students through all four attributes. Have students respond with their own choices.

6. Play music softly in the background and have students practice all four of their unique movement ideas in sequence. Cue one movement idea to the next with a single clap.

7. After a few rehearsals, invite students to show their movement to the class. After they have shown the class their movement, allow them time to share about the choices they made and why.

8. Highlight how each student has made unique choices—some movements may have been similar, but all are unique to each student. Tell students this is how we are as a community of people. We each have an idea that responds to a larger idea.

9. **Extension**: Once students understand the structure of this strategy, they can find other images, scenes, or ideas in the text and build more four-part movement sequences to the poem. This can be done as solos or small groups working together.

10. Debrief, using the Discussion Questions.

Discussion Questions

▸ How did the poet organize this poem around four main ideas?

▸ How did movement help you understand the organization of the poem?

▸ How can movement be an important tool in visualizing poetic imagery?

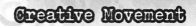

Answer Me in Movement *(cont.)*

Sample Motion Ideas

Movement Prompt	Sample Movement Ideas for Students
One sun	Appear to be peeking over a mountain range Move as if running/charging forward
One light	Place palms in front of them as if framing a window, and then move their head in and out of the frame as if many faces were looking through the same window; freeze after four or five times Hold hands out in front of them, opening and closing their hands for the blinking rhythm of traffic lights
One ground	Move as if they are digging a trench; freeze in stillness after two digs Gesture as if brushing dust off of their clothes for "the dust of farms"
One sky	Turn their face upward, reach their arms overhead, and make twinkling motions with their fingers; freeze in that position Wrap themself in a hug

Answer Me in Movement *(cont.)*

Specific Grade-Level Ideas

Grades K–2

Select a character from a text you are reading. Ask students, "Answer me in movement: What is a character trait of ____?"

Grades 6–8

Select a sculpture that suggests movement such as Constantin Brancusi's *Bird in Space* (1923). Ask students: "Answer me in movement: How is the motion of flight represented in this sculpture?"

Grades 3–5

Select a photograph such as Dorothea Lange's 1936 "Migrant Mother." Ask students to isolate details (both human beings and clothing) in the image. Notice, for example, the mother's hand cupped around her chin, how her sleeve is pushed up, and how the folds of the blanket are gathered around the baby. Ask students: "Answer me in movement: What is one detail that you notice?"

Grades 9–12

Have students read across a text set of paintings by Van Gogh. Have groups choose a painting and identify its style and theme. Display a painting, such as *Starry Night*. Ask students: "Answer me in movement: What is the mood evoked in this painting?"

Movement Strings

Model Lesson: "One Today" Movement Strings

Overview

In this lesson, students read the poem "One Today" by Richard Blanco and use the Movement Strings strategy to identify how information is communicated sequentially and to what effect. Students create individual movements and then link them to form a sequence of movements to communicate the sequential order of the ideas.

Materials

▸ "One Today" by Richard Blanco (available as a picture book, on **Poets.org**, or as a video of the 2013 Inaugural Reading)

▸ markers

▸ copy of "One Today" for each student *(optional)*

▸ two different color pencils for each student *(optional)*

▸ United States map *(optional)*

Standards

Grades K–2

▸ Describes how words and phrases (regular beats, alliteration, rhymes, repeated lines) supply rhythm and meaning in a story, poem, or song

▸ Chooses movements that express a main idea or emotion or follow a musical phrase

Grades 3–5

▸ Determines the meaning of words and phrases as they are used in a text, including figurative language such as metaphors and similes

▸ Develops a dance phrase that expresses and communicates an idea or feeling

Grades 6–8

▸ Determines the meaning of words and phrases as they are used in a text, including figurative and connotative meanings; analyzes the impact of specific word choices on meaning and tone, including analogies or allusions to other texts

▸ Implements movement from a variety of stimuli to develop dance content for an original dance study or dance

Grades 9–12

▸ Determines the meaning of words and phrases as they are used in a text, including figurative and connotative meanings; analyzes the impact of specific word choices on meaning and tone, including words with multiple meanings or language that is particularly fresh, engaging, or beautiful

▸ Explores a variety of stimuli for sourcing movement to develop an improvisational or choreographed dance study

Movement Strings *(cont.)*

Preparation

Have students practice using the Movement Strings strategy (page 208) before beginning this lesson. This strategy also builds on what was learned from the Answer Me in Movement strategy (pages 219–223). If students are not familiar with that strategy, practice it with them first before beginning Movement Strings. Additional ideas are provided in the Specific Grade-Level Ideas.

Procedure

1. Reread "One Today" with students. After a general discussion about the poem, display and direct the student's attention to how the poet builds on ideas. Use the opening lines as an example for investigation:

   "One sun rose on us today, kindled over our shores, / peeking over the Smokies, greeting the faces / of the Great Lakes, spreading a simple truth / across the Great Plains, then charging across the Rockies."

2. Point out that you arrived at the stopping point because of the period at the end of the four lines of the poem. Circle each comma with one color, and then circle the verb in each phrase with another color. As a class, discuss how to turn each verb into its "to" (infinitive) form.

   Examples:

   kindled: to kindle

   peeking: to peek

   greeting: to greet

   spreading: to spread

   charging: to charge

3. Have students use a dictionary to look up the meaning of each word, with the goal of gathering rich words or alternate definitions. **Optional**: Use a map of the United States to trace the path of the poem from the eastern shore to the Rocky Mountains. See if students can note how the poem moves from east to west, just like the path of the sun.

4. Place students into small groups. Ask groups to think of a movement to represent each separate verb, and then do those movements as a string sequence all together.

   kindle peek greet spread charge

5. Have each group decide on a beginning still position and an ending still position. These positions could be discrete or connected human sculptures (tableaux) with everyone in the group as part of the sculpture.

   Example:

   Students start by forming a circle holding hands with one another, because they want to start out as the sun. Then they turn to the person to their right and rub their hands together as if they are making heat to kindle a fire (kindle). Next they line up in two rows facing the audience. The front row is on their knees, and the back row "hides" behind them; on a cue the back row peeks over the front row (peek). Then the students all stand up and begin to wave and gesture silent "hellos" to one another, leading them into a long line all holding hands (greet). From this line they move their held hands forward and back as if to spread the air in front of them (spread). With a burst of energy they let go of hands and charge around the room (charge) until they are all in one clump as if they were a mountain range. They stay frozen in this final human sculpture.

Movement Strings *(cont.)*

6. **Extension**: Assign students to find another sequence in the poem where the nouns or verbs create a sequence of movement from which they could create a movement string.

7. Debrief, using the Discussion Questions.

Discussion Questions

▸ How do poets create a sense of movement with motion words (verbs)?

▸ Did identifying the verbs in movement give you new insight into the poem?

Specific Grade-Level Ideas

Grades K–2

Read aloud the poem "Sick" by Shel Silverstein. Ask students to make a list on a different topic (things that make them happy, foods they like) and end the list with the craft strategy of a surprise ending. Have students create a movement for each item on the list. Then ask them to perform the movements in a sequence from the first to the last.

Grades 3–5

Read aloud or have students read the book *I Am Every Good Thing* by Derrick Barnes. Ask students to make their own list about who they are, in the same format. Have them create a movement for each item on the list. Then invite them to perform the movements in a sequence from the first to the last.

Grades 6–8

Choose a poem from Nikki Grimes's book *One Last Word: Wisdom from the Harlem Renaissance*. Have students use this poem to inspire their movement string.

Grades 9–12

Read Joy Harjo's poem "For Calling the Spirit Back from Wandering the Earth in Its Human Feet." Ask students to isolate the ideas listed in the poem and invent a movement for each. Then have them perform these in a sequence.

Progressions

Model Lesson: "One Today" Progressions

Overview

Progressions are similar to movement strings, in that movements are put together in a sequential sequence; but in progressions, students focus on the emotional development and transitions of how one thing evolves into the next. In this lesson, students read the poem "One Today" by Richard Blanco and use movement to analyze the emotional progression of the poem as the author combines collective words to personal words.

Materials

▸ "One Today" by Richard Blanco (available as a picture book, on **Poets.org**, or as a video of the 2013 Inaugural Reading)

▸ markers

▸ copy of "One Today" for each student *(optional)*

▸ two different color pencils for each student *(optional)*

Standards

Grades K–2

▸ Describes the connection between two individuals, events, ideas, or pieces of information in a text

▸ Chooses movements that express a main idea or emotion, or follow a musical phrase

Grades 3–5

▸ Describes the relationship between a series of historical events, scientific ideas or concepts, or steps in technical procedures in a text, using language that pertains to time, sequence, and cause/effect

▸ Develops a dance phrase that expresses and communicates an idea or feeling

Grades 6–8

▸ Analyzes in detail how a key individual, event, or idea is introduced, illustrated, and elaborated in a text

▸ Implements movement from a variety of stimuli to develop dance content for an original dance study or dance

Grades 9–12

▸ Analyzes how the author unfolds an analysis or series of ideas or events, including the order in which the points are made, how they are introduced and developed, and the connections that are drawn between them

▸ Explores a variety of stimuli for sourcing movement to develop an improvisational or choreographed dance study

Progressions *(cont.)*

Preparation

Have students practice using the Progressions strategy (pages 209–210) before beginning this lesson. This strategy builds on what was learned from the Answer Me in Movement (pages 219–223) and Movement Strings (pages 224–226) strategies. If students are not familiar with those strategies, practice them first before beginning this Progressions strategy. Additional ideas are provided in the Specific Grade-Level Ideas.

Procedure

1. Reread Richard Blanco's poem "One Today" with students.

2. Display the poem and distribute copies of the poems, if desired. Focus students' attention on the sequence that begins "My face, your face, millions of faces in morning's mirrors . . ." and ends ". . . for twenty years, so I could write this poem."

3. As a class, identify the pronouns in that portion of the poem. Circle the pronouns with one color and note where the pronouns shift from collective to singular (*our/us to my/I*). Have students do the same on their copy of the poem if you choose to have them follow along.

   "My face, your face, millions of faces in morning's mirrors, / each one yawning to life, crescendoing into our day: ..."

4. Using the basic idea of progressions, discuss with students how moving from collective to singular pronouns affects the mood of the poem by telling us something about the author. Discuss the idea of empathy.

5. In small groups have students create a movement idea for each cluster they have identified. Students may find slight variations within this suggestion.

Cluster examples:

Cluster 1: "My face . . . our day:"

Cluster 2: "pencil-yellow . . . fruit stands:"

Cluster 3: "apples . . . begging our praise."

Cluster 4: "Silver trucks . . . paper—"

Cluster 5: "Bricks or milk . . . alongside us,"

Cluster 6: "On our way . . . save lives—"

Cluster 7: "to teach geometry . . . write this poem."

Progressions *(cont.)*

6. Have groups think of one movement idea for each cluster. To transition from one cluster to the next, have them focus on the emotional energy.

   Example:

   Cluster 1: "My face . . . our day": Students stand in two lines facing each other like a mirror and yawn at each other.

   Transition: Taking the verb "crescendo" as a suggestion, they crescendo into the next movement.

   Cluster 2: "pencil-yellow . . . fruit stands": Students make a line; with hands on the shoulders of the students in front of them, they bounce along like a school bus stopping and going in a rhythm.

   Transition: The bouncing stops abruptly for the stillness of a fruit stand.

   Cluster 3: "apples . . . begging our praise": Students stretch out like a rainbow.

   Transition: Taking the verb "begging" as a suggestion, they look around for the audience's praise.

   Cluster 4: "Silver trucks . . . paper—": Students form one solid shape with everyone packed together like a heavy truck.

   Transition: Students change their motion from heavy and weighted to quickly moving ("teeming over highways") as they move like many vehicles traversing many highways, becoming cluster five.

   Cluster 5: "Bricks or milk . . . alongside us": Students make imaginary piles around themselves.

   Transition: Students stop making piles and move straight into the next movements in cluster six.

   Cluster 6: "On our way . . . save lives—": Students take on individual tasks of either cleaning, adding up figures/cash register, or taking pulses (nursing, healing).

   Transition: All the action slows down, and all students focus on one lone student.

   Cluster 7: "to teach geometry . . . write this poem": The lone student stands in the center of a circle of the other students, sitting on the ground around them. The student in the center does a motion as if writing a poem.

7. Debrief, using the Discussion Questions.

Discussion Questions

- How did the poet's use of collective and singular pronouns affect how you related to the poem?

- Why are punctuation and line breaks important to a poet?

- How did you use punctuation and line breaks to make decisions about your movement choices?

Progressions *(cont.)*

Specific Grade-Level Ideas

Grades K–2

Invite students to explore animal migration using the text *Going Home: The Mystery of Animal Migration* by Marianne Berkes. Explore through movement the migration of loggerhead turtles, monarch butterflies, manatees, and more.

Grades 3–5

Explore ideas in a scientific process such as the water cycle or how different types of rocks are formed. Ask students to invent movements that depict different phases in the scientific process they chose and how they are related.

Grades 6–8

Explore the causes of a historical event such as the Industrial Revolution, embodying key events through movement and showing how history evolves over time.

Grades 9–12

Create a progression of ideas for the evolution of a character in a text such as the *Maltese Falcon* by Dashiell Hammett, showing the arc of a character's life choices through movement.

Sensory Movement

Model Lesson: "One Today" Sensory Movement

Overview

In this lesson, students read the poem "One Today" by Richard Blanco and examine the text to see how imagery is used to communicate information. They explore this imagery by translating the rich sensory details into movements. Motion is included as a sixth sense. With sensory movement, students become aware of how language evokes the senses.

Materials

▸ "One Today" by Richard Blanco (available as a picture book, on **Poets.org**, or as a video of the 2013 Inaugural Reading)

▸ copy of "One Today" for each student

Standards

Grades K–2

▸ Identifies words and phrases in stories or poems that suggest feelings or appeal to the senses

▸ Explores movement inspired by a variety of stimuli and suggests additional sources for movement ideas

Grades 3–5

▸ Determines the meaning of words and phrases as they are used in a text, distinguishing literal from nonliteral language

▸ Builds content for choreography using several stimuli

Grades 6–8

▸ Determines the meaning of words and phrases as they are used in a text, including figurative and connotative meanings; analyzes the impact of a specific word choice on meaning and tone

▸ Relates similar or contrasting ideas to develop choreography using a variety of stimuli

Grades 9–12

▸ Determines the meaning of words and phrases as they are used in the text, including figurative and connotative meanings; analyzes the cumulative impact of specific word choices on meaning and tone

▸ Explores a variety of stimuli for sourcing movement to develop an improvisational or choreographed dance study; analyzes the process and the relationship between the stimuli and the movement

Sensory Movement *(cont.)*

Preparation

Have students practice using the Sensory Movement strategy (page 211) before beginning this lesson. This strategy also builds on what was learned from the Answer Me in Movement (pages 219–223), Movement Strings (pages 224–226), and Progressions (pages 227–230) strategies. If students are not familiar with those strategies, practice them first before beginning the Sensory Movement strategy. Additional ideas are provided in the Specific Grade-Level Ideas.

Procedure

1. Explain to students that sensory language is language the uses the five senses: sight, taste, sound, touch, and smell. For this strategy, tell students they also will consider motion as a sixth sense, but motion words can carry sensory images with them. For example: "Cutting sugarcane" has the action of cutting and a sound and smell to go with it.

2. Reread the poem "One Today" by Richard Blanco aloud. Display and direct students to the stanza that begins "Hear: squeaky playground swings, trains whistling..."

3. As a class, make a list of words or phrases that are directly sensory (for example, "trains whistling") and implicitly sensory (for example, "doors we open").

4. Have students respond to the following prompts:
   ‣ Show me what "a squeaky playground swing" sound *looks* like in movement.
   ‣ Show me what a train whistle *looks* like as a movement.

   ‣ Show me what a whisper across a table *looks* like. Not the action of whispering, but the whisper itself.
   ‣ The author asks us to "hear the doors we open." What is that sound, and how can we turn that sound into a movement?

5. Ask students to suggest other movements based on the rest of the stanza.

6. Place students into small groups. Have groups make sequences of sensory movement imagery drawn from the poem. After each group has created and practiced their dance, provide time for each group to perform it for the rest of the class.

7. Use the Discussion Questions to debrief with students after each group shares.

Sensory Movement *(cont.)*

Discussion Questions

▸ How does a writer use sensory words and motion words to create interest?

▸ What did you learn about sensory words by translating them into movement? For example, what did it feel like to do a sound word without the sound?

▸ What did you love about what you saw? Why?

▸ Was there anything that this group did that sparked an idea of something you would like to use in your next dance?

▸ If you were to keep working on this dance, what would you add, take away, or change?

Specific Grade-Level Ideas

Grades K–2

Explore color with the book *What Color Is Night?* by Grant Snider. Choose one or more moments of the book to have students experience through movement.

Or, choose a text with different subject matter, such as *Outside In* by Deborah Underwood and Cindy Derby and explore it through movement.

Grades 3–5

Explore through movement color poems and writing exercises from the University of Arizona Poetry Center's website, **poetry.arizona.edu/blog/colors-colors-everywhere-poems-writing-exercises-kids**.

Grades 6–8

Invite students to create movement to experience the extended metaphor in a poem, such as "'Hope' is the thing with feathers" by Emily Dickinson. Discuss how hope is like a bird.

Grades 9–12

Locate the poem called "Colors passing through us" by Marge Piercy on the Poetry Foundation's website. Create movement to explore key concepts in the poem.

Choreographic Structure

Model Lesson: "One Today" Choreography

Overview

For each previous creative movement strategy (Answer Me in Movement, Movement Strings, Progressions, and Sensory Movement), students have essentially choreographed short creative movement dances. In this strategy, students generate movement ideas, develop those ideas using choreographic tools, and place them in the choreographic structure known as a suite.

Materials

▸ "One Today" by Richard Blanco (available as a picture book, on **Poets.org**, or as a video of the 2013 Inaugural Reading)

▸ *"One Today" Choreography Planning Guide* (pages 240–251)

▸ copy of "One Today" for each student *(optional)*

Standards

Grades K–2

▸ Describes the connection between two individuals, events, or ideas in a text

▸ Participates in collaborative conversations with diverse partners about grade-level topics and texts with peers and adults

▸ Demonstrates a range of locomotor and nonlocomotor movements, body patterning, and dance sequences that require moving through space using a variety of pathways

Grades 3–5

▸ Explains the relationships or interactions between individuals, events, or concepts in a historical, scientific, or technical text based on information in the text

▸ Engages effectively in a range of collaborative discussions with diverse partners on grade-level topics and texts, building on others' ideas and expressing their own clearly

▸ Recalls and executes a series of dance phrases using fundamental dance skills

Grades 6–8

▸ Analyzes how a text makes connections among and distinctions between individuals, ideas, or events

▸ Engages effectively in a range of collaborative discussions (one-on-one, in groups, and teacher led) with diverse partners on grade-level topics and texts, building on others' ideas and expressing their own clearly

▸ Embodies technical dance skills to replicate, recall, and execute spatial designs and musical or rhythmical dance phrases

Grades 9–12

▸ Analyzes a complex set of ideas or sequence of events and explains how specific individuals, ideas, or events interact and develop over the course of a text

▸ Engages effectively in a range of collaborative discussions with diverse partners on grade-level topics and texts, building on others' ideas and expressing their own clearly and persuasively

▸ Embodies technical dance skills to retain and execute dance choreography

Choreographic Structure (cont.)

Preparation

Have students practice using Choreographic Structure (pages 212–214) before beginning this lesson. This strategy also builds on what students learned from the Answer Me in Movement (pages 219–223), Movement Strings (pages 224–226), Progressions (page 227–230), and Sensory Movement (page 231–233) strategies. If students are not familiar with those strategies, practice them first before beginning Choreographic Structure. Review the Planning Questions ahead of time so that you are able to prompt students/groups as needed throughout the entire lesson. Find additional ideas in the Specific Grade-Level Ideas.

Procedure

1. Explain to students that they will explore the poem "One Today" by Richard Blanco and create an entire group of movements that go along with each stanza of the poem. This is called a *dance suite*.

2. Reread the poem "One Today." Place students into groups of five (or four or six, depending on your class size). Distribute a copy of the *"One Today" Choreography Planning Guide* to each student.

Stanza One

1. Remind students that they already practiced movement for the first stanza of the poem during the Movement Strings strategy. Explain that they will use those verbs for stanza one and the choreographic tool Call and Response to create their dance suite.

2. Remind students of the selected verbs from stanza one.

> Kindled: to kindle
> Peeking: to peek
> Greeting: to greet
> Spreading: to spread
> Charging: to charge

3. In their groups, have students select a movement to go with each verb and record it on their *"One Today" Choreography Planning Guide*.

4. Prompt students to consider formation for the Call and Response. Is the caller in the center of a circle, with the responders around them? Or does the caller stand in front of the responders in a row? Will just one person be the caller, or will different students have a turn? Have students record information about their formation in their planning guides.

5. Allow students time to practice this until they can perform it with confidence.

Stanza Two

1. Remind students that in the Progressions strategy they created a choreographic structure for the second stanza, which they will use for stanza two here as well. This is an example of how a creative movement strategy can also be a choreographic tool.

2. Have students revisit the phrase clusters and create a movement idea for each cluster. These can be the same ones they used before, or they can develop new ideas.

   Clusters:
   Cluster 1: "My face . . . our day"
   Cluster 2: "pencil-yellow . . . fruit stands:"
   Cluster 3: "apples . . . begging our praise."
   Cluster 4: "Silver trucks . . . paper—"
   Cluster 5: "Bricks or milk . . . alongside us,"
   Cluster 6: "On our way . . . save lives—"
   Cluster 7: "to teach geometry . . . write this poem."

Choreographic Structure (cont.)

3. Have students record the movements in their planning guides.

4. Allow students time to practice until they can perform these movements with confidence.

Stanza Three

1. Read and display the third stanza of the poem. As a class, identify the five "lessons for the day."

2. In their groups, have students create a single movement for each "lesson." Students should all agree on the same movement (for example, all students do the same movement for "equations to solve"). Prompt students to consider the formation they want to use—everyone facing front? Two lines facing one another? A circle? A diagonal?

3. Have students record the actions and formation(s) in their planning guides.

4. Using the choreographic tool Unison, have each group practice performing their selected movements at the same time together until they can perform them with confidence.

Stanza Four

1. Read and display the fourth stanza of the poem. As a class, identify the actions that "hands" are doing in the poem.

   A. Wheat sown

   B. Gleaning coal

   C. Planting windmills

   D. Digging trenches

   E. Routing pipes

   F. Cutting sugarcane

2. Explain to students that they will use the choreographic tool Rondo to perform these movements. In their groups, have students decide on a movement to represent each of the six actions that "hands" are doing in the poem and record them in their planning guides.

3. Remind students that in Rondo, each student performs the sequence in a different order, but all at the same time. Have students use the table in their planning guides to create the movement sequence for each person in their group.

   Example:
   Student A: 1, 2, 3, 4, 5, 6

   Student B: 2, 3, 4, 5, 6, 1

   Student C: 3, 4, 5, 6, 1, 2

   Student D: 4, 5, 6, 1, 2, 3

   Student E: 5, 6, 1, 2, 3, 4

   Student F: 6, 1, 2, 3, 4, 5

4. Allow students time to practice until they can perform these movements with confidence.

Choreographic Structure *(cont.)*

Stanza Five

1. Read and display the fifth stanza of the poem. As a class, identify the six images that the author asks readers "to hear."

2. Remind students how to complete the movement sequence of the choreographic tool Fan.

3. In their groups, have students create one movement idea for each image that the author asks readers to hear. Have students record those movements in their planning guides.

4. Allow students time to practice until they can perform these movements with confidence.

Stanza Six

1. Read and display stanza six from the poem. Revisit the list of sensory words from the Sensory Movement lesson (pages 231–233).

2. Have students share choreography ideas they remember from that lesson to go with each of the sensory images from the stanza.

3. In their groups, have students make sequences of sensory movement imagery drawn from the list of sensory words/ images from the stanza. Have students record their movement choices in their planning guides.

4. Allow students time to practice until they can perform these movements with confidence.

Stanza Seven

1. Read and display stanza seven from the poem.

2. Explain to students that they will use the choreographic tool called Counter Unison, where each student does a unique movement.

3. Explain to students that within each group, each student must choose four words or short phrases from the stanza that they like. Have students create a unique movement for each of their words/phrases and record them in their planning guides.

4. Reread the stanza, and when students hear the words/phrases they selected, they should complete the movement they selected. Students must understand that even within each group, each student has four distinct words/phrases; some may use the same ones, but each student has selected unique movements. All students should perform their unique movements at the same time.

5. Reread the stanza several times so that students can have additional practice and can perform their movements with confidence.

Choreographic Structure *(cont.)*

Stanza Eight

1. Explain to students that for this stanza, they are returning to the tool Unison.

2. Reread and display stanza eight from the poem.

3. Have groups create a sequence of movements where everyone is doing the same movement to express the following ideas from the stanza:

   - lift our eyes tired from work

   - giving thanks for a love that loves you back

   - praising a mother who knew how to give

   - forgiving a father who couldn't give what you wanted

4. Have students record their movements for each phrase in their planning guides.

5. Allow students time to practice until they can perform these movements with confidence.

Stanza Nine

1. Reread and display stanza nine from the poem.

2. Explain to students that they will use the choreographic tools of Call and Response and Recurrence for this stanza. Remind them that Recurrence is the repetition of something that has been done before, but usually with a slight twist.

3. Explain that they will use the same Call and Response technique and movements from stanza one, but with stanza nine. Have groups work together to decide what kinds of twists they want to put on the original movements.

4. Once groups have decided on their movements, have them record the information in their planning guides.

5. Allow students time to practice until they can perform these movements with confidence.

Putting It Together

1. Explain to students that now it is time to put everything together to share the work with others.

2. Allow groups time to review all the movements and practice them in sequence. It may be helpful to provide students access to a recording of the poem so that they can practice in sequence and align the spoken word with the choreography.

Choreographic Structure *(cont.)*

This dance suite could be performed for an audience. To do this, assign a student or teacher to read the poem with the performance. The speaker must rehearse with the class to make sure that the speaker pauses to best align the spoken word with the choreography. Alternatively, the stanza could be read, then danced, read, then danced, and so on through all nine stanzas. It may be helpful to use music as background as well.

Planning Questions

▸ What formation will the group take in relationship to one another? You could all be in a circle, in two rows facing the audience, in a single line facing the audience, in a random pattern, and so on. Draw various formations that dancers could take. Use a dot to represent each dancer. This could be done on individual paper or you can come to the white board and share an idea.

> **Example:** dancers could all be in a circle.
> **Example:** dancers could be in two rows
> **Example:** dancers could be lined up behind one another
> **Example:** dancers could be scattered randomly

▸ Will the movements all be done in one place, or will the movements cause the dancer to move from one location to another? In dance, we call this "traveling" or "locomotion." You could walk, skip, run, crawl, leap, and so on to get from one place to another.

▸ The suite form is in distinct sections, but what kinds of transitions will link all five sections together? How will the dancers get from one formation to another?

Specific Grade-Level Ideas

Grades K–2

Gather a text set of books about the water cycle such as *Water Is Water: A Book About the Water Cycle* by Miranda Paul; *The Snowflake: A Water Cycle Story* by Neil Waldman; *All the Water in the World* by George Ella Lyon and Katherine Tillotson; and *Water Dance* by Thomas Locker. Explore the water cycle through a choreographed dance.

Grades 3–5

Bring to life the importance of the honeybees in a choreographed dance as a call to action, using the text *Honeybee: The Busy Life of Apis Mellifera* by Candace Fleming. Visit *The Classroom Bookshelf* blog to locate additional resources about bees.

Grades 6–8

Explore choreography as a call to action by inviting small groups of students to choose an issue that is important to them and communicate advocacy through a choreographed dance.

Grades 9–12

In addition to the advocacy ideas for grades 6–8, students can choreograph a dance to communicate the life of an activist, the life of a subject in a memoir or biography, a scientific process, processes in the social-emotional realm, the passage of time throughout a historical period, and more.

Name: _____ Date: _____

"One Today" Choreography Planning Guide

Directions: Draw or describe the movements you and your group select for each stanza.

Stanza One: Call and Response

Draw or describe a movement for each verb.

kindled: to kindle

peeking: to peek

greeting: to greet

spreading: to spread

charging: to charge

Name: _____ Date: _____

"One Today" Choreography Planning Guide (cont.)

Directions: Draw or describe the movements you and your group select for each stanza.

Stanza One: Call and Response (continued)

Draw a diagram that describes how you will use Call and Response.

Who will be the "caller"? Will the caller always be the same?

What is the formation (circles, lines, random, and so on)? Will the formation always be the same?

Name: _____ Date: _____

"One Today" Choreography Planning Guide (cont.)

Stanza Two: Progressions

Draw or describe a movement for each cluster of words from the stanza.

Cluster 1: "My face . . . our day"

Cluster 2: "pencil-yellow . . . fruit stands"

Cluster 3: "apples . . . begging our praise"

Name: _____ Date: _____

"One Today" Choreography Planning Guide (cont.)

Stanza Two: Progressions (continued)

Draw or describe a movement for each cluster of words from the stanza.

Cluster 4: "Silver trucks . . . paper—"

Cluster 5: "Bricks or milk . . . alongside us"

Cluster 6: "On our way . . . save lives—"

Cluster 7: "to teach geometry . . . write this poem"

Name: _____ Date: _____

"One Today" Choreography Planning Guide *(cont.)*

Stanza Three: Unison

Draw or describe a movement for each "lesson." Also describe the formation you will use for each lesson.

Lesson 1: equations to solve

Lesson 2: history to question

Lesson 3: atoms to imagine

Lesson 4: "I have a dream" to keep dreaming

Lesson 5: the impossible vocabulary of sorrow

Name: _____ Date: _____

"One Today" Choreography Planning Guide *(cont.)*

Stanza Four: Rondo

Draw or describe a movement for each action the "hands" are doing in the stanza.

1. wheat sown

2. gleaning coal

3. planting windmills

4. digging trenches

5. routing pipes

6. cutting sugarcane

Name: _____ Date: _____

"One Today" Choreography Planning Guide (cont.)

Stanza Four: Rondo (cont.)

Use the chart to record the order in which the group will perform the movements.

Student A Sequence	Student B Sequence	Student C Sequence	Student D Sequence	Student E Sequence

117848—Integrating the Arts in Language Arts

Name: _____ Date: _____

"One Today" Choreography Planning Guide *(cont.)*

Stanza Five: Fan

Draw or describe a movement for each image the poet asks us to "hear."

1. the dust of farms and deserts, cities and plains

2. our breath

3. honking cabs

4. buses launching down avenues

5. symphony of footsteps, guitars, and screeching subways

6. the unexpected song bird on your clothes line

Write the order in which your group will perform the fan:

Name: _____ Date: _____

"One Today" Choreography Planning Guide (cont.)

Stanza Six: Sensory Movement

Make a sequence of sensory movement imagery drawn from the list of sensory words or images brainstormed from the stanza.

Draw or describe the sequence that your group created.

Name: _____ Date: _____

"One Today" Choreography Planning Guide *(cont.)*

Stanza Seven: Counter Unison

Choose four words or short phrases that you like from the stanza.

Create your own unique movement for each of the words/phrases you chose.

Word/Phrase 1: _____
Movement description:

Word/Phrase 2: _____
Movement description:

Word/Phrase 3: _____
Movement description:

Word/Phrase 4: _____
Movement description:

Name: _____ Date: _____

"One Today" Choreography Planning Guide *(cont.)*

Stanza Eight: Unison

Draw or describe a movement for each phrase shown below. Also describe the formation you will use for each phrase.

1. lift our eyes tired from work

2. giving thanks for a love that loves you back

3. praising a mother who knew how to give

4. forgiving a father who couldn't give what you wanted

Name: _____ Date: _____

"One Today" Choreography Planning Guide *(cont.)*

Stanza Nine: Call and Response with Recurrence

Rewrite the movements from stanza one. Make sure to include a "twist" with at least two of the movements.

Draw a diagram that describes how you will use Call and Response.

Who will be the "caller"? Will the caller always be the same?

What is the formation (circles, lines, random, and so on)? Will the formation always be the same?

References Cited

Academy of American Poets. n.d. "Glossary of Poetic Terms." Accessed October 1, 2021. poets.org/glossary.

Acevedo, Elizabeth. 2018. "*The Poet X* Live Performance." www.youtube.com/watch?v=YH4gIM6TZkQ.

———. 2019. *The Poet X*. New York: Harper Collins.

Albers, Peggy, and Jerome C. Harste. 2007. "The Arts, New Literacies, and Modality." *English Education* 40 (1): 6–20.

Alexander, Kwame. 2019. *The Write Thing*. Huntington Beach, CA: Shell Education.

Andersen, Christopher. 2004. "Learning in 'As-If' Worlds: Cognition in Drama in Education." *Theory into Practice* 43 (4): 281–286.

Association of College and Research Libraries. 2011. "ACRL Visual Literacy Competency Standards for Higher Education." www.ala.org/acrl/standards/visualliteracy.

Beare, Kenneth. 2020. "Grammar Chants to Learn English." *Thought Co.*, January 10, 2020. www.thoughtco.com/grammar-chants-to-learn-english-1211063.

Beckett, Marcia. 2015. "Making an Assemblage and Learning about Louise Nevelson." *Art is Basic* (blog), April 17, 2015. www.artisbasic.com/2015/04/making-an-assemblage-learning-about-louise-nevelson.html.

Bellisario, Kerrie, and Lisa Donovan with Monica Prendergast. 2012. "Voices from the Field: Teachers' Views on the Relevance of Arts Integration." Unpublished manuscript. Cambridge, MA: Lesley University.

Berea Public Art. 2009. "Assemblage Art Made from 'Throwaways.'" www.bereapublicart.com/wp-content/uploads/2015/06/5th-and-up-assemblage-art.pdf.

Bigelow, Bill, and Linda Christensen. 2001. "Promoting Social Imagination Through Interior Monologues." *The Quarterly* 23 (1): 28–31.

Blanco, Richard. 2019. "Richard Blanco: How to Love a Country." Interview by Krista Tippet. *On Being with Krista Tippet*, November 27, 2019. onbeing.org/programs/richard-blanco-how-to-love-a-country/.

Boal, Augusto. 2002. *Games for Actors and Non-actors*. London: Routledge.

Bodensteiner, Kirsten. 2019. "Do You Wanna Dance? Understanding the Five Elements of Dance." The Kennedy Center. www.kennedy-center.org/education/resources-for-educators/classroom-resources/media-and-interactives/media/dance/do-you-wanna-dance/.

Bogard, Jennifer M., and Mary C. McMackin. 2015. *Writing Is Magic, or Is It? Using Mentor Texts to Develop the Writer's Craft*. Huntington Beach, CA: Shell.

References Cited (cont.)

Borris, Chris. 2016. "The Power of Poetry." *Scholastic Teacher* 25 (5): 44–45. www.scholastic.com/teachers/articles/teaching-content/power-poetry/.

Brouillette, Liane, and Lynne Jennings. 2010. "Helping Children Cross Cultural Boundaries in the Borderlands: Arts Integration at Freese Elementary Creates Cultural Bridges." *Journal for Learning through the Arts* 6 (1). www.escholarship.org/uc/item/1kf6p9th.

Bruce, Eloise, Maureen Heffernan, Sanaz Hojreh, Wendy Liscow, Shawna Longo, Michelle L. Marigliano, Erica Nagel, et al. 2020. *New Jersey's Arts Integration Think and Do Workbook: A Practical Guide to Think about and Implement Arts Integration.* Morristown, NJ: Geraldine R. Dodge Foundation. njpsa.org/documents/ArtsIntLdshpInst2020/artsintegrationWorkbook2020.pdf.

Cahill, Bryon. 2006. "Ready, Set, Write!" *Writing* 29 (1): 12.

Cappiello, Mary Ann, and Erika Thulin Dawes. 2013. *Teaching with Text Sets.* Huntington Beach, CA: Shell Education.

Carpenter, Siri. 2011. "Body of Thought: How Trivial Sensations Can Influence Reasoning, Social Judgment, and Perception." *Scientific American Mind*, January 2011, 38–45.

Cash, Justin. n.d. "The 12 Dramatic Elements." *The Drama Teacher* (blog). Accessed October 1, 2021. thedramateacher.com/wp-content/uploads/2008/02/The-12-Dramatic-Elements.pdf.

Center for Applied Special Technology. n.d. "About CAST." Accessed October 10, 2012. www.cast.org/about/index.html.

Ciecierski, Lisa, and William Bintz. 2012. "Using Chants and Cadences to Promote Literacy Across the Curriculum: Chants and Cadences Engage Students in Creative Writing and Critical Thinking." *Middle School Journal* 44 (2): 22–29. DOI:10.2307/41763116.

Collins, Polly. 2008. "Using Poetry throughout the Curriculum." *Kappa Delta Pi Record* 44 (2): 81–84.

Concept Art Empire. 2021. "Introduction to Thumbnailing." conceptartempire.com/intro-to-thumbnail-sketching/.

Cougar Dramatics. n.d. "Improvisation." Accessed May 7, 2021. cougardramatics.weebly.com/uploads/5/0/0/4/5004863/chapter_1_power_point.pptx.

Coulter, Cathy, Charles Michael, and Leslie Poynor. 2007. "Storytelling as Pedagogy: An Unexpected Outcome of Narrative Inquiry." *Curriculum Inquiry* 37 (2): 103–122.

Craven, Jackie. 2018. "What Is Ekphrastic Poetry? How Poets Engage with Art." www.thoughtco.com/ekphrastic-poetry-definition-examples-4174699.

Cremin, Teresa, Kathy Goouch, Louise Blakemore, Emma Goff, and Roger Macdonald. 2006. "Connecting Drama and Writing: Seizing the Moment to Write." *Research in Drama Education* 11 (3): 273–291.

DeBlase, Gina. 2005. "Teaching Literature and Language through Guided Discovery and Informal Classroom Drama." *The English Journal* 95 (1): 29–32.

Dehner, Megan. n.d. "Collograph in the Classroom at a Glance." Osage, IA: The Art of Education University. Accessed September 13, 2021. theartofeducation.edu/2019/11/12/collagraph-in-the-classroom-at-a-glance/.

DeMichele, Mary. 2019. "23 Reasons for Teachers to Apply Improv in the Classroom." *One Rule Improv* (blog), July 24, 2019. www.oneruleimprov.com/2019/07/24/apply-improv-in-the-classroom/.

Diaz, Gene, Lisa Donovan, and Louise Pascale. 2006. "Integrated Teaching through the Arts." Presentation given at the UNESCO World Conference on Arts Education, Lisbon, Portugal, March 8, 2006.

Donovan, Lisa, and Louise Pascale. 2022. *Integrating the Arts Across the Curriculum, Second Edition.* Huntington Beach, CA: Shell Education.

Dunn, Geoffrey. 2003. "Photographic License." *New Times.* www.newtimesslo.com/archive/2003-12-03/archives/cov_stories_2002/cov_01172002.html.

Elliott-Johns, Susan E., David Booth, Jennifer Rowsell, Enrique Puig, and Jane Paterson. 2012. "Using Student Voices to Guide Instruction." *Voices from the Middle* 19 (3): 25–31.

Estrella, Espie. 2019. "An Introduction to the Elements of Music." *LiveAbout.* November 4, 2019. www.liveabout.com/the-elements-of-music-2455913.

Facing History and Ourselves. n.d. "Found Poems." Accessed August 9, 2021. www.facinghistory.org/resource-library/teaching-strategies/found-poems.

Ferlazzo, Larry. 2020a. "Five Ways to Use Music in Lessons." *Education Week Classroom Q & A* (blog), July 13, 2020. www.edweek.org/teaching-learning/opinion-five-ways-to-use-music-in-lessons/2020/07.

———. 2020b. "Teaching Poetry in 'Playful' Ways." *Education Week Classroom Q & A* (blog), May 21, 2020. www.edweek.org/teaching-learning/opinion-teaching-poetry-in-playful-ways/2020/05.

Gallo, Carmine. 2019. "A Novel Program at VA Hospitals Uses an Old-World Tradition to Advance Patient Care." *Forbes*, August 25, 2019. www.forbes.com/sites/carminegallo/2019/08/25/a-novel-program-at-va-hospitals-uses-an-old-world-tradition-to-advance-patient-care/?sh=704d8d305165.

Gardner, Howard. 2011. *Frames of Mind: The Theory of Multiple Intelligences.* 3rd ed. New York: Basic Books.

Glatstein, Jeremy. 2019. "Formal Visual Analysis: The Elements and Principles of Composition." The Kennedy Center. www.kennedy-center.org/education/resources-for-educators/classroom-resources/articles-and-how-tos/articles/educators/formal-visual-analysis-the-elements-and-principles-of-compositon/.

References Cited (cont.)

Gorman, Amanda. 2016. "Using Your Voice Is a Political Choice." www.youtube.com/watch?v=plU-QpcEswo&feature=emb_title.

Griss, Susan. 1994. "Creative Movement: A Language for Learning." *Educational Leadership* 51 (5): 78–80.

Hamilton, Martha, and Mitch Weiss. 2005. *Children Tell Stories: Teaching and Using Storytelling in the Classroom.* Katonah, NY: Richard C. Owen Publishers.

Harjo, Joy. 2019. "An Interview with Joy Harjo, U.S. Poet Laureate." *Poets.org*, March 31, 2019. poets.org/text/interview-joy-harjo-us-poet-laureate.

Heagle, Amie I., and Ruth Anne Rehfeldt. 2006. "Teaching Perspective—Taking Skills to Typically Developing Children through Derived Relational Responding." *Journal of Early and Intensive Behavior Intervention* 3 (1): 1–34.

Hetland, Lois. 2009. "Nilaja Sun's 'No Child' . . . Revealing Teaching and Learning through Theater." *Teaching Artist Journal* 7 (1): 34–39.

Hetland, Lois, Ellen Winner, Shirley Veenema, and Kimberly Sheridan. 2007. *Studio Thinking: The Real Benefits of Visual Arts Education.* New York: Teachers College Press.

Hipp, Jamie, and Margaret-Mary Sulentic Dowell. 2021. "Arts Integrated Teacher Education Benefits Elementary Students and Teachers Alike." *EdNote* (blog), February 1, 2021. ednote.ecs.org/arts-integrated-teacher-education-benefits-elementary-students-and-teachers-alike/.

Hollander, John. 2014. "Speaking Pictures: Poetry Addressing Works of Art." National Gallery of Art. www.nga.gov/audio-video/audio/poetry-hollander.html.

Hopkins, Lee Bennett, ed. 2018. *World Make Way: New Poems Inspired by Art from the Metropolitan Museum of Art.* New York: Abrams Books for Young Readers with the Metropolitan Museum of Art.

Hourcade, Juan Pablo, Benjamin B. Bederson, and Allison Druin. 2004. "Building KidPad: An Application for Children's Collaborative Storytelling." *Software: Practice & Experience* 34 (9): 895–914.

Huff, Hannah. 2018. "Dear Bad Writers, Read This Poetic Line Breaks Guide." notesofoak.com/discover-literature/poetic-line-breaks-guide/.

Hughes, Janette. 2007. "Poetry: A Powerful Medium for Literacy and Technology Development." *What Works? Research into Practice* (October). www.edu.gov.on.ca/eng/literacynumeracy/inspire/research/hughes.pdf.

International School of Athens. n.d. "Drama Handbook." Accessed May 4, 2021. isa.edu.gr/files/319/Drama_Handbook.pdf.

J. Paul Getty Museum. n.d.-a "Elements of Art." Accessed October 1, 2021. www.getty.edu/education/teachers/building_lessons/formal_analysis.html/.

J. Paul Getty Museum. n.d.-b "Principles of Design." Accessed October 1, 2021. www.getty.edu/ education/teachers/building_lessons/formal_analysis2.html/.

Jacobsen, Daniel Christopher. 1992. *A Listener's Introduction to Music.* Dubuque, Iowa: Wm. C. Brown Publishers.

Jensen, Eric. 2001. *Arts with the Brain in Mind.* Alexandria, VA: Association for Supervision and Curriculum Development.

Johnson, Joshua. 2011. "Close Photoshop and Grab a Pencil: The Lost Art of Thumbnail Sketches." *Design Shack* (blog), November 10, 2011. designshack.net/articles/inspiration/close-photoshop-and-grab-a-pencil-the-lost-art-of-thumbnail-sketches/.

Kay, Sarah. 2011. "If I Should Have a Daughter." TED Talk. www.ted.com/talks/sarah_kay_if_i_should_have_a_daughter?language=en.

Kennedy, Randy. 2006. "Guggenheim Study Suggests Arts Education Benefits Literacy Skills." *New York Times*, July 27, 2006.

KET. 2014. "Principles of Design." PBS Learning Media. pbslearningmedia.org/resource/459077ac-6d7d-4eef-bd7e-e38d12e7ce97/principals-of-design/

Kindermusik International. n.d. "The Impact of Music on Language and Early Literacy: A Research Summary in Support of Kindermusik's ABC Music & Me" (white paper). Accessed August 9, 2021. kindermusik.tammysings.com/docs/ABCWhitepaper.pdf.

KQED Art School. 2015. "The Five Elements of Dance." PBS Learning Media. pbslearningmedia.org/ resource/d7fcd19b-ee9b-4d90-a550-833fbe22865c/the-five-elements-of-dance/.

Kurzawski, Kristen S. 2011. "Demystifying Poetry Using Women's Ekphrasis." teachers.yale.edu/ curriculum/viewer/initiative_10.01.11_g.

Kuta, Katherine. 2003. "And Who Are You?" *Writing* 25 (5): 30–31.

LaBonty, Jan, and Kathy Everts Danielson. 2004. "Reading and Writing Poetry in Math." *Reading Horizon*s 45 (1): 39–54.

Lane, Barry. 1992. After *THE END: Teaching and Learning Creative Revision.* Portsmouth, NH: Heinemann.

Library of Congress. n.d. "Primary Source Set: Found Poetry." Accessed September 13, 2021. www.loc. gov/classroom-materials/found-poetry/.

Library of Congress Research Guides. n.d. "Dorothea Lange's 'Migrant Mother' Photographs in the Farm Security Administration Collection." Accessed August 9, 2021. guides.loc.gov/migrant-mother/ introduction.

Lindwall, Courtney. 2019. "Watch These Young Spoken-Word Poets Take on Climate Change." www. nrdc.org/onearth/watch-these-young-spoken-word-poets-take-climate-change.

References Cited *(cont.)*

Ludwig VanDerwater, Amy. 2018. *Poems Are Teachers: How Studying Poetry Strengthens Writing in All Genres.* Portsmouth, NH: Heinemann.

Lyon, George Ella. 2010. "Where I'm From." www.georgeellalyon.com/where.html.

Maples, Joellen. 2007. "English Class at the Improv: Using Improvisation to Teach Middle School Students Confidence, Community, and Content." *The Clearing House* 80 (6): 273–277.

Marzano, Robert J. 2007. *The Art and Science of Teaching: A Comprehensive Framework for Effective Instruction.* Alexandria, VA: Association for Supervision and Curriculum Development.

McKim, Elizabeth, and Judith W. Steinbergh. 1992. *Beyond Words: Writing Poems with Children: A Guide for Parents and Teachers.* Brookline, MA: Talking Stone Press.

McKitrich, Ann. 2016. "The Significance of Creative Movement for Kids." *Nurtured Noggins* (blog), March 14, 2016. nurturednoggins.com/creative-movement/.

Murphy, Shannon. 2012. "Tableaux Vivant: History and Practice." *Art Museum Teaching: A Forum for Reflecting on Practice.* (blog), December 6, 2012. artmuseumteaching.com/2012/12/06/tableaux-vivant-history-and-practice/.

National Coalition for Core Arts Standards. 2014. "Glossary of Terms: Theatre." https://docplayer.net/29830664-Glossary-for-national-core-arts-theatre-standards.html.

National Governors Association Center for Best Practices & Council of Chief State School Officers. 2010. *Common Core State Standards for English Language Arts and Literacy in History/Social Studies, Science, and Technical Subjects.* Washington, DC: Authors.

National Storytelling Network. n.d. "What Is Storytelling?" Accessed April 30, 2021. storynet.org/what-is-storytelling/.

Neelands, Jonothan, and Tony Goode, n.d. 2021. "Role on the Wall." *Drama-Based Instruction: Activating Learning through the Arts.* dbp.theatredance.utexas.edu/content/role-wall-0#:~:text=Role%20on%20the%20Wall%20is,outline%20of%20a%20human%20figure.

Neelands, Jonothan, and Tony Goode. n.d. "Guided Imagery." *Drama-Based Instruction: Activating Learning through the Arts.* dbp.theatredance.utexas.edu/content/guided-imagery.

Norfolk, Sherry, Jane Stenson, and Diane Williams. 2006. *The Storytelling Classroom.* Westport, CT: Libraries Unlimited.

Oliver, Mary, 1994. *A Poetry Handbook: A Prose Guide to Understanding and Writing Poetry.* Orlando, FL: Mariner Books.

O'Neill, Cecily. 1995. *Drama Worlds: A Framework for Process Drama.* Portsmouth, NH: Heinemann.

Panckridge, Jo. 2020. "Storytelling: The Power of Oral Narratives." *Practical Literacy* 25(3).

References Cited (cont.)

Paquette, Kelli R., and Sue A. Rieg. 2008. "Using Music to Support the Literacy Development of Young English Language Learners." *Early Childhood Education Journal* 36 (3): 227–232.

Partnership for 21st Century Learning. 2019. "Framework for 21st Century Learning." static. battelleforkids.org/documents/p21/P21_Framework_Brief.pdf.

Pascale, Louise. 2014. "Returning Music to the Children of Afghanistan." TEDx Talk. www.youtube.com/watch?v=t1UWvPJ5WcU.

Perpich Center for Arts Education. 2009. "The Elements of Dance." www.nationalartsstandards.org/sites/default/files/Dance_resources/ElementsOfDance_organizer.pdf.

Perret, Peter, and Janet Fox. 2006. *A Well-Tempered Mind: Using Music to Help Children Listen and Learn.* New York: Dana Press.

Phelan, Ben. 2014. "The Story of the 'Migrant Mother.'" *Antiques Roadshow,* April 14, 2014. www.pbs.org/wgbh/roadshow/stories/articles/2014/4/14/migrant-mother-dorothea-lange/.

Poetry Foundation. 2015. "Forms and Features: Found Poetry." www.poetryfoundation.org/events/73989/forms-and-features-found-poetry.

Poetry Foundation. n.d. "Glossary of Poetic Terms." www.poetryfoundation.org/learn/glossary-terms.

Poetry Out Loud. 2012. "Tips on Reciting." poetryoutloud.org/poems-and-performance/tips-on-reciting.

Poetry Out Loud. n.d. "Lesson Plan: The Tone Map." Accessed October 15, 2020. www.poetryoutloud.org/wp-content/uploads/sites/2/2019/07/Tone-Map-Terms.pdf.

Powell, Mary Clare. 1997. "The Arts and the Inner Lives of Teachers." *Phi Delta Kappan* 78 (6): 450–453.

President's Committee on the Arts and the Humanities. 2011. "Reinvesting in Arts Education: Winning America's Future Through Creative Schools." www.pcah.gov/sites/default/files/PCAH_Reinvesting_4web_0.pdf.

Rasinski, Timothy. 2014. "Tapping the Power of Poetry." *Educational Leadership* 72 (3): 30–34.

The Red Piano Art Gallery. n.d. "Jonathan Green." Accessed August 9, 2021. redpianoartgallery.com/artists/painters/jonathan-green.

reDesign. n.d. "Guided Imagery." Accessed May 6, 2021. www.redesignu.org/resources/guided-imagery/.

Reed, Stephen K. 2010. *Cognition: Theories and Application.* 8th ed. Belmont, CA: Wadsworth Cengage Learning.

Reeves, Douglas. 2007. "Academics and the Arts." *Educational Leadership* 64 (5): 80–81.

Riley, Susan. 2017. "The Elements of Art Anchor Charts." Institute for Arts Integration and STEAM. July 1, 2017. artsintegration.com/2017/07/01/elements-art-anchor-charts/.

Rinne, Luke, Emma Gregory, Julia Yarmolinskyay, and Mariale Hardiman. 2011. "Why Arts Integration Improves Long-Term Retention of Content." *Mind, Brain, and Education* 5 (2): 89–96.

Rose, Todd. 2012. "Learner Variability and Universal Design for Learning." *Universal Design for Learning Series*. udlseries.udlcenter.org/presentations/learner_variability.html.

Schafer, R. Murray. 1977. *Tuning of the World*. New York: Knopf.

Schafer, R. Murray. 1992. *A Sound Education*. Indian River, ON: Arcana Editions.

Scharner, Samara. 2019. "Storytelling for Oral Language Fluency." *Practical Literacy* 24 (2). link.gale.com/apps/doc/A589966989/AONE?u=mlin_w_masscol&sid=AONE&xid=66f37e35.

School Curriculum and Standards Authority. 2014. "Drama Elements." k10outline.scsa.wa.edu.au/home/teaching/curriculum-browser/the-arts/visual-arts2/arts-overview/glossary/elements-of-drama#.

Segaren, Sharuna. 2019. "Is Arts Integration in Schools All It's Cracked Up To Be?" *Study International*, January 14, 2019. www.studyinternational.com/news/is-arts-integration-in-schools-all-its-cracked-up-to-be/.

Seneca Academy. n.d. "Arts Integration in School: 10 Reasons Why It's Important." Accessed September 13, 2021. www.senecaacademy.org/10-reasons-why-integrating-art-is-important-in-school/.

Skoning, Stacey. 2008. "Movement in Dance in the Inclusive Classroom." *TEACHING Exceptional Children Plus* 4 (6). files.eric.ed.gov/fulltext/EJ967723.pdf.

Smithsonian Magazine. 2002. "Migrant Madonna." www.smithsonianmag.com/arts-culture/migrant-madonna-60096830/.

South, Helen. 2018. "How to Use Thumbnail Sketching to Help With Drawing." *LiveAbout*, December 23, 2018. www.liveabout.com/thumbnail-sketching-to-help-with-drawing-4077911.

Stojkovic, Anika. 2017. "Using Drama and Theater in the Classroom to Promote Literacy." *Early Childhood Education* (blog), Novak Djokovic Foundation, August 17, 2017. novakdjokovicfoundation.org/using-drama-theater-classroom-promote-literacy/.

Talisse, Chesley. 2018. "Building a Sense of Community With Music." *Edutopia*, June 20, 2018. www.edutopia.org/article/building-sense-community-music.

Tate. n.d. "Assemblage." Accessed September 13, 2021. www.tate.org.uk/art/art-terms/a/assemblage.

Torf, Victoria. n.d. "Thumbnail Sketches: Shorthand Drawing for Artists." Accessed May 4, 2021. victoriatorf.com/media_design/thumbnails_sketches.html

Toth, Natasha Anne. 2015. "Altered Books as a Form of Student Reflection about Constructivist Learning Experiences." Master's thesis, Vancouver Island University. viurrspace.ca/bitstream/handle/10613/2624/Toth.pdf.

Turner, Bret. 2018. "Building Classroom Community Through Storytelling." *Educational Leadership* 76 (1): 72–76.

References Cited *(cont.)*

Umansky, Leah. 2020. "Find Poetry in the Pages of a Newspaper." *New York Times*, June 7, 2020. www.nytimes.com/2020/06/07/books/coronavirus-find-poetry-in-the-pages-of-a-newspaper.html.

Varlas, Laura. 2012. "It's Complicated: Common Core State Standards Focus on Text Complexity." *Education Update* 54 (4).

Venkat, Srividhya. 2020. "Using Oral Storytelling Techniques in Reading Sessions." *Knowledge Quest* 48 (5).

Walker, Elaine, Carmine Tabone, and Gustave Weltsek. 2011. "When Achievement Data Meet Drama and Arts Integration." *Language Arts* 88 (5).

West, Keith. 2011. *Inspired Drama Teaching: A Practical Guide for Teachers*. New York: Bloomsbury Publishing.

Windmill Theatre Company. n.d. "Elements of Drama." Accessed October 1, 2021. windmill.org.au/wp-content/uploads/2018/09/Elements-of-Drama.pdf.

Wohlberg, Meagan. 2012. "Don't Let the Facts Spoil a Good Story: Storyteller Jim Green to Release Album on Yellowknife's Gold Range." *Slave River Journal*, 18.

Woodson, Jacqueline. 2015. "Lift Every Voice." www.poetryfoundation.org/articles/70271/lift-every-voice.

Yellin, David, Mary Blake Jones, and Beverly A. DeVries. 2007. *Integrating the Language Arts*. Scottsdale, AZ: Holcomb Hathaway Publishers.

Yew, Jude. 2005. "Collaborative Narratives: Collaborative learning in Blogosphere." Master's thesis, University of Michigan. DOI:2027.42/39368.

Zull, James E. 2002. *The Art of Changing the Brain: Enriching Teaching by Exploring the Biology of Learning*. Sterling, VA: Stylus.

Digital Resources

Accessing the Digital Resources

The digital resources can be downloaded by following these steps:

1. Go to **www.tcmpub.com/digital**

2. Use the ISBN to redeem the digital resources.

> **ISBN 978-0-7439-7032-7**

3. Respond to the question using the book.

4. Follow the prompts on the Content Cloud website to sign in or create a new account.

5. Choose the digital resources you would like to download. You can download all the files at once, or a specific group of files.

Please note: Some files provided for download have large file sizes. Download times for these larger files vary based on your internet speed.